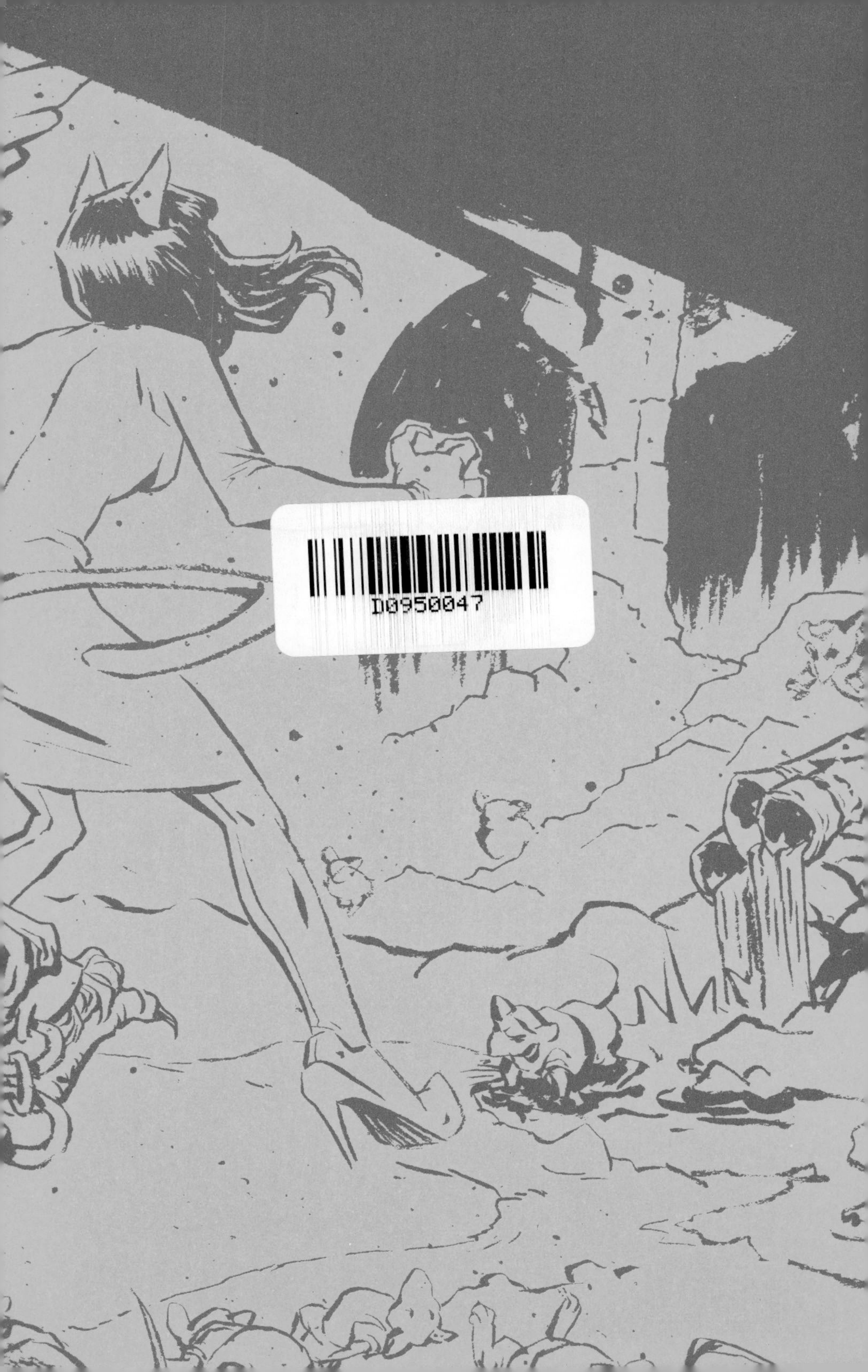

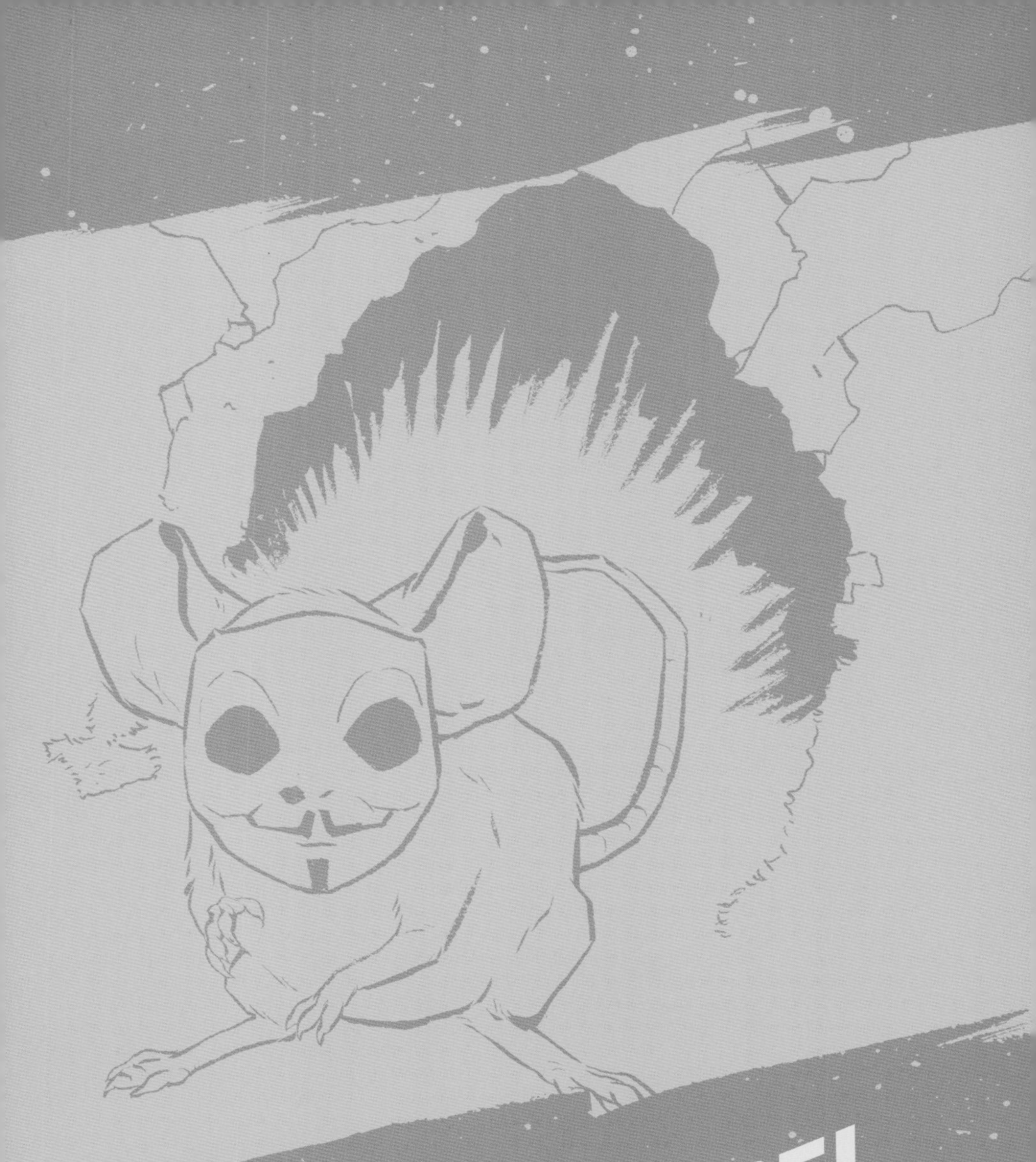

ANGEL CATBIRD™

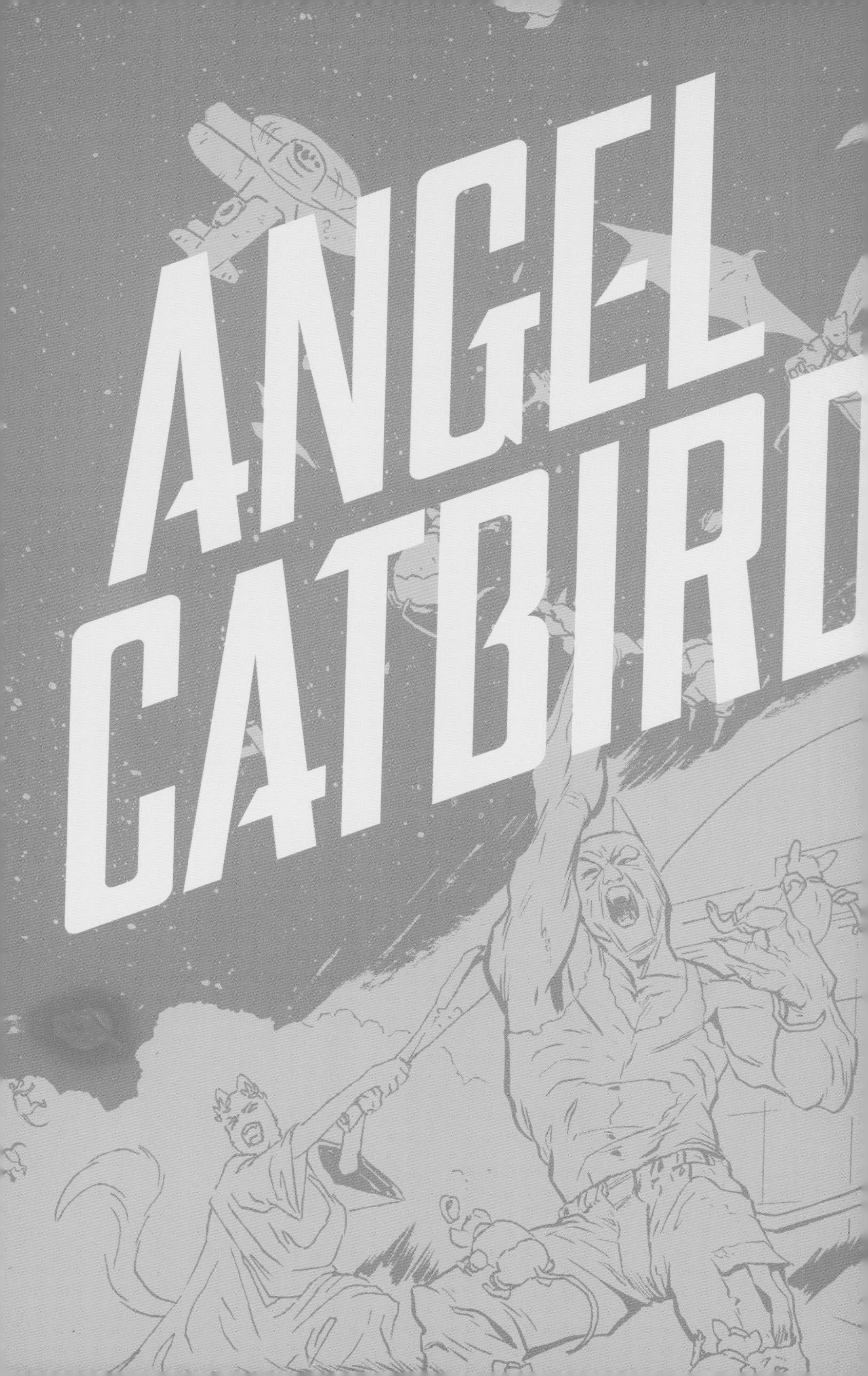
ANGEL
CATBIRD

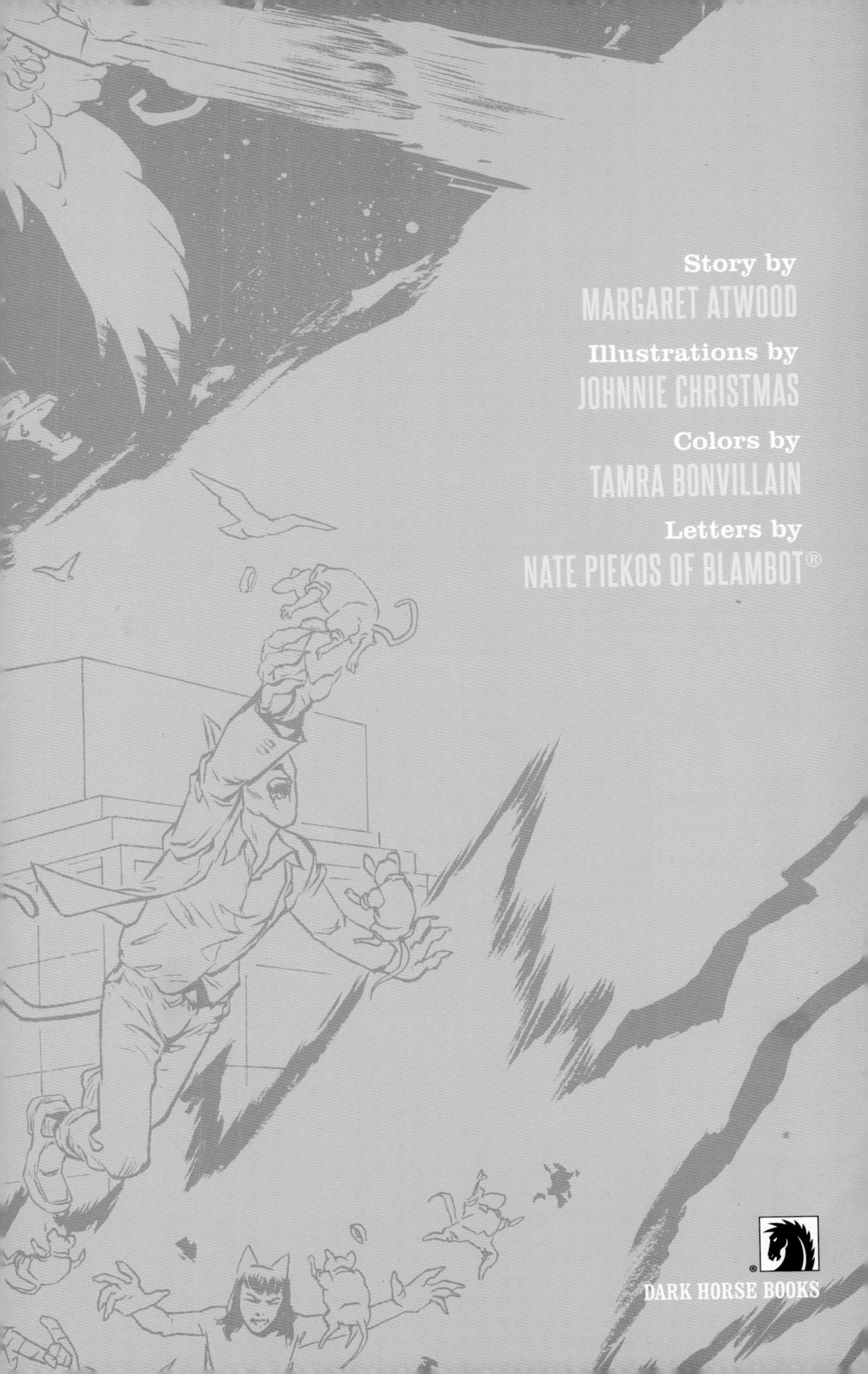

Story by
MARGARET ATWOOD

Illustrations by
JOHNNIE CHRISTMAS

Colors by
TAMRA BONVILLAIN

Letters by
NATE PIEKOS OF BLAMBOT®

DARK HORSE BOOKS

President and Publisher MIKE RICHARDSON

Editor DANIEL CHABON

Assistant Editors CARDNER CLARK AND RACHEL ROBERTS

Project Adviser HOPE NICHOLSON

Designer BRENNAN THOME

Digital Art Technician CONLEY SMITH

Special thanks to Sarah Cooper.

NEIL HANKERSON Executive Vice President • TOM WEDDLE Chief Financial Officer •
RANDY STRADLEY Vice President of Publishing • MATT PARKINSON Vice President of
Marketing • DAVID SCROGGY Vice President of Product Development • DALE LaFOUNTAIN
Vice President of Information Technology • CARA NIECE Vice President of Production and
Scheduling • NICK McWHORTER Vice President of Media Licensing • MARK BERNARDI
Vice President of Book Trade and Digital Sales • KEN LIZZI General Counsel • DAVE
MARSHALL Editor in Chief • DAVEY ESTRADA Editorial Director • SCOTT ALLIE Executive
Senior Editor • CHRIS WARNER Senior Books Editor • CARY GRAZZINI Director of Specialty
Projects • LIA RIBACCHI Art Director • VANESSA TODD Director of Print Purchasing •
MATT DRYER Director of Digital Art and Prepress • SARAH ROBERTSON Director of
Product Sales • MICHAEL GOMBOS Director of International Publishing and Licensing

Published by Dark Horse Books
A division of Dark Horse Comics, Inc.
10956 SE Main Street
Milwaukie, OR 97222

First edition: July 2017
ISBN 978-1-50670-170-7

10 9 8 7 6 5 4 3 2 1
Printed in China

International Licensing: (503) 905-2377 | Comic Shop Locator Service: (888) 266-4226

ANGEL CATBIRD VOLUME 3: THE CATBIRD ROARS

KELLY SUE DeCONNICK

FOREWORD

A *foreword* is part of a book's *front matter*. It's usually written by someone other than the main author, and its purpose (these days, anyway) is more as a marketing aid than anything else. The idea is to get an esteemed person of some variety—an expert in a related field or perhaps a successful author of a similar book—to lend an air of credibility to the launch.

You see the problem, don't you?

The book you hold in your hands is by Margaret Atwood and Johnnie Christmas, with colors by Tamra Bonvillain. Christmas and Bonvillain may be new to you, but the Margaret Atwood in question is THE Margaret Atwood. Margaret Atwood of *The Handmaid's Tale*. Margaret Atwood of the MaddAddam Trilogy. Literary Grand Dame Margaret Atwood. Margaret Atwood: *Companion of the Order of Canada*. Unless this is, I dunno, the very first book you've ever read, chances are you've heard of her. Hell, if you're a woman of my generation, I'd lay odds you either have a *nolite te bastardes carborundorum* tattoo or you've seriously considered one. So, as proud as I am of my work and what I've accomplished as the author of *Captain Marvel*, *Bitch Planet*, and *Pretty Deadly*, there is no universe in which I have any credibility whatsoever to lend to MARGARET ATWOOD'S BOOK LAUNCH.

Then why am I here? Why are you reading this, and not jumping right into the further adventures of Angel Catbird? Because I'm constitutionally incapable of saying no to Margaret Atwood, is the short answer. But I'd like to justify my presence with something more useful than that. So what can I do?

As a comic book writer of some renown and a comic book *consumer* of thirty-plus years, it occurs to me that I might be able to offer you a little context. Some of you—perhaps even many of you—may have followed Ms. Atwood from her prose work to this medium. It may be new to you and maybe—maybe!—I can add to your appreciation by filling you in on a little bit of our history. There are two areas I want to address: Golden Age Comics and Comics as Pedagogy.

GOLDEN AGE COMICS

Both in substance and style, *Angel Catbird* is a playful nod to the period of comics publishing from 1938 to 1955, referred to as the "Golden Age." Though the superhero genre had come to dominate the medium by the end of the Golden Age (and that rise is a significant part of how we define it), through most of the period, genres like horror, western, romance, war, and "funny animal" comics were equally popular. Atwood herself, in her introduction to the first *Angel Catbird* collection, cites Walt Kelly's talking-animal strip *Pogo* as an influence.

Pogo, which launched in 1941 in the premiere issue of Dell's creatively titled *Animal Comics*, is an unsurprising favorite for Atwood—like the woman and her work, it's both erudite and mischievous. Through the eyes of an "everyman possum," *Pogo* uses allegory to comment on human nature in a manner that reminds me of Greek mythology more than anything else. Sadly, it isn't remembered by as many people as it ought to be.

But back to the rise and rapid dominance of the superhero genre, which is what most of us think of when we think of the Golden Age. *Angel Catbird*, while full of *Pogo*-esque talking animals, is constructed primarily as a superhero tale. Though books of that genre in that period were mercifully devoid of relatable villains or devilish antiheroes—good was good, evil was evil, and the closest thing to moral ambiguity one encountered was a femme fatale torn between her attraction to the hero and the necessity of her plot against him (she wasn't *really* bad; she was just drawn that way)—Golden Age comics were also more sophisticated and sexier than the moralistic and goofy comics that followed in the Silver Age. This was, remember, before the Comics Code. (I don't have the time to get into that here, but if you're interested, I highly recommend *The Ten-Cent Plague: The Great Comic-Book Scare and How It Changed America* by David Hajdu.) Angel Catbird's feather booty shorts and sculpted nude torso would have been right at home among the virile heroes of the Golden Age.

Note that I am American and I write this overview from an American perspective. Atwood is Canadian. As it happens, this period was also a "Golden Age" for Canadian comics, since American comics were banned from import to Canada under WECA, or the War Exchange Conservation Act. During the six years the act was in effect, what came to be known as "Canadian Whites" (because they were printed in black and white) flourished. Titles such as *Triumph Comics* and *Better Comics* (which is almost as good a title as *Animal Comics*) unfortunately folded once WECA was lifted and their American counterparts flooded back into the market.

Americans: ruining Canadian comics since 1946. You're welcome.

COMICS AS PEDAGOGY

Comics are both multimodal and interactive.

"Multimodal" is a word academics use in a few different ways, but in this instance, Professor Ben Saunders, who heads the Comics Studies program at the University of Oregon, explained it to mean that comics "mix semiotic registers." Of course, that's so much more confusing than "multimodal" that Ben wrote "(ugh)" right after it in our correspondence on the matter. (Ben's a good egg.)

"Semiotic registers" basically means "ways of communicating." It's a little more complicated than that, but my search for understanding led me down a rabbit hole of mathematical language and Jungian approaches to literature and I want to spare you that folly. So, basically—just go with me on this—comics are multimodal because they communicate ideas using both written text (a series of symbols representing sounds, which, when "heard" together in your head, have meaning) and pictures (I'm not going to break down what pictures are and how they communicate meaning. I am also a good egg, see?). That two-pronged attack makes comics a very powerful way to engage the brain in story.

Comics are also *interactive*. What do I mean by that? Well, when you consume a movie or television show, your role is passive—the pace is prescribed; you simply sit and take it in as it's served. With comics, the reader controls the pace. Even more than that, the reader's participation is *required* to fill in the action that happens between the panels—the space we call "the gutters." When we see a drawing of a woman ten feet from a door and then another picture of a woman's hand on a doorknob,

something much more active than persistence of vision is required for our brains to understand that the lady from the first illustration walked to the door and raised her hand to open it—all in the gutter. You follow?

Combine multimodal and interactive and what you get is a storytelling medium that is so cognitively engaging as to be a powerful tool for education . . . or persuasion. *Angel Catbird* does both for bird conservation—educating us on the dangers of free-roaming cats, for example, and using statistics and suggestions to try to alter our behavior.

Comics have a long and fascinating history as a means of propaganda or persuasion. In World War II, the US Office of War Information published a comic called *The Nightmares of Lieutenant Ichi; or, Juan Posong Gives Ichi the Midnight Jitters* and distributed it throughout the Pacific theater to boost morale among the Filipinos and denigrate the occupying Japanese. In 1984, the CIA developed a comic and airdropped it over Grenada prior to the US invasion. I guess they viewed that book as successful, because in 1985 the CIA made another one for the Contras in Nicaragua! Think too of the fire-and-brimstone scare comics Jack Chick produced or, on a more pleasant note, *Martin Luther King and the Montgomery Story*, the comic that helped kick off nonviolent protest movements across the American South, and later, as far away as the Middle East.

Okay, so let's bring this home: I promised a bit of comics history to contextualize *Angel Catbird* and I think I've delivered, but there's one more idea I want to sneak in: in combining the traditions of Golden Age Comics and Comics as Pedagogy, Atwood has done something very modern: she's made a genre mash-up.

What was it I called her up there—erudite and mischievous? I stand by both.

Kelly Sue DeConnick
Portland, OR
2017

Our Story So Far...

GENETIC ENGINEER STRIG FELEEDUS WAS HIRED BY MUROID LABS TO PERFECT A D.N.A. SUPER-SPLICER.

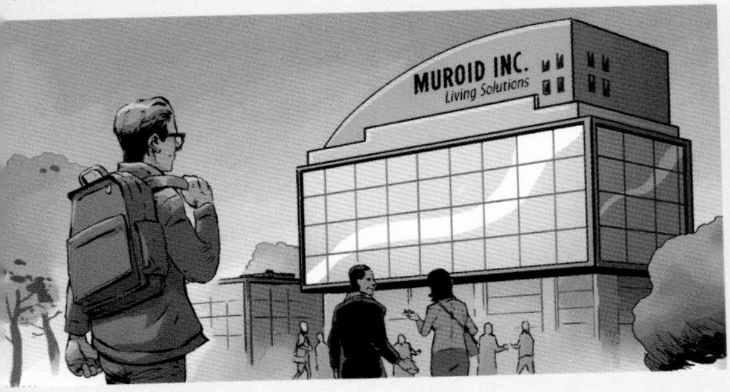
MUROID INC.
Living Solutions

AFTER CRACKING THE FORMULA HE HEADED OUT--FLASK IN HAND--AND WAS INVOLVED IN A CAR ACCIDENT.

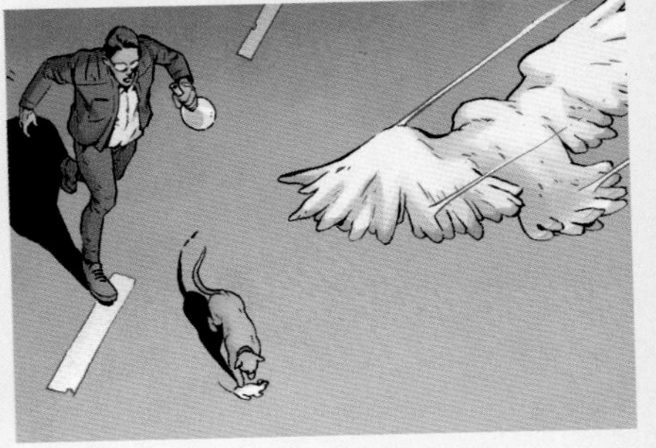

T FOR DEAD IN A PUDDLE OF THE SPILLED SUPER-
ICER, STRIG UNDERWENT A METAMORPHOSIS
D EMERGED AS PART OWL AND PART CAT.

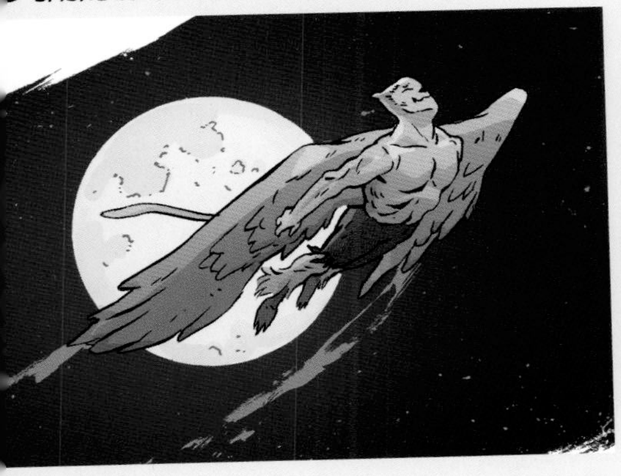

STRIG'S COWORKER CATE SNIFFED OUT HIS CAT SECRET. CATE IS HALF-CAT, AND WAS SPYING ON THEIR ENEMY, THE HALF-RAT MUROID, WHO NEEDED THE FORMULA TO TURN HIS RATS INTO RAT-MEN AND COMPLETE HIS PLAN FOR GLOBAL DOMINATION.

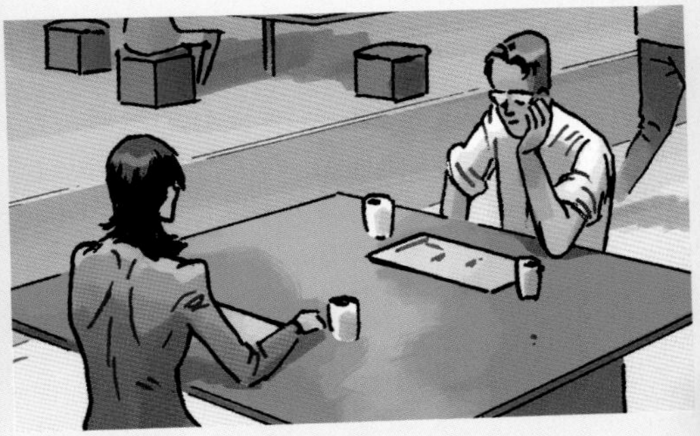

CATE INTRODUCED STRIG TO AN UNDERGROUND HALF-CAT CULTURE, BUT THEY WERE ALL BEING WATCHED BY MUROID THROUGH SPYCAMS...

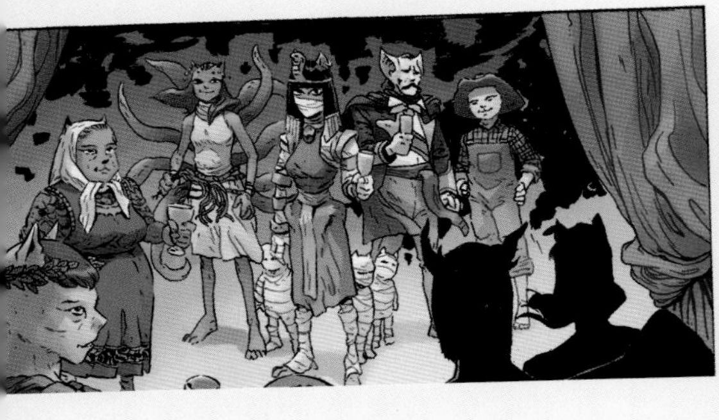

COUNT CATULA, IN HIS BAT FORM, FOLLOWED A RAT BACK TO MUROID'S LAB, WHERE HE STOLE A COPY OF MUROID'S EVIL PLANS TO BLOW UP THE HALF-CAT STRONGHOLD. ANGEL AND COMPANY SET OUT TO STOP HIM, BUT THEY WERE TOO LATE.

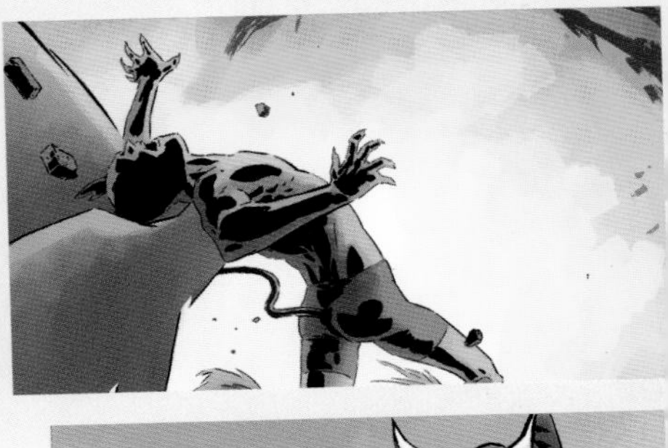

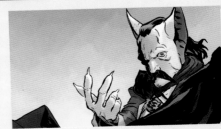

CATULA INVITED THEM ALL TO HIS CASTLE DEEP IN THE FOREST, A SAFE PLACE TO REGROUP. MEANWHILE, MUROID PREPARED TO UNLEASH HIS RAT ARMY.

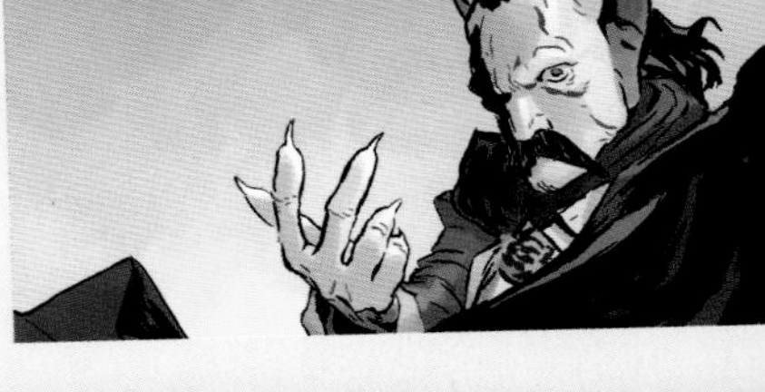

ON THE WAY TO THE COUNT'S CASTLE, THEY FOUND A NEW ALLY: THE GODDESS ATHEEN-OWL. SHE TRIED TO PUT THE MOVES ON ANGEL, BUT CATE INTERVENED.

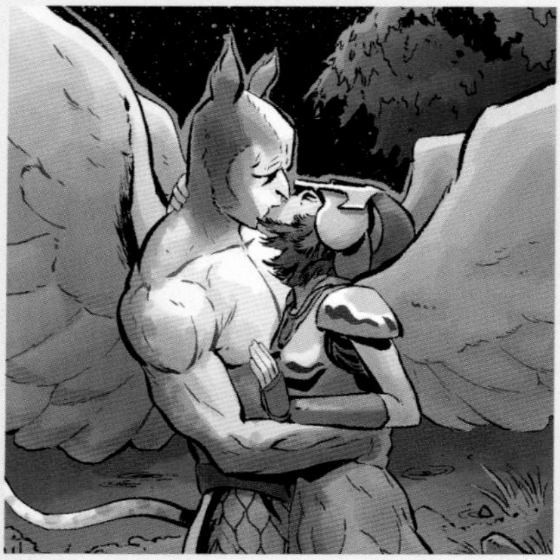

MEANWHILE MUROID PLANNED TO CAPTURE CATE AND U
HER PAIN TO EXTRACT THE FORMULA FROM ANGEL.

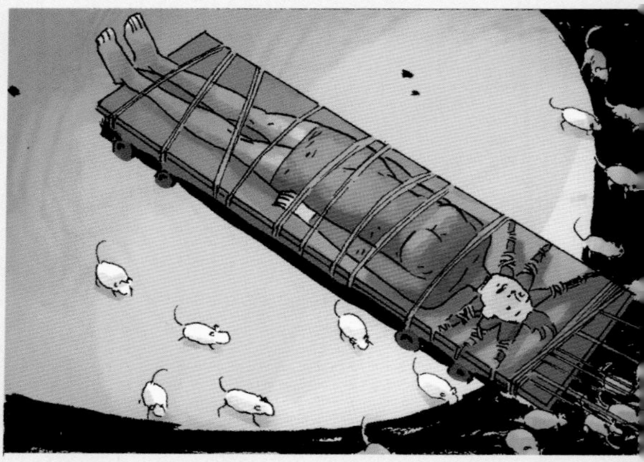

RAY ROUNDED UP SOME SURVIVORS, INCLUDING MUMMYCAT-- ALSO KNOWN AS THE ANCIENT EGYPTIAN QUEEN NEFERKITTI!

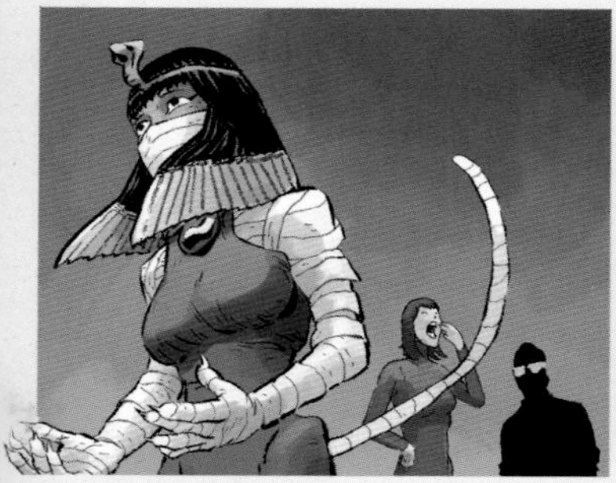

THE HALF-CATS FOUGHT OFF AN ATTACK BY THE RATS, AND FIN
REACHED CASTLE CATULA. THEY WERE GREETED BY THE MANY W
OF CATULA AND SETTLED DOWN FOR A CATNAP.

BUT MUROID DEPLOYED THE DRAT--A GIANT CAT TOY/MISSILE
AND THE CASTLE WAS UNDER ATTACK!

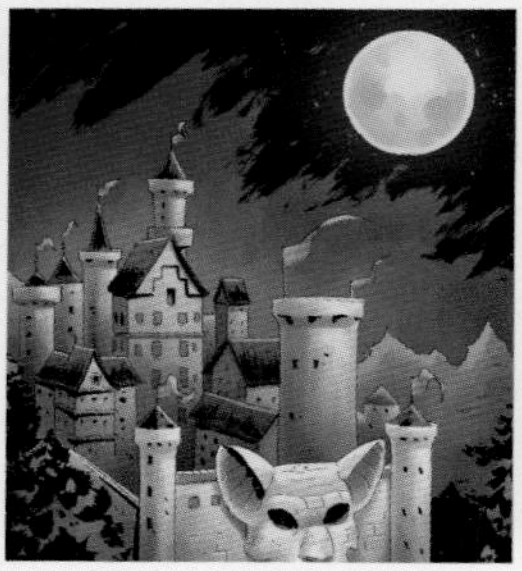

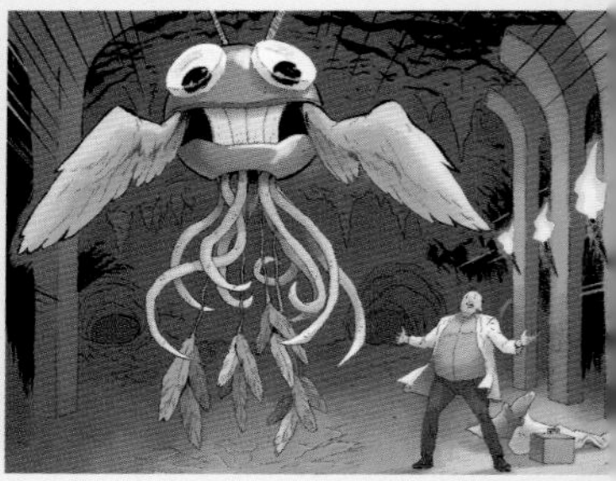

AN AERIAL BATTLE FOLLOWED, BUT THE DRAT LURED ANGEL CATBIRD INTO A TRAP AND MUROID PUT HIM IN A CAGE.

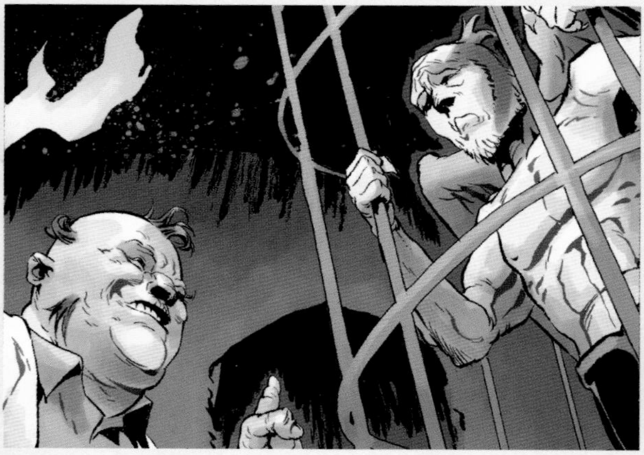

NOW OUR HEROES ARE POISED TO RESCUE ANGEL AS...THE CATBIRD ROARS!

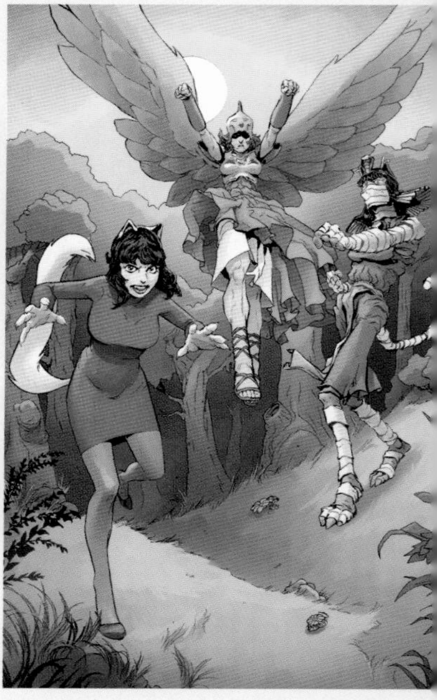

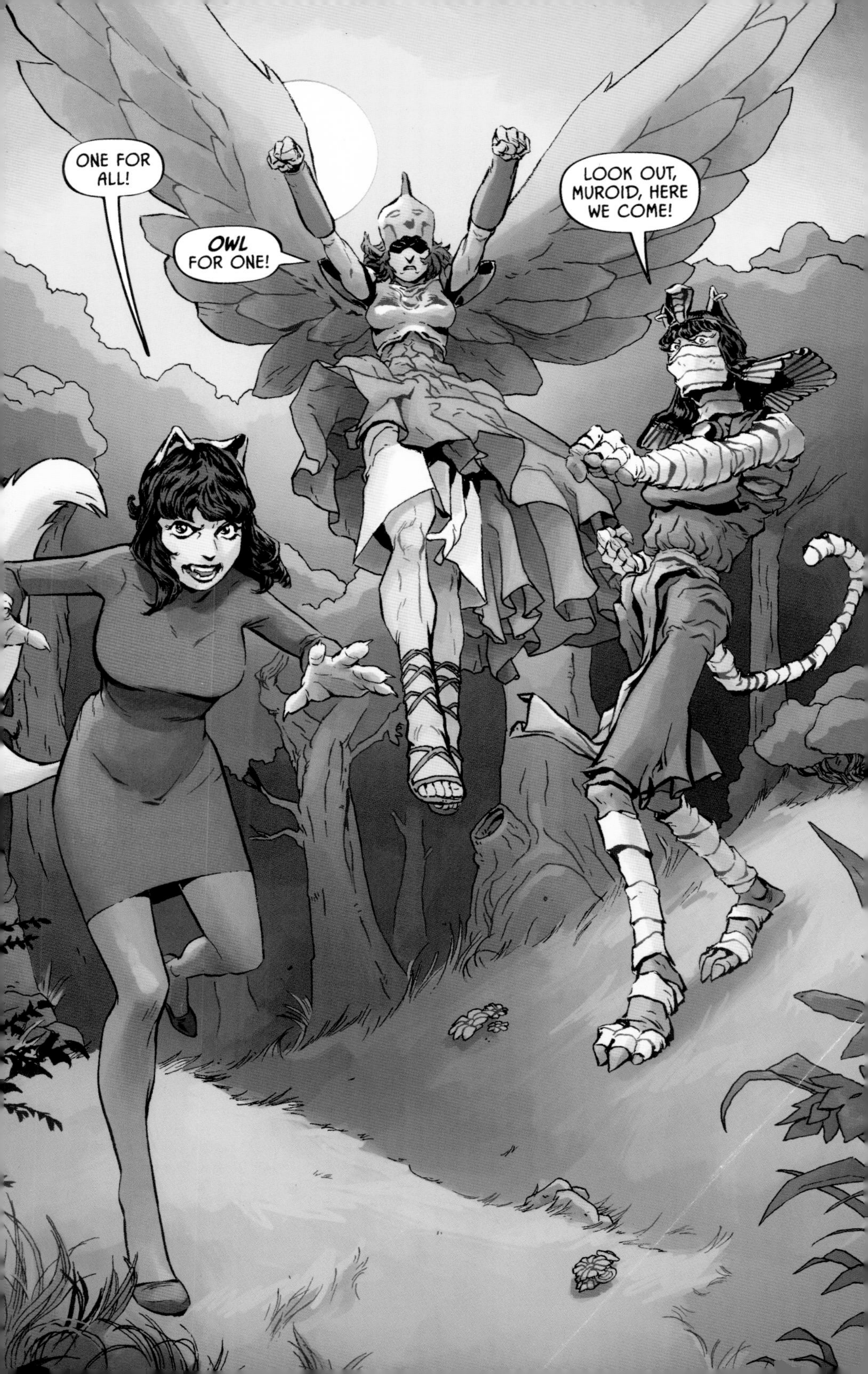
ONE FOR ALL!
OWL FOR ONE!
LOOK OUT, MUROID, HERE WE COME!

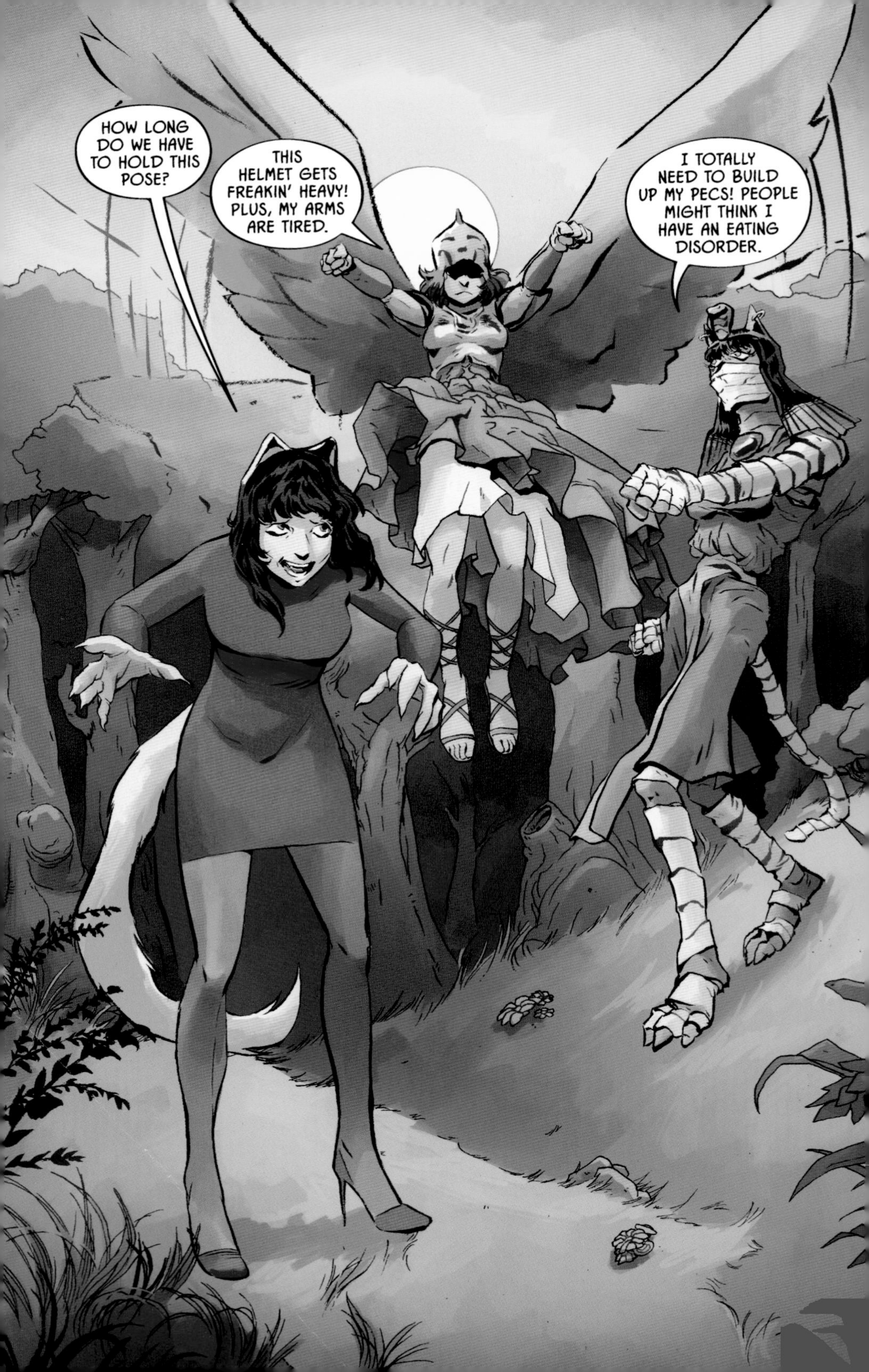
HOW LONG DO WE HAVE TO HOLD THIS POSE?
THIS HELMET GETS FREAKIN' HEAVY! PLUS, MY ARMS ARE TIRED.
I TOTALLY NEED TO BUILD UP MY PECS! PEOPLE MIGHT THINK I HAVE AN EATING DISORDER.

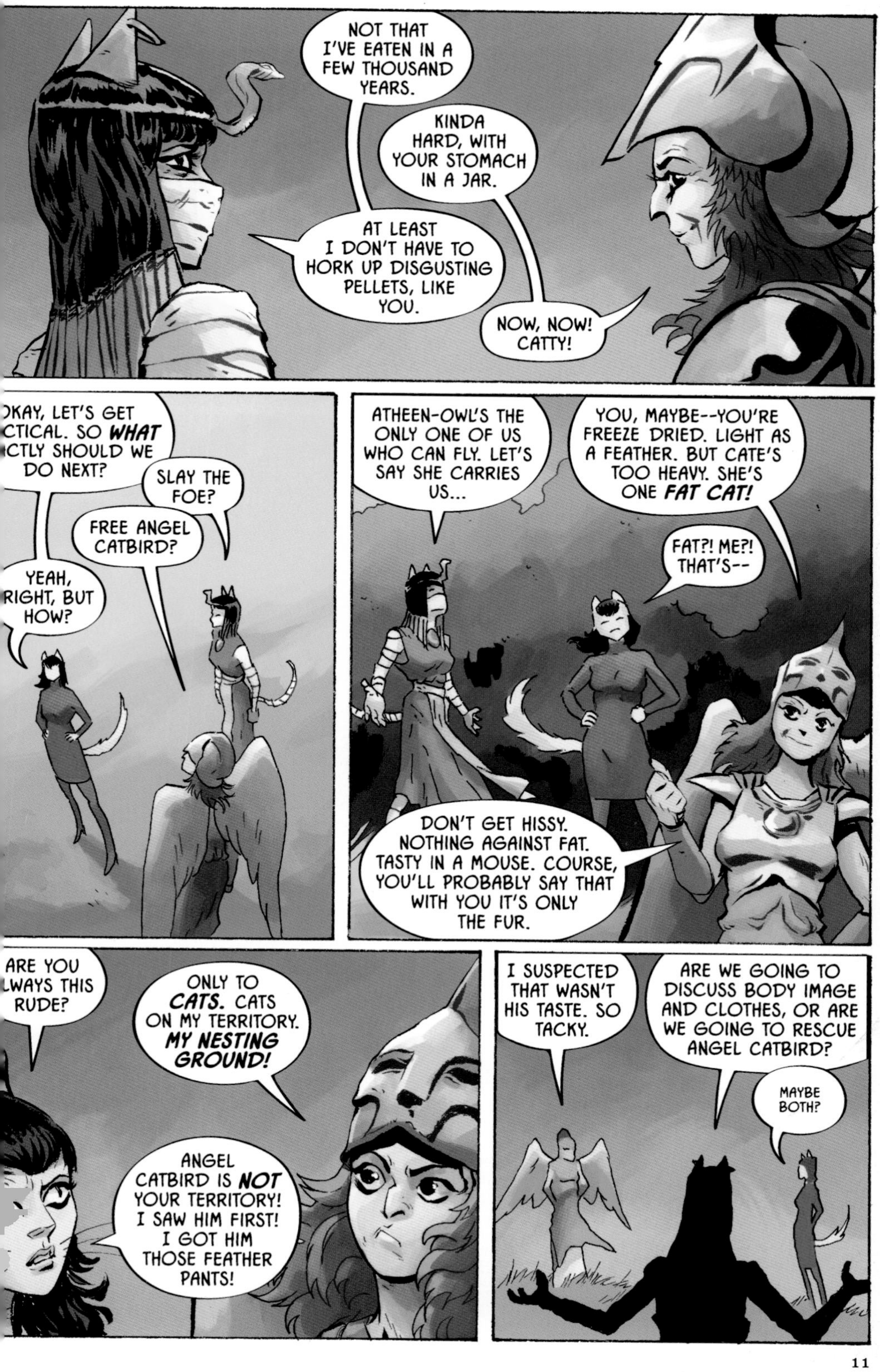
NOT THAT I'VE EATEN IN A FEW THOUSAND YEARS.
KINDA HARD, WITH YOUR STOMACH IN A JAR.
AT LEAST I DON'T HAVE TO HORK UP DISGUSTING PELLETS, LIKE YOU.
NOW, NOW! CATTY!
OKAY, LET'S GET CTICAL. SO WHAT CTLY SHOULD WE DO NEXT?
SLAY THE FOE?
FREE ANGEL CATBIRD?
YEAH, RIGHT, BUT HOW?
ATHEEN-OWL'S THE ONLY ONE OF US WHO CAN FLY. LET'S SAY SHE CARRIES US...
YOU, MAYBE--YOU'RE FREEZE DRIED. LIGHT AS A FEATHER. BUT CATE'S TOO HEAVY. SHE'S ONE FAT CAT!
FAT?! ME?! THAT'S--
DON'T GET HISSY. NOTHING AGAINST FAT. TASTY IN A MOUSE. COURSE, YOU'LL PROBABLY SAY THAT WITH YOU IT'S ONLY THE FUR.
ARE YOU LWAYS THIS RUDE?
ONLY TO CATS. CATS ON MY TERRITORY. MY NESTING GROUND!
ANGEL CATBIRD IS NOT YOUR TERRITORY! I SAW HIM FIRST! I GOT HIM THOSE FEATHER PANTS!
I SUSPECTED THAT WASN'T HIS TASTE. SO TACKY.
ARE WE GOING TO DISCUSS BODY IMAGE AND CLOTHES, OR ARE WE GOING TO RESCUE ANGEL CATBIRD?
MAYBE BOTH?

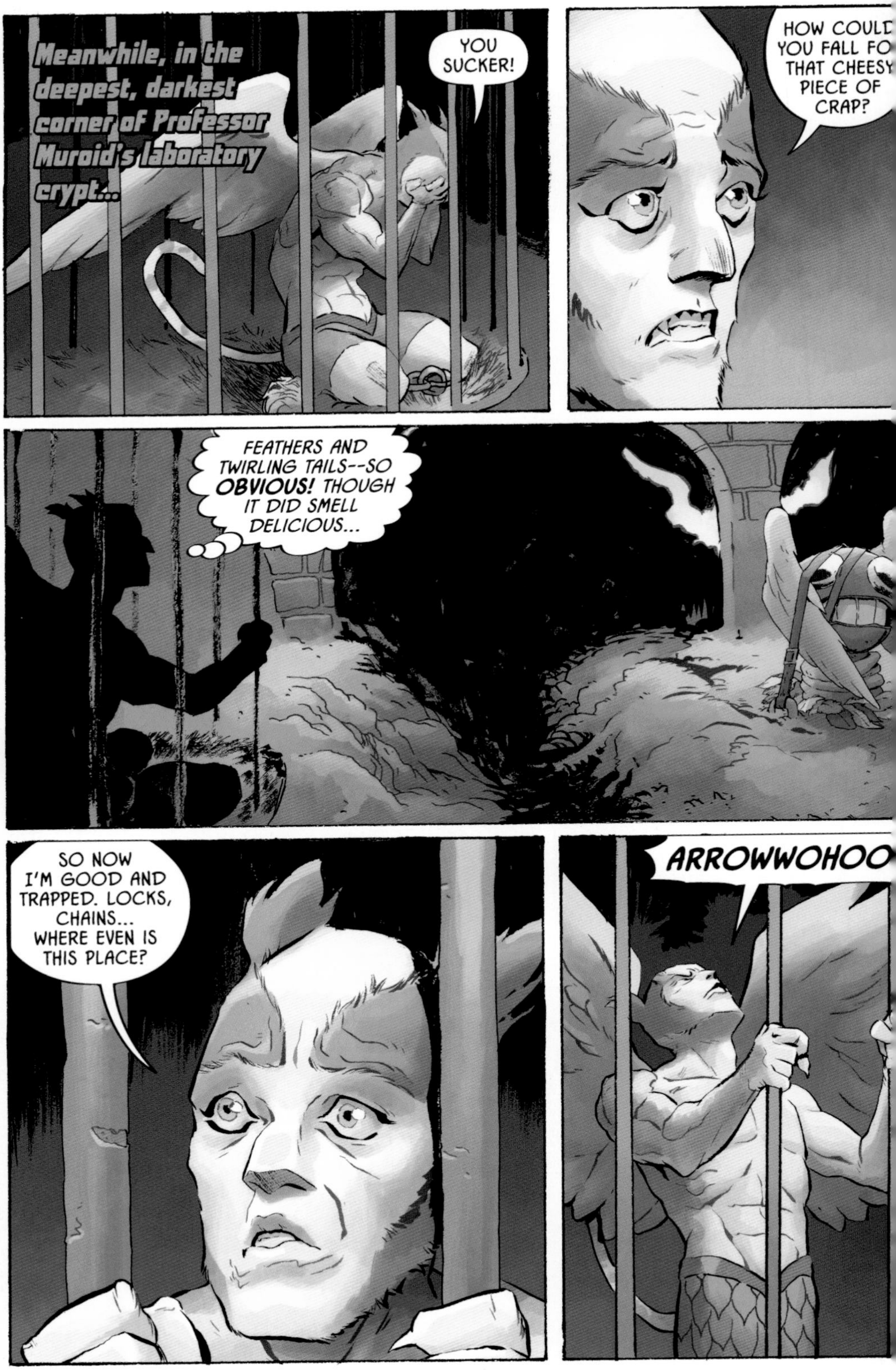
Meanwhile, in the deepest, darkest corner of Professor Muroid's laboratory crypt...
YOU SUCKER!
HOW COULD YOU FALL FO THAT CHEESY PIECE OF CRAP?
FEATHERS AND TWIRLING TAILS--SO OBVIOUS! THOUGH IT DID SMELL DELICIOUS...
SO NOW I'M GOOD AND TRAPPED. LOCKS, CHAINS... WHERE EVEN IS THIS PLACE?
ARROWWOHOO

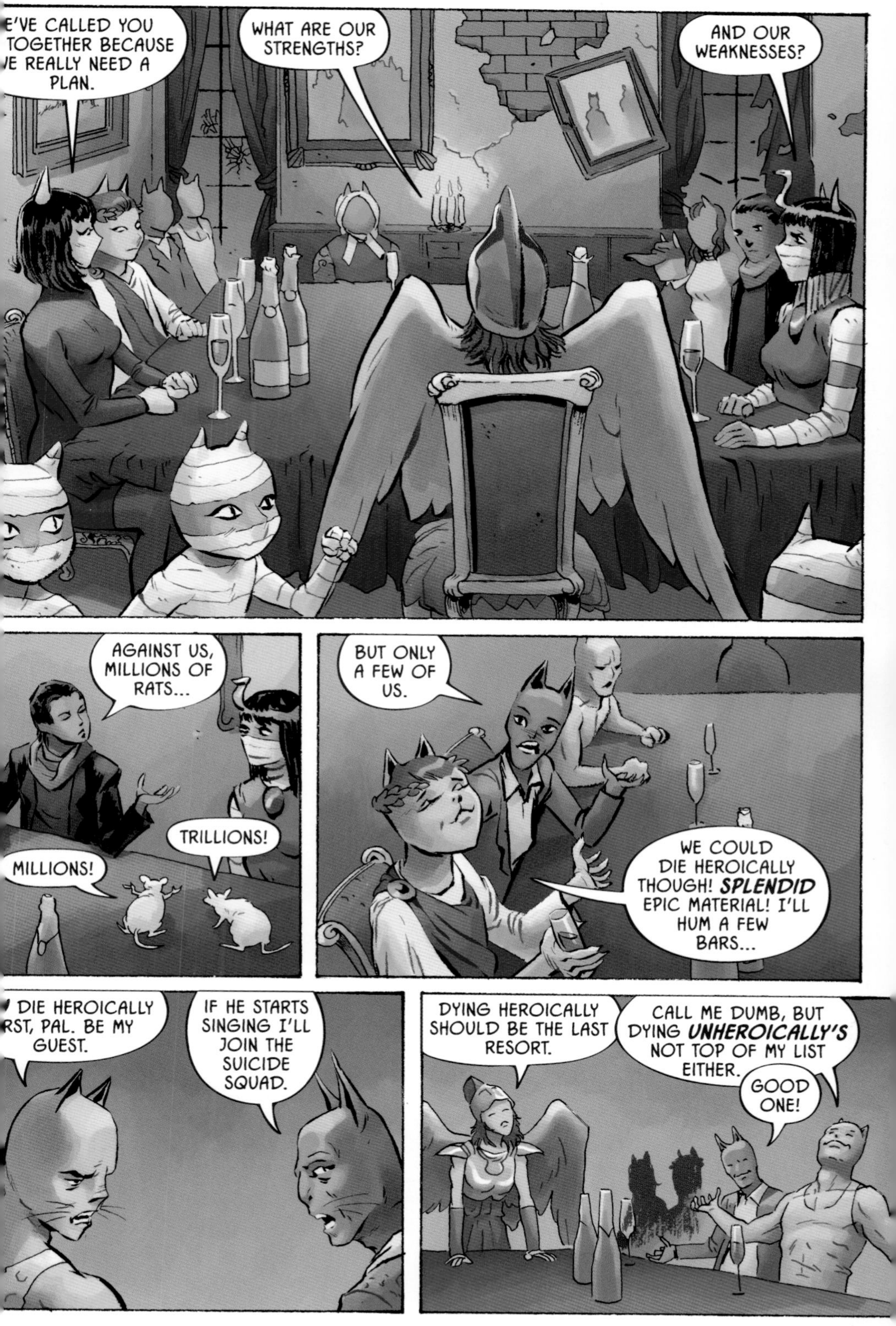
E'VE CALLED YOU TOGETHER BECAUSE E REALLY NEED A PLAN.
WHAT ARE OUR STRENGTHS?
AND OUR WEAKNESSES?
AGAINST US, MILLIONS OF RATS...
MILLIONS!
TRILLIONS!
BUT ONLY A FEW OF US.
WE COULD DIE HEROICALLY THOUGH! ***SPLENDID*** EPIC MATERIAL! I'LL HUM A FEW BARS...
DIE HEROICALLY RST, PAL. BE MY GUEST.
IF HE STARTS SINGING I'LL JOIN THE SUICIDE SQUAD.
DYING HEROICALLY SHOULD BE THE LAST RESORT.
CALL ME DUMB, BUT DYING ***UNHEROICALLY'S*** NOT TOP OF MY LIST EITHER.
GOOD ONE!

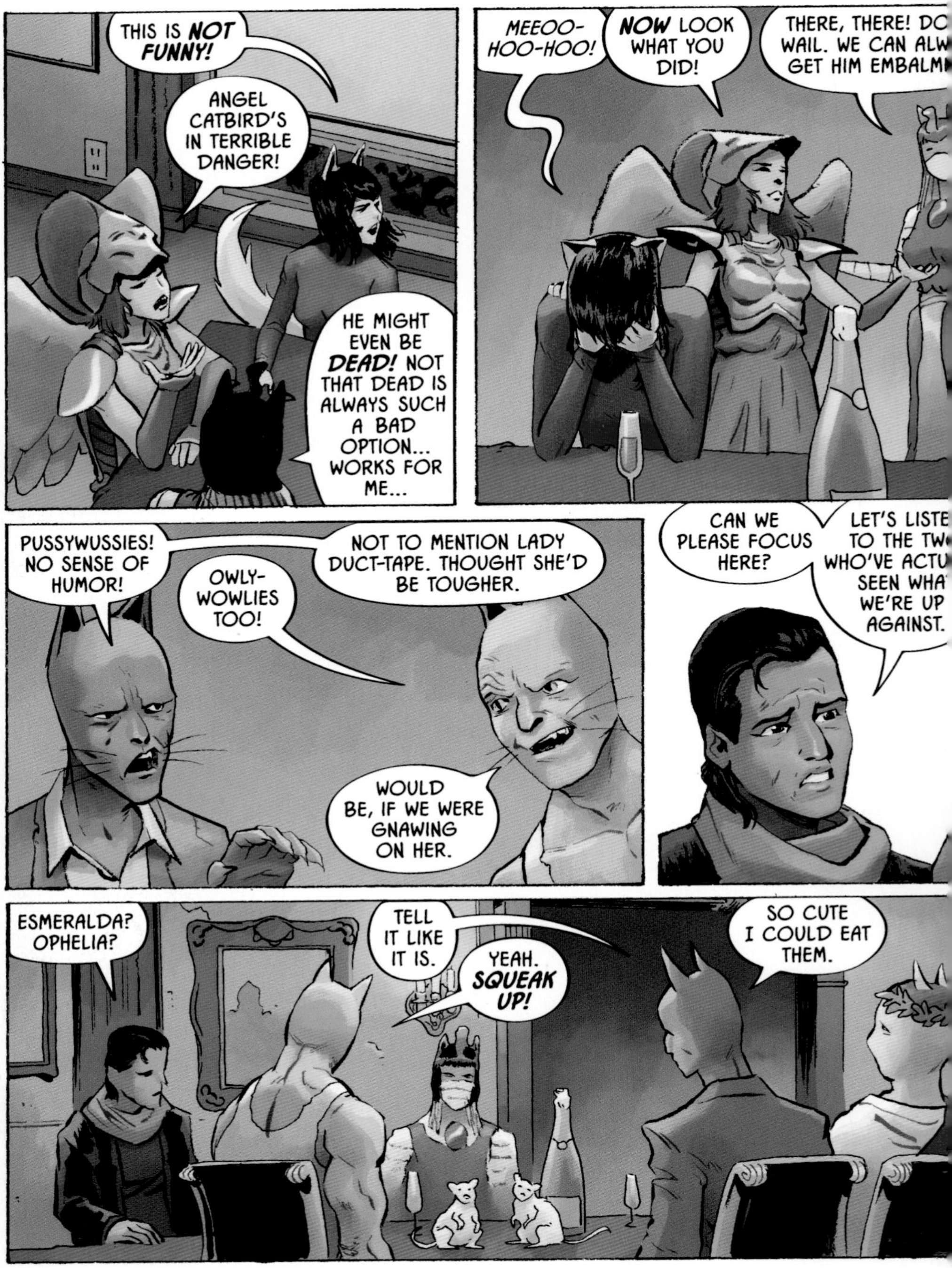
THIS IS NOT FUNNY!
ANGEL CATBIRD'S IN TERRIBLE DANGER!
HE MIGHT EVEN BE DEAD! NOT THAT DEAD IS ALWAYS SUCH A BAD OPTION... WORKS FOR ME...
MEEOO-HOO-HOO!
NOW LOOK WHAT YOU DID!
THERE, THERE! DO
WAIL. WE CAN ALW
GET HIM EMBALM
PUSSYWUSSIES! NO SENSE OF HUMOR!
OWLY-WOWLIES TOO!
NOT TO MENTION LADY DUCT-TAPE. THOUGHT SHE'D BE TOUGHER.
WOULD BE, IF WE WERE GNAWING ON HER.
CAN WE PLEASE FOCUS HERE?
LET'S LISTE
TO THE TW
WHO'VE ACTU
SEEN WHA
WE'RE UP
AGAINST.
ESMERALDA? OPHELIA?
TELL IT LIKE IT IS.
YEAH. SQUEAK UP!
SO CUTE I COULD EAT THEM.

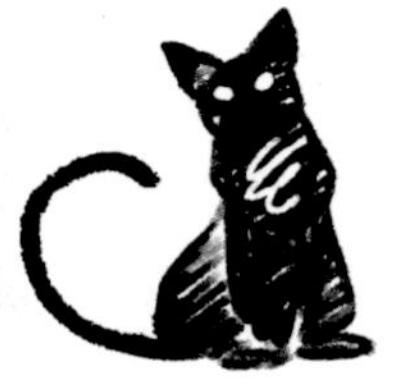

WHAT THEY'RE UP AGAINST

Cats are strong and resilient creatures, but they don't really have nine lives. Outd cats frequently get hit by cars and are at much higher risk of disease, getting lost fights with wildlife and other cats, poisoning, and parasites. Read more at www.catsandbirds.ca

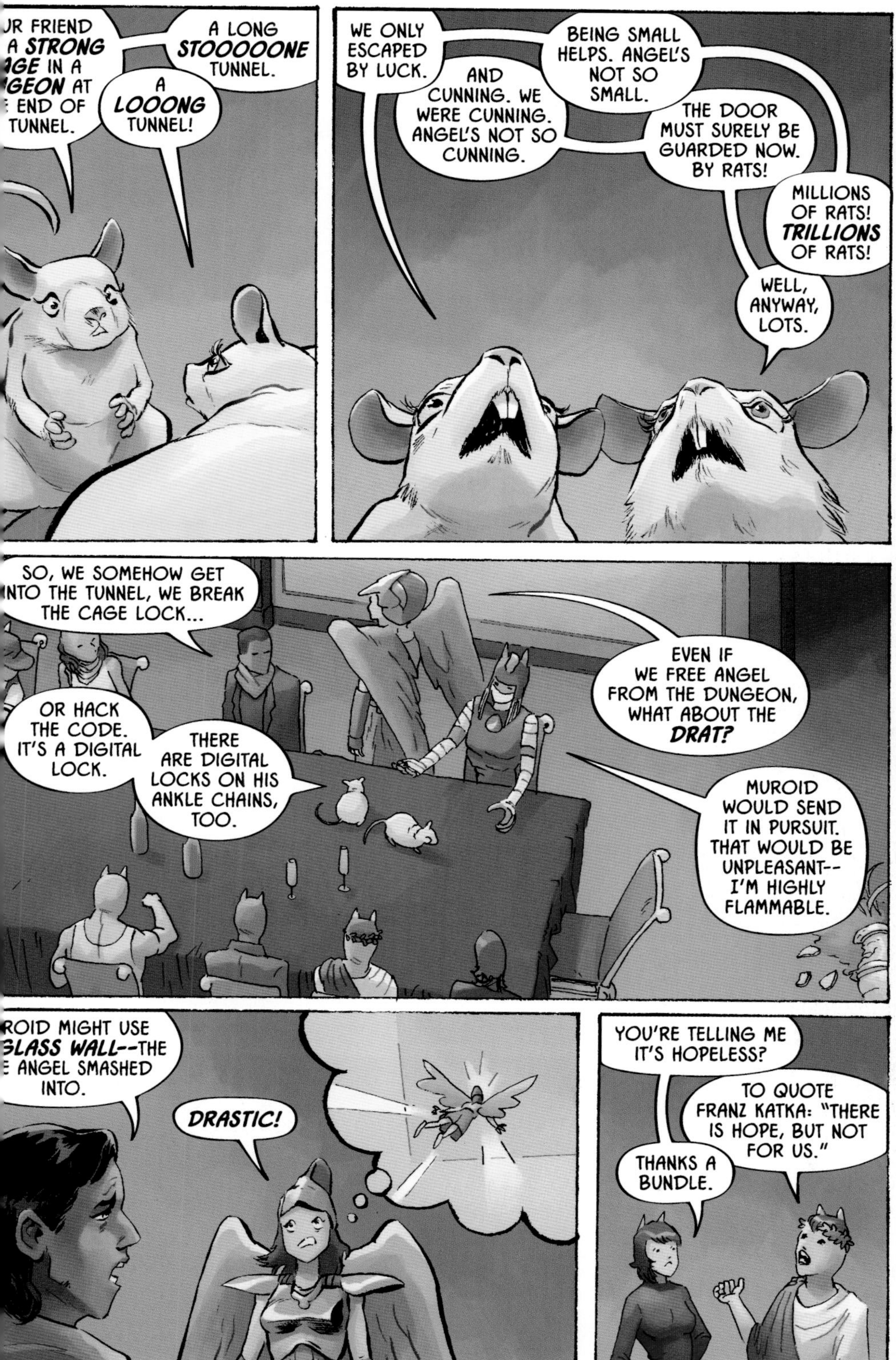

...R FRIEND ...A STRONG ...GE IN A ...GEON AT ...END OF ...TUNNEL.
A LONG STOOOOONE TUNNEL.
A LOOONG TUNNEL!
WE ONLY ESCAPED BY LUCK.
AND CUNNING. WE WERE CUNNING. ANGEL'S NOT SO CUNNING.
BEING SMALL HELPS. ANGEL'S NOT SO SMALL.
THE DOOR MUST SURELY BE GUARDED NOW. BY RATS!
MILLIONS OF RATS! TRILLIONS OF RATS!
WELL, ANYWAY, LOTS.
SO, WE SOMEHOW GET INTO THE TUNNEL, WE BREAK THE CAGE LOCK...
OR HACK THE CODE. IT'S A DIGITAL LOCK.
THERE ARE DIGITAL LOCKS ON HIS ANKLE CHAINS, TOO.
EVEN IF WE FREE ANGEL FROM THE DUNGEON, WHAT ABOUT THE DRAT?
MUROID WOULD SEND IT IN PURSUIT. THAT WOULD BE UNPLEASANT-- I'M HIGHLY FLAMMABLE.
...ROID MIGHT USE ...GLASS WALL--THE ...ANGEL SMASHED INTO.
DRASTIC!
YOU'RE TELLING ME IT'S HOPELESS?
TO QUOTE FRANZ KATKA: "THERE IS HOPE, BUT NOT FOR US."
THANKS A BUNDLE.

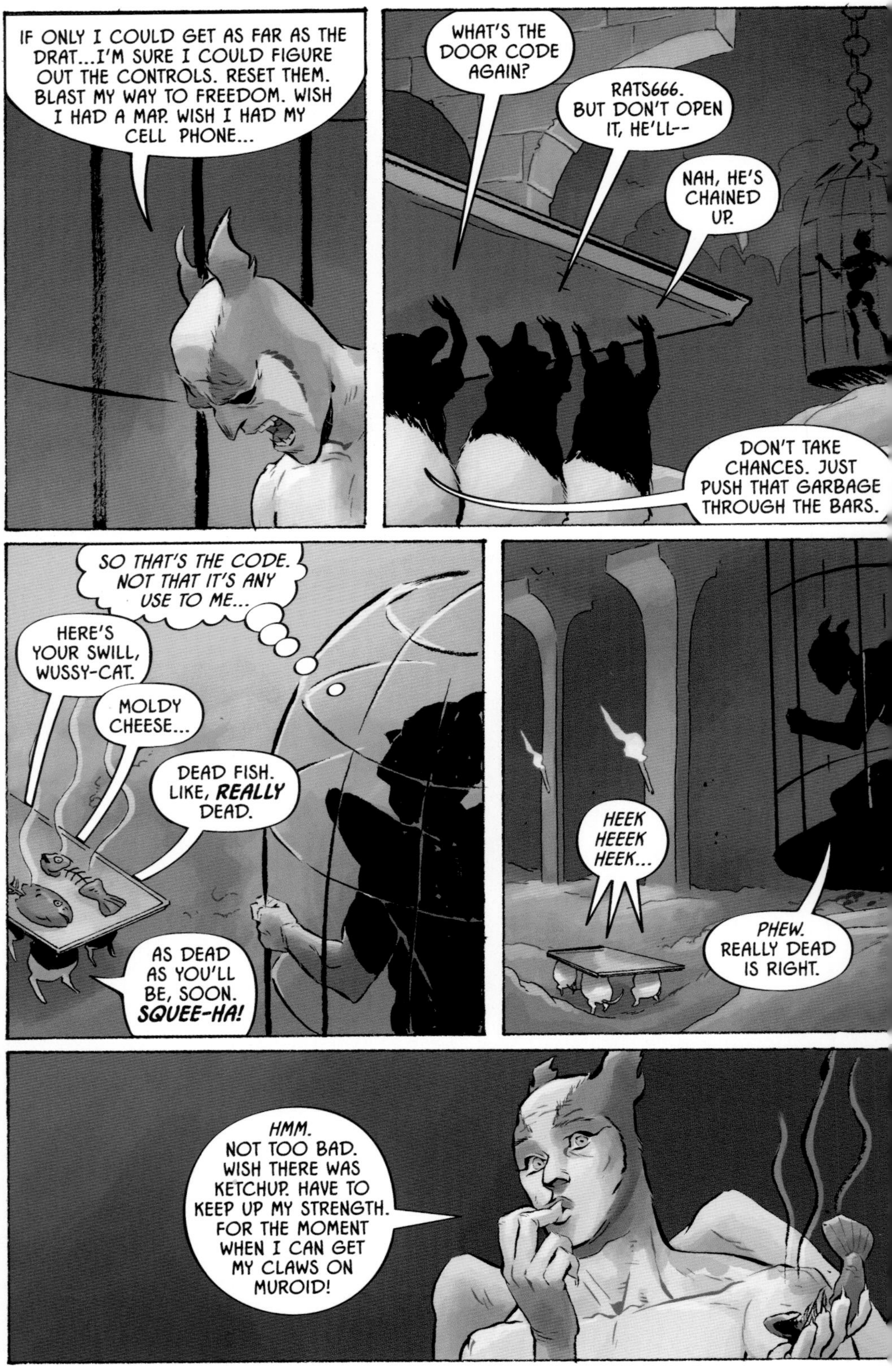
IF ONLY I COULD GET AS FAR AS THE DRAT...I'M SURE I COULD FIGURE OUT THE CONTROLS. RESET THEM. BLAST MY WAY TO FREEDOM. WISH I HAD A MAP. WISH I HAD MY CELL PHONE...
WHAT'S THE DOOR CODE AGAIN?
RATS666. BUT DON'T OPEN IT, HE'LL--
NAH, HE'S CHAINED UP.
DON'T TAKE CHANCES. JUST PUSH THAT GARBAGE THROUGH THE BARS.
SO THAT'S THE CODE. NOT THAT IT'S ANY USE TO ME...
HERE'S YOUR SWILL, WUSSY-CAT.
MOLDY CHEESE...
DEAD FISH. LIKE, ***REALLY*** DEAD.
AS DEAD AS YOU'LL BE, SOON. ***SQUEE-HA!***
HEEK HEEEK HEEK...
PHEW. REALLY DEAD IS RIGHT.
HMM. NOT TOO BAD. WISH THERE WAS KETCHUP. HAVE TO KEEP UP MY STRENGTH. FOR THE MOMENT WHEN I CAN GET MY CLAWS ON MUROID!

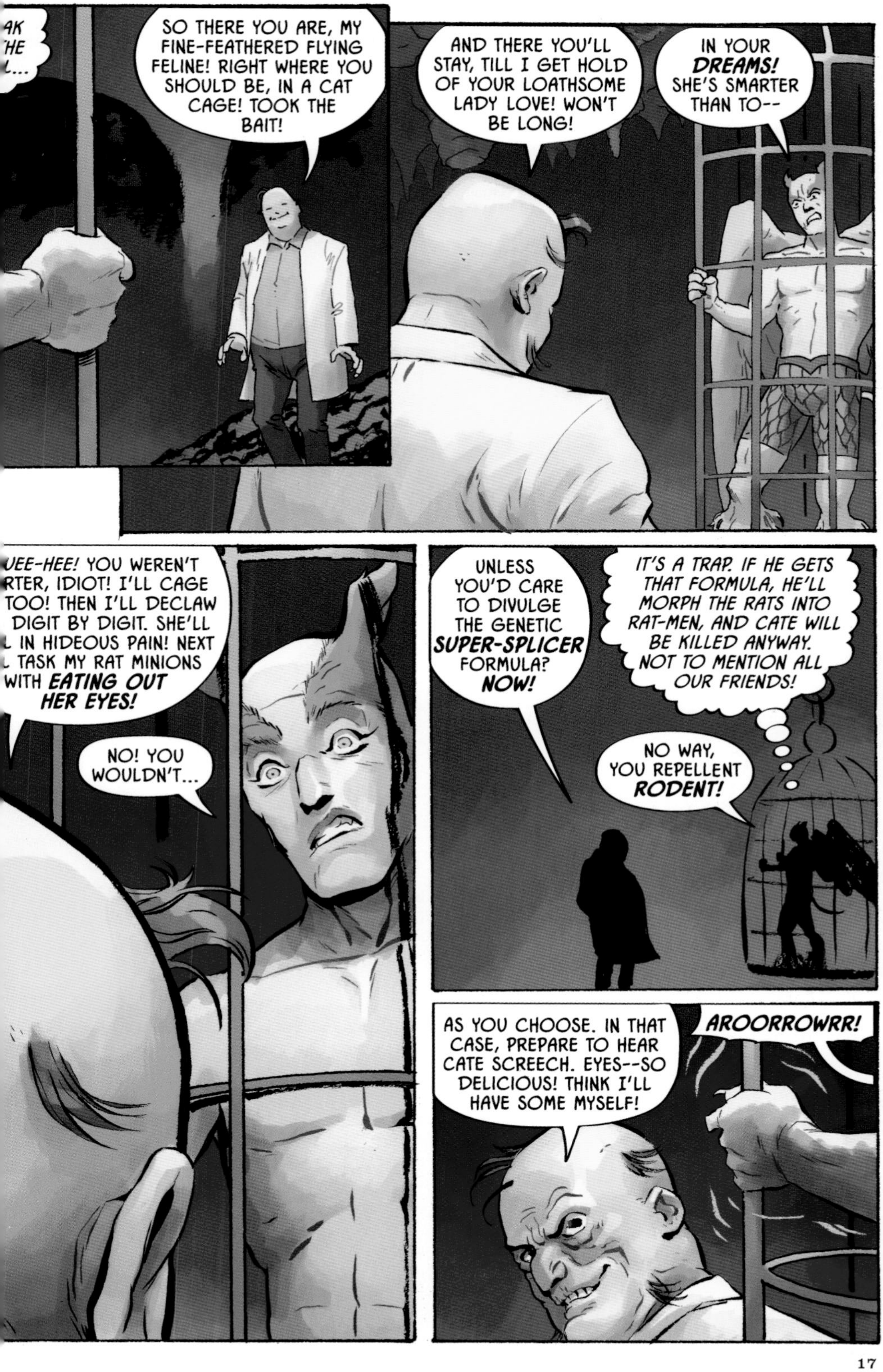
SO THERE YOU ARE, MY FINE-FEATHERED FLYING FELINE! RIGHT WHERE YOU SHOULD BE, IN A CAT CAGE! TOOK THE BAIT!
AND THERE YOU'LL STAY, TILL I GET HOLD OF YOUR LOATHSOME LADY LOVE! WON'T BE LONG!
IN YOUR *DREAMS!* SHE'S SMARTER THAN TO--
UEE-HEE! YOU WEREN'T RTER, IDIOT! I'LL CAGE TOO! THEN I'LL DECLAW DIGIT BY DIGIT. SHE'LL IN HIDEOUS PAIN! NEXT TASK MY RAT MINIONS WITH *EATING OUT HER EYES!*
NO! YOU WOULDN'T...
UNLESS YOU'D CARE TO DIVULGE THE GENETIC *SUPER-SPLICER* FORMULA? *NOW!*
IT'S A TRAP. IF HE GETS THAT FORMULA, HE'LL MORPH THE RATS INTO RAT-MEN, AND CATE WILL BE KILLED ANYWAY. NOT TO MENTION ALL OUR FRIENDS!
NO WAY, YOU REPELLENT *RODENT!*
AS YOU CHOOSE. IN THAT CASE, PREPARE TO HEAR CATE SCREECH. EYES--SO DELICIOUS! THINK I'LL HAVE SOME MYSELF!
AROORROWRR!

SO, MUROID'S OFFICE IS HERE...

AND THE DOOR TO THE DUNGEON IS HERE...

BUT THERE'S A GROUND-LEVEL ENTRANCE, HERE...

AND A TUNNEL FOR THE *DRAT*--IT GOES TO THE ROOFTOP-- HERE...

SO IF WE COULD GET TO THE ROOFTOP WE MIGHT BE ABLE TO USE THE *DRAT* TUNNEL TO GET DOWN TO THE DUNGEON?

MAYBE. MUROID WOULDN'T BE EXPECTING THAT.

THE ROOFTOP ENTRANCE MIGHT NOT BE HEAVILY GUARDED.

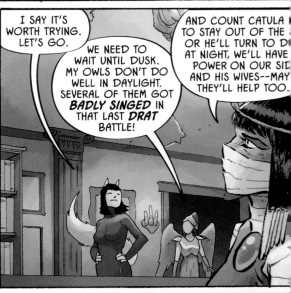

I SAY IT'S WORTH TRYING. LET'S GO.

WE NEED TO WAIT UNTIL DUSK. MY OWLS DON'T DO WELL IN DAYLIGHT. SEVERAL OF THEM GOT *BADLY SINGED* IN THAT LAST *DRAT* BATTLE!

AND COUNT CATULA TO STAY OUT OF THE OR HE'LL TURN TO D AT NIGHT, WE'LL HAVE POWER ON OUR SI AND HIS WIVES--MAY THEY'LL HELP TOO.

IT HAS TO BE NOW! EVERY MINUTE WE WAIT, TERRIBLE THINGS COULD BE HAPPENING TO ANGEL!

IF WE GO NOW, WE RISK *FAILURE!*

FINE. THEN I'LL TRY IT ALONE.

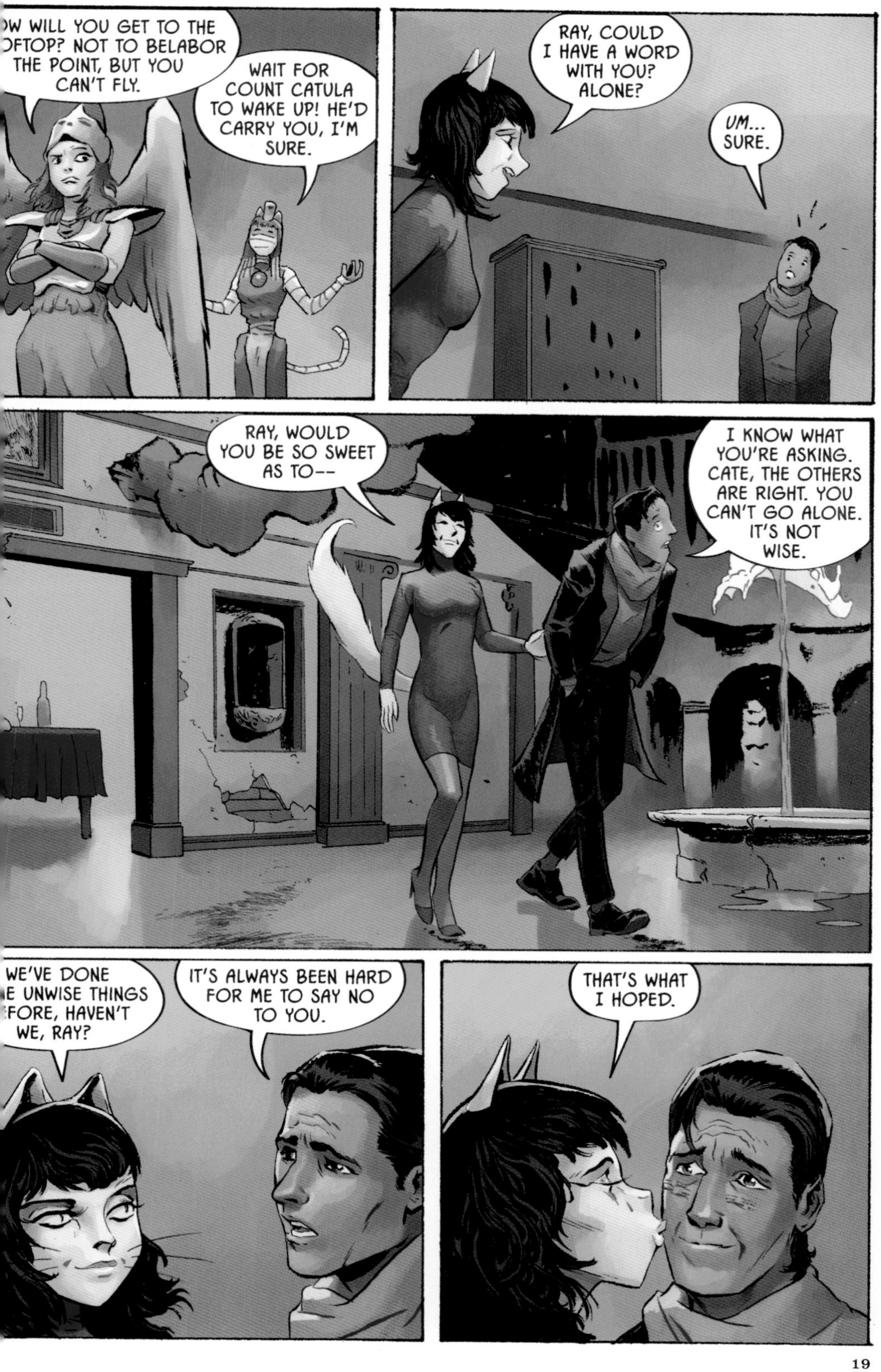

OW WILL YOU GET TO THE OFTOP? NOT TO BELABOR THE POINT, BUT YOU CAN'T FLY.
WAIT FOR COUNT CATULA TO WAKE UP! HE'D CARRY YOU, I'M SURE.
RAY, COULD I HAVE A WORD WITH YOU? ALONE?
UM... SURE.
RAY, WOULD YOU BE SO SWEET AS TO--
I KNOW WHAT YOU'RE ASKING. CATE, THE OTHERS ARE RIGHT. YOU CAN'T GO ALONE. IT'S NOT WISE.
WE'VE DONE E UNWISE THINGS FORE, HAVEN'T WE, RAY?
IT'S ALWAYS BEEN HARD FOR ME TO SAY NO TO YOU.
THAT'S WHAT I HOPED.

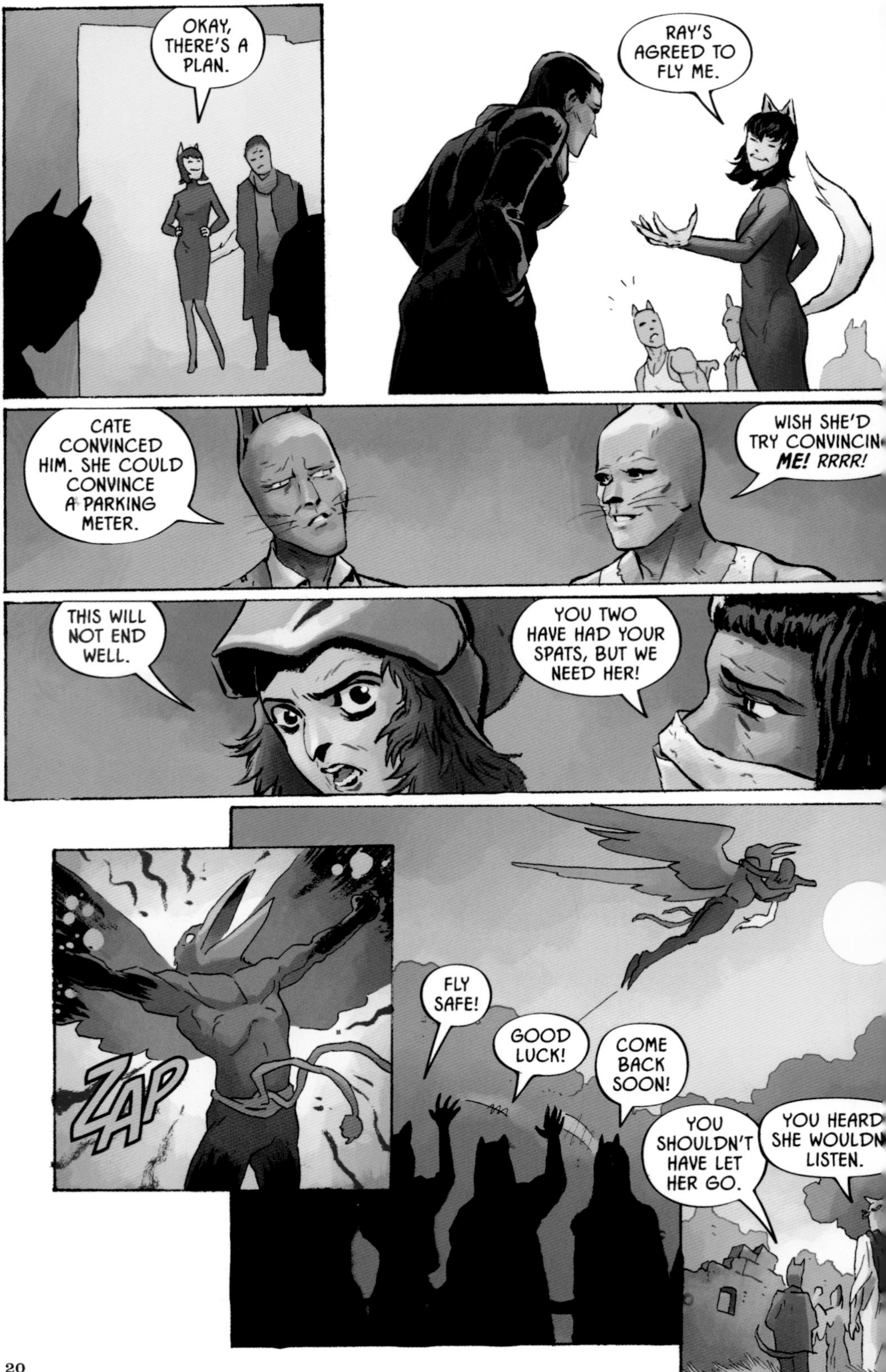
OKAY, THERE'S A PLAN.
RAY'S AGREED TO FLY ME.
CATE CONVINCED HIM. SHE COULD CONVINCE A PARKING METER.
WISH SHE'D TRY CONVINCIN ME! RRRR!
THIS WILL NOT END WELL.
YOU TWO HAVE HAD YOUR SPATS, BUT WE NEED HER!
ZAP
FLY SAFE!
GOOD LUCK!
COME BACK SOON!
YOU SHOULDN'T HAVE LET HER GO.
YOU HEARD SHE WOULDN LISTEN.

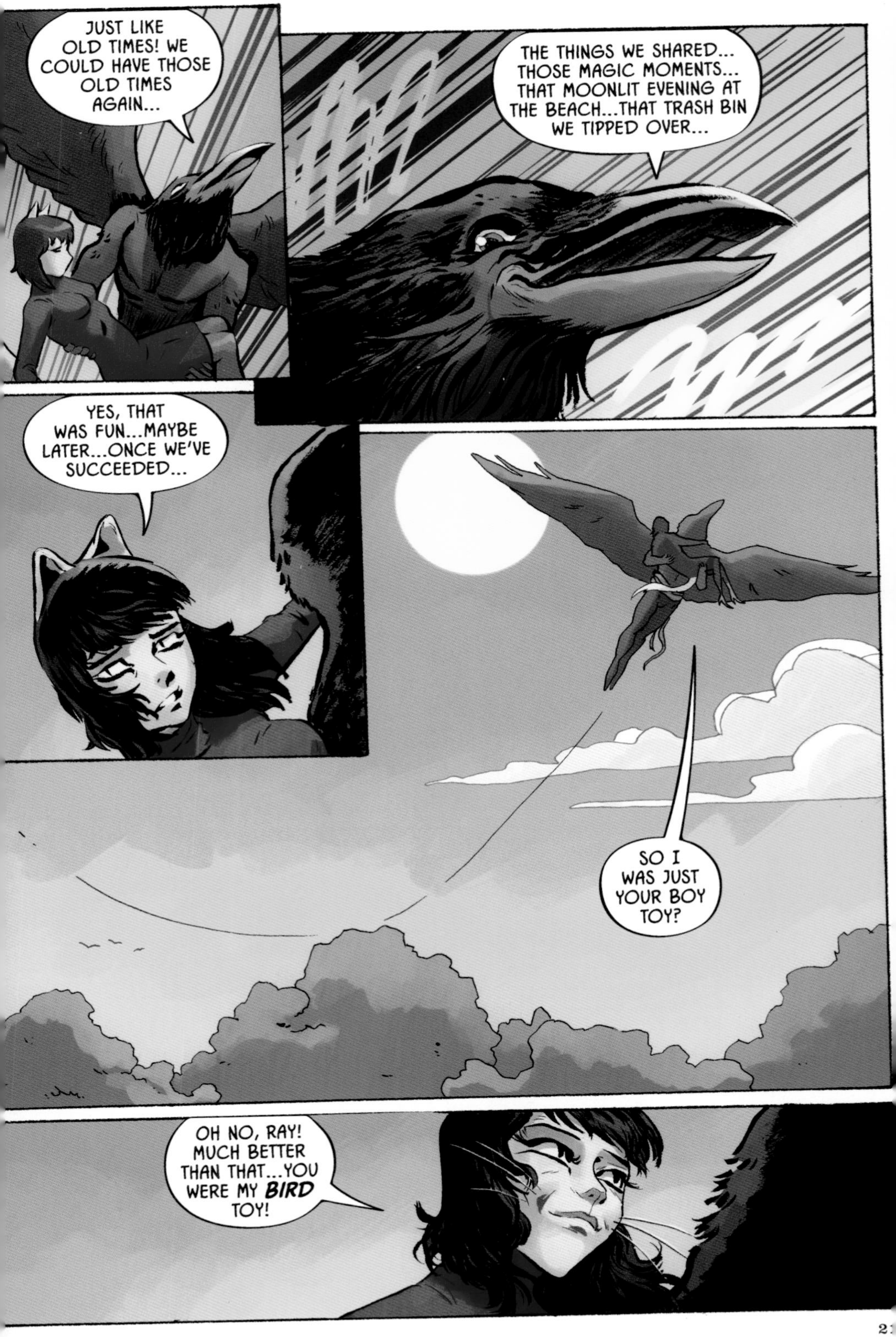
JUST LIKE OLD TIMES! WE COULD HAVE THOSE OLD TIMES AGAIN...
THE THINGS WE SHARED... THOSE MAGIC MOMENTS... THAT MOONLIT EVENING AT THE BEACH...THAT TRASH BIN WE TIPPED OVER...
YES, THAT WAS FUN...MAYBE LATER...ONCE WE'VE SUCCEEDED...
SO I WAS JUST YOUR BOY TOY?
OH NO, RAY! MUCH BETTER THAN THAT...YOU WERE MY **BIRD** TOY!

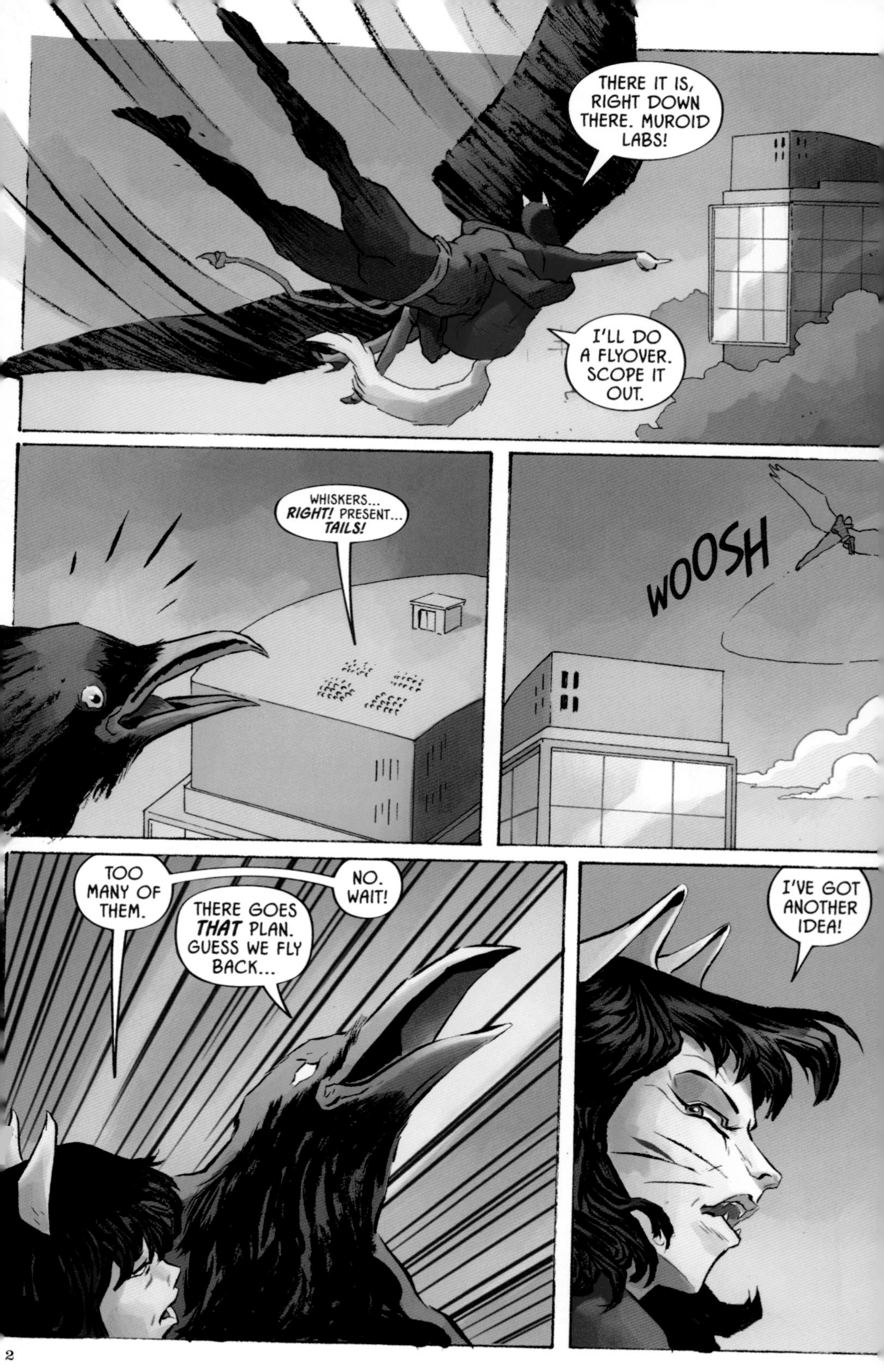
THERE IT IS, RIGHT DOWN THERE. MUROID LABS!
I'LL DO A FLYOVER. SCOPE IT OUT.
WHISKERS... **RIGHT!** PRESENT... **TAILS!**
WOOSH
TOO MANY OF THEM.
NO. WAIT!
THERE GOES **THAT** PLAN. GUESS WE FLY BACK...
I'VE GOT ANOTHER IDEA!

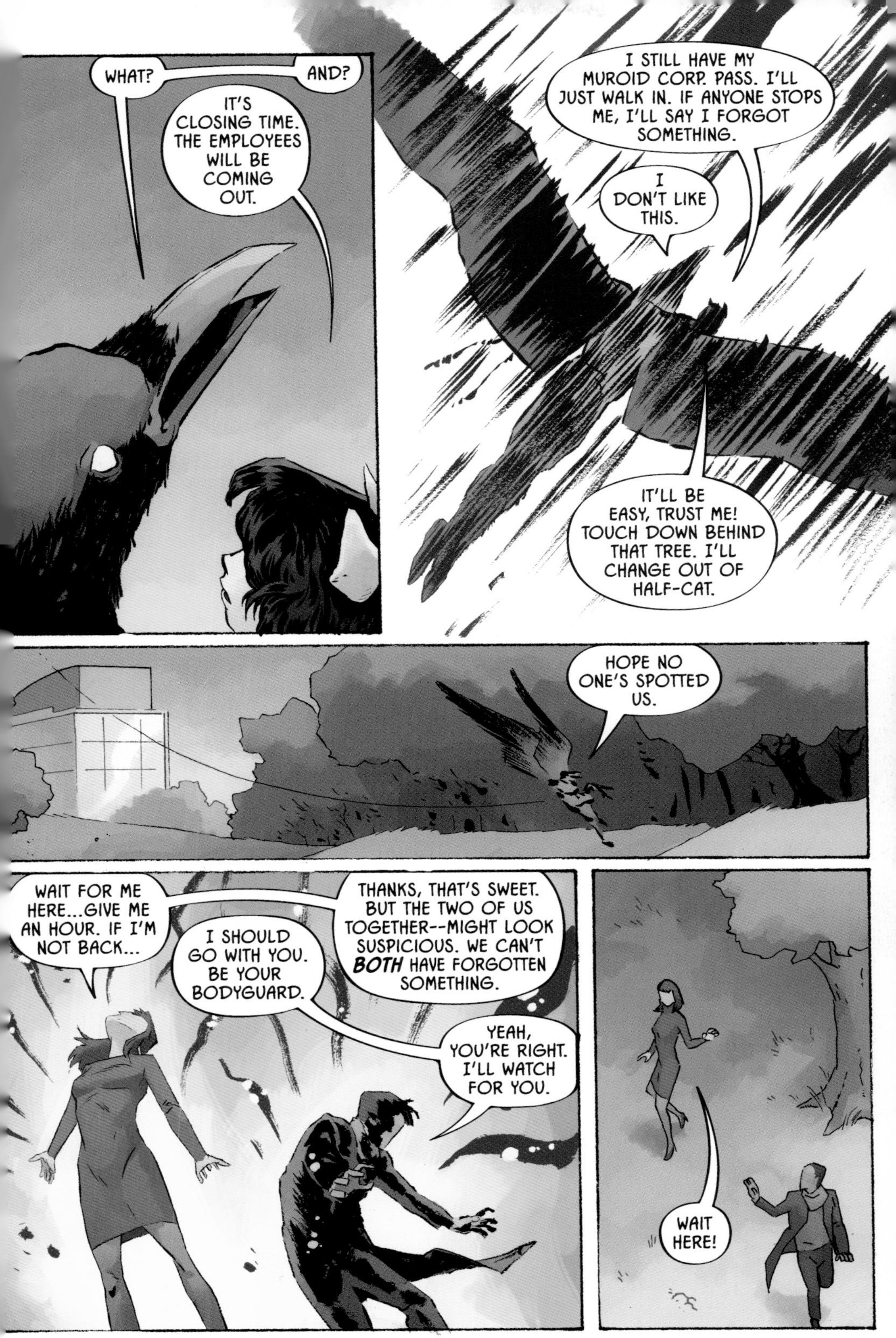
WHAT?
AND?
IT'S CLOSING TIME. THE EMPLOYEES WILL BE COMING OUT.
I STILL HAVE MY MUROID CORP. PASS. I'LL JUST WALK IN. IF ANYONE STOPS ME, I'LL SAY I FORGOT SOMETHING.
I DON'T LIKE THIS.
IT'LL BE EASY, TRUST ME! TOUCH DOWN BEHIND THAT TREE. I'LL CHANGE OUT OF HALF-CAT.
HOPE NO ONE'S SPOTTED US.
WAIT FOR ME HERE...GIVE ME AN HOUR. IF I'M NOT BACK...
I SHOULD GO WITH YOU. BE YOUR BODYGUARD.
THANKS, THAT'S SWEET. BUT THE TWO OF US TOGETHER--MIGHT LOOK SUSPICIOUS. WE CAN'T BOTH HAVE FORGOTTEN SOMETHING.
YEAH, YOU'RE RIGHT. I'LL WATCH FOR YOU.
WAIT HERE!

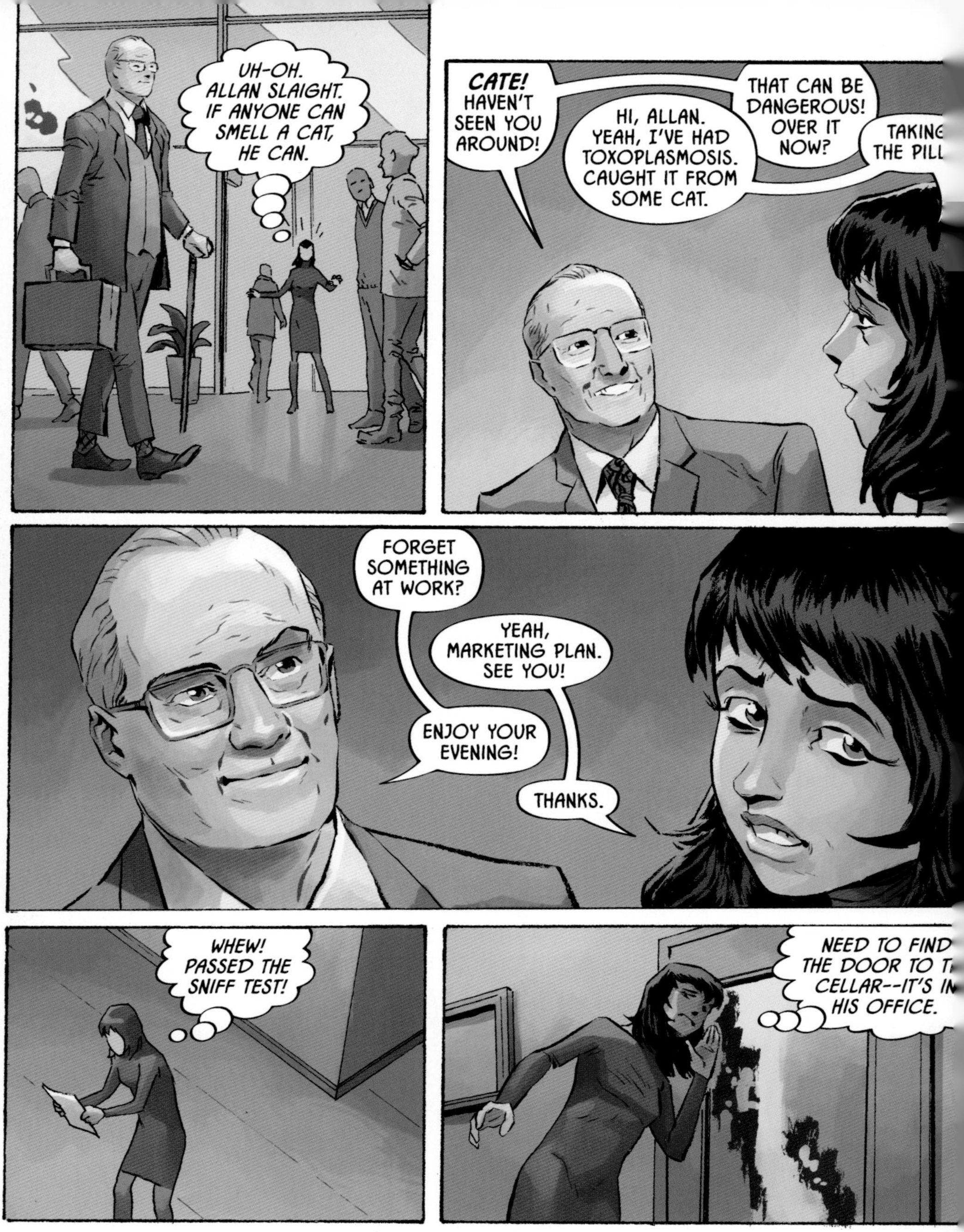

UH-OH. ALLAN SLAIGHT. IF ANYONE CAN SMELL A CAT, HE CAN.
CATE! HAVEN'T SEEN YOU AROUND!
HI, ALLAN. YEAH, I'VE HAD TOXOPLASMOSIS. CAUGHT IT FROM SOME CAT.
THAT CAN BE DANGEROUS! OVER IT NOW?
TAKING THE PILL
FORGET SOMETHING AT WORK?
YEAH, MARKETING PLAN. SEE YOU!
ENJOY YOUR EVENING!
THANKS.
WHEW! PASSED THE SNIFF TEST!
NEED TO FIND THE DOOR TO T CELLAR--IT'S IN HIS OFFICE.

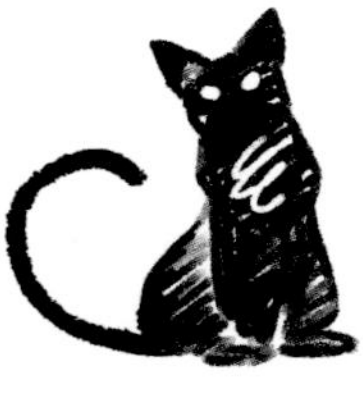

TOXOPLASMOSIS

Toxoplasma gondii is a parasite carried by cats. It has no effect on most people but can cause problems for those with weak immune systems, especially unborn babies. Keeping your cat indoors and changing the litter daily are two of the best ways to avoid infection. Read more at www.catsandbirds.ca

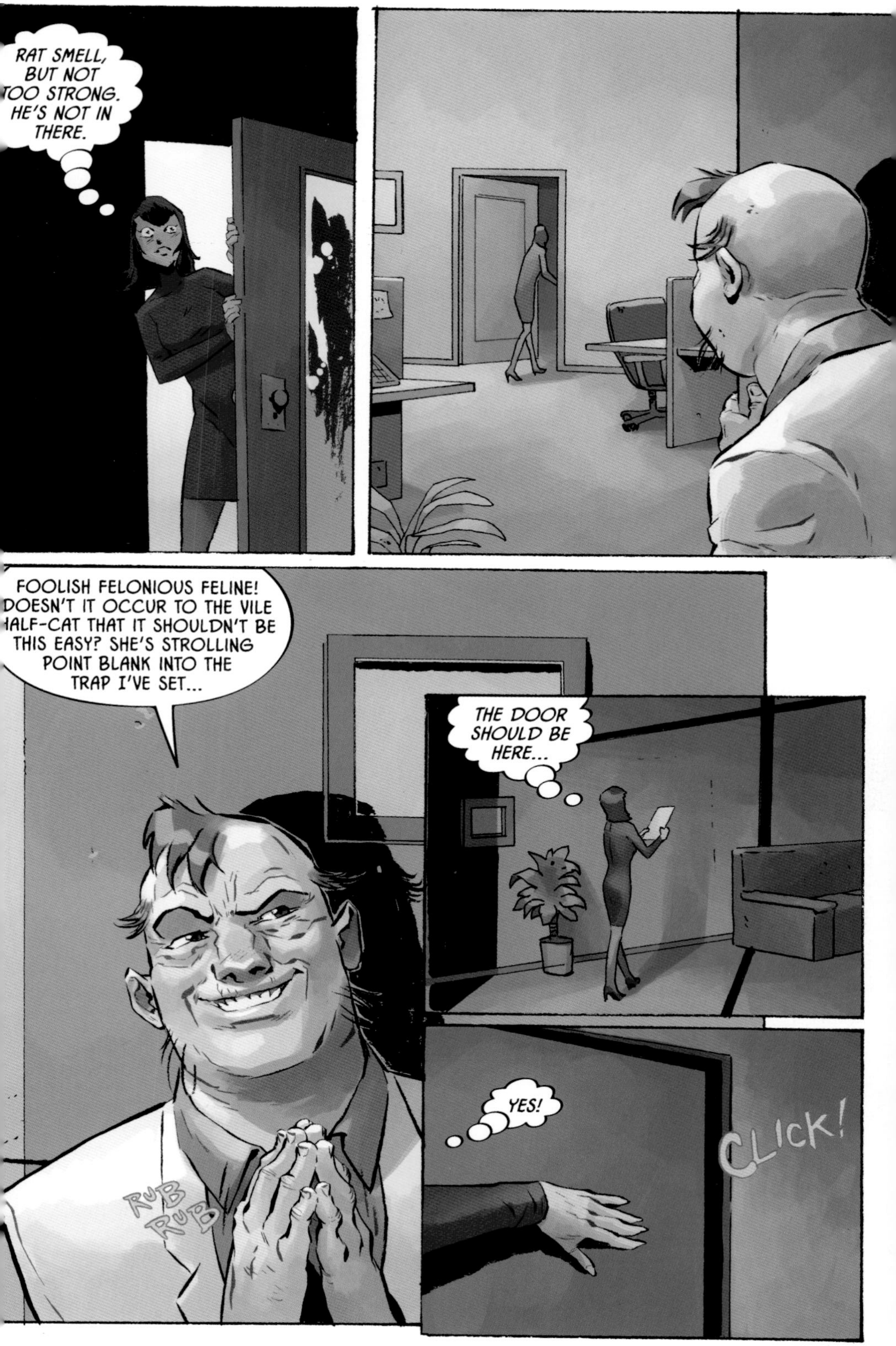
RAT SMELL, BUT NOT TOO STRONG. HE'S NOT IN THERE.
FOOLISH FELONIOUS FELINE! DOESN'T IT OCCUR TO THE VILE HALF-CAT THAT IT SHOULDN'T BE THIS EASY? SHE'S STROLLING POINT BLANK INTO THE TRAP I'VE SET...
RUB RUB
THE DOOR SHOULD BE HERE...
YES!
CLICK!

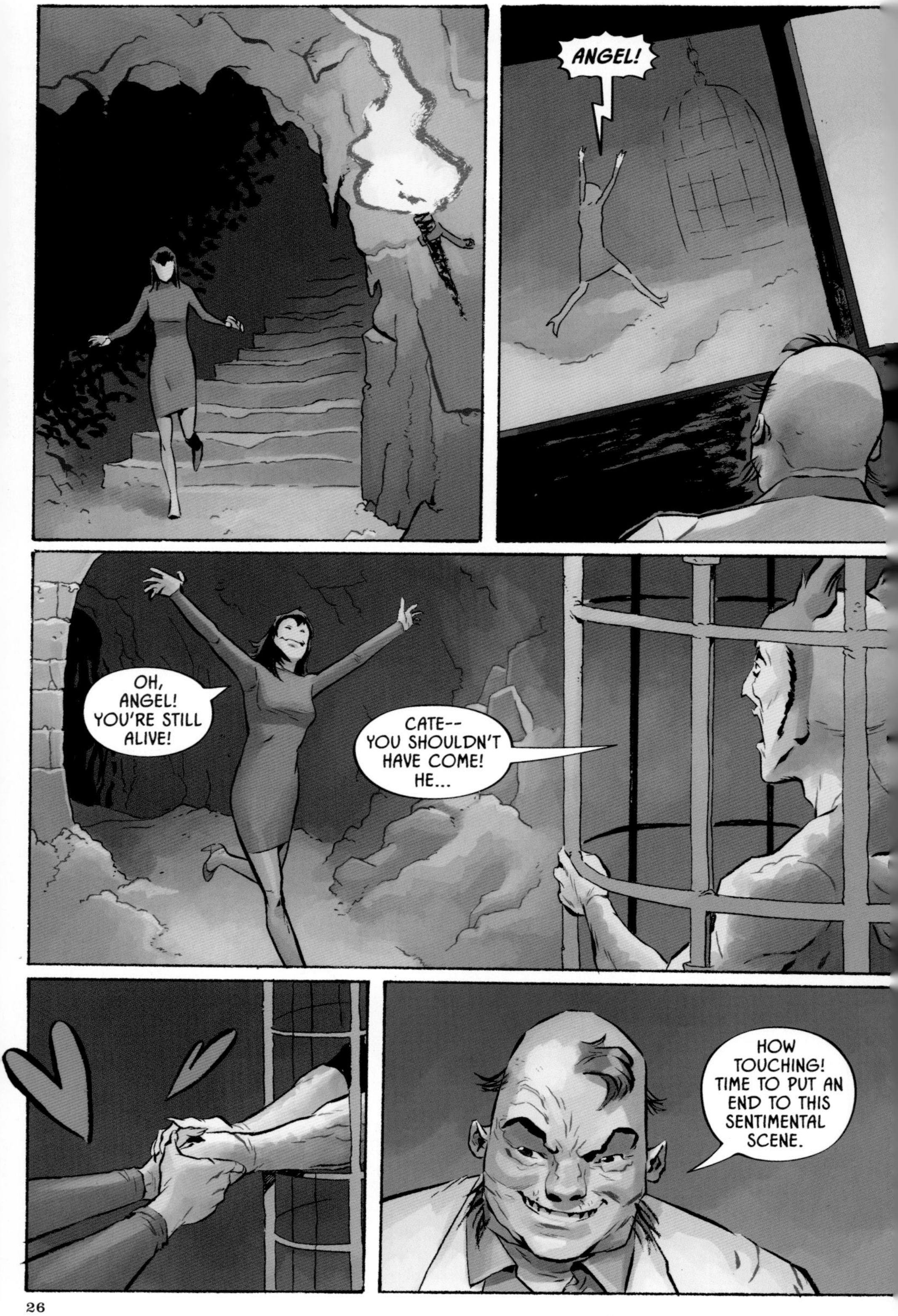
ANGEL!
OH, ANGEL! YOU'RE STILL ALIVE!
CATE-- YOU SHOULDN'T HAVE COME! HE...
HOW TOUCHING! TIME TO PUT AN END TO THIS SENTIMENTAL SCENE.

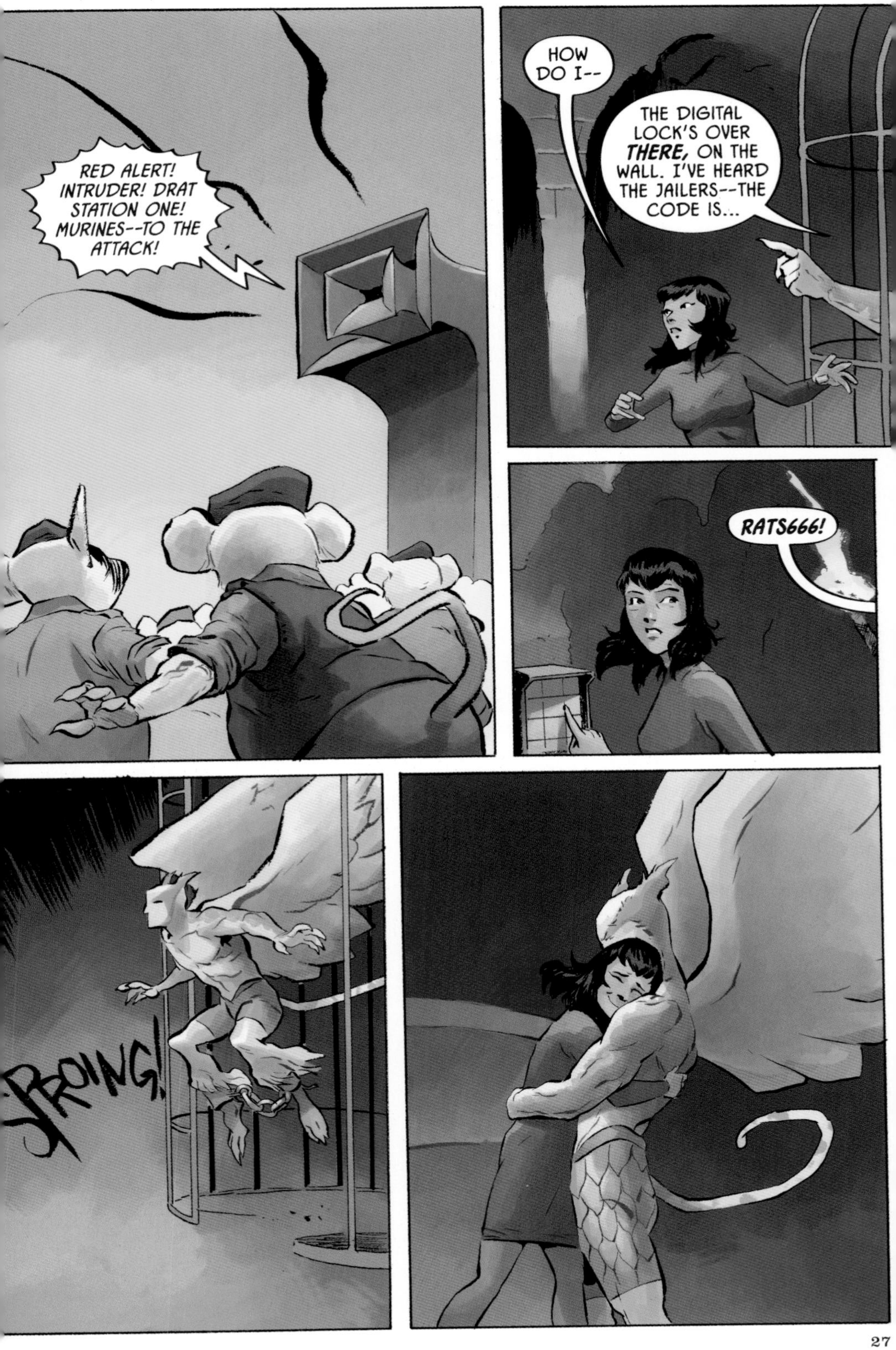
RED ALERT! INTRUDER! DRAT STATION ONE! MURINES--TO THE ATTACK!
HOW DO I--
THE DIGITAL LOCK'S OVER THERE, ON THE WALL. I'VE HEARD THE JAILERS--THE CODE IS...
RATS666!
SPROING!

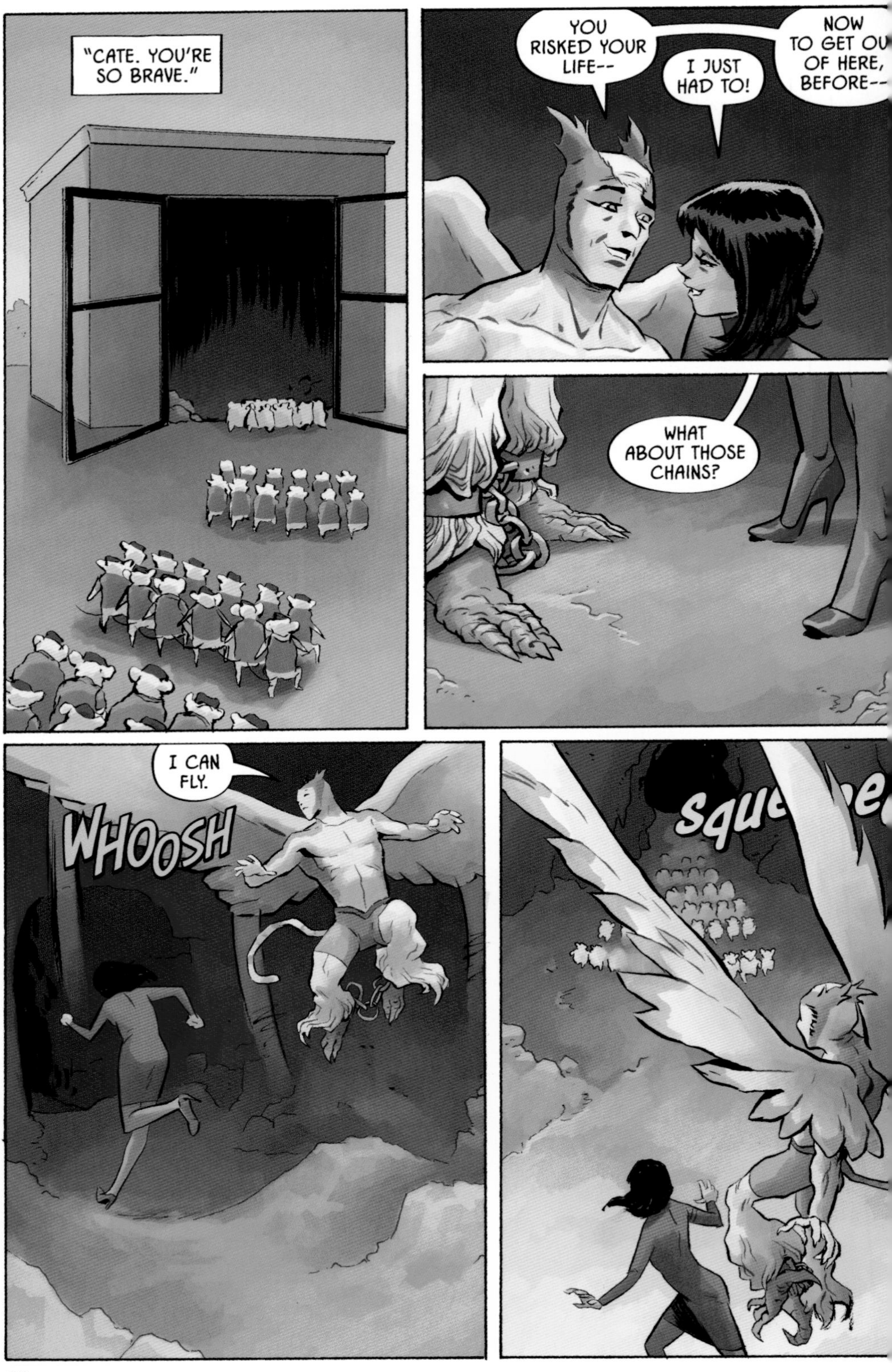
"CATE. YOU'RE SO BRAVE."
YOU RISKED YOUR LIFE--
I JUST HAD TO!
NOW TO GET OU OF HERE, BEFORE--
WHAT ABOUT THOSE CHAINS?
I CAN FLY.
WHOOSH

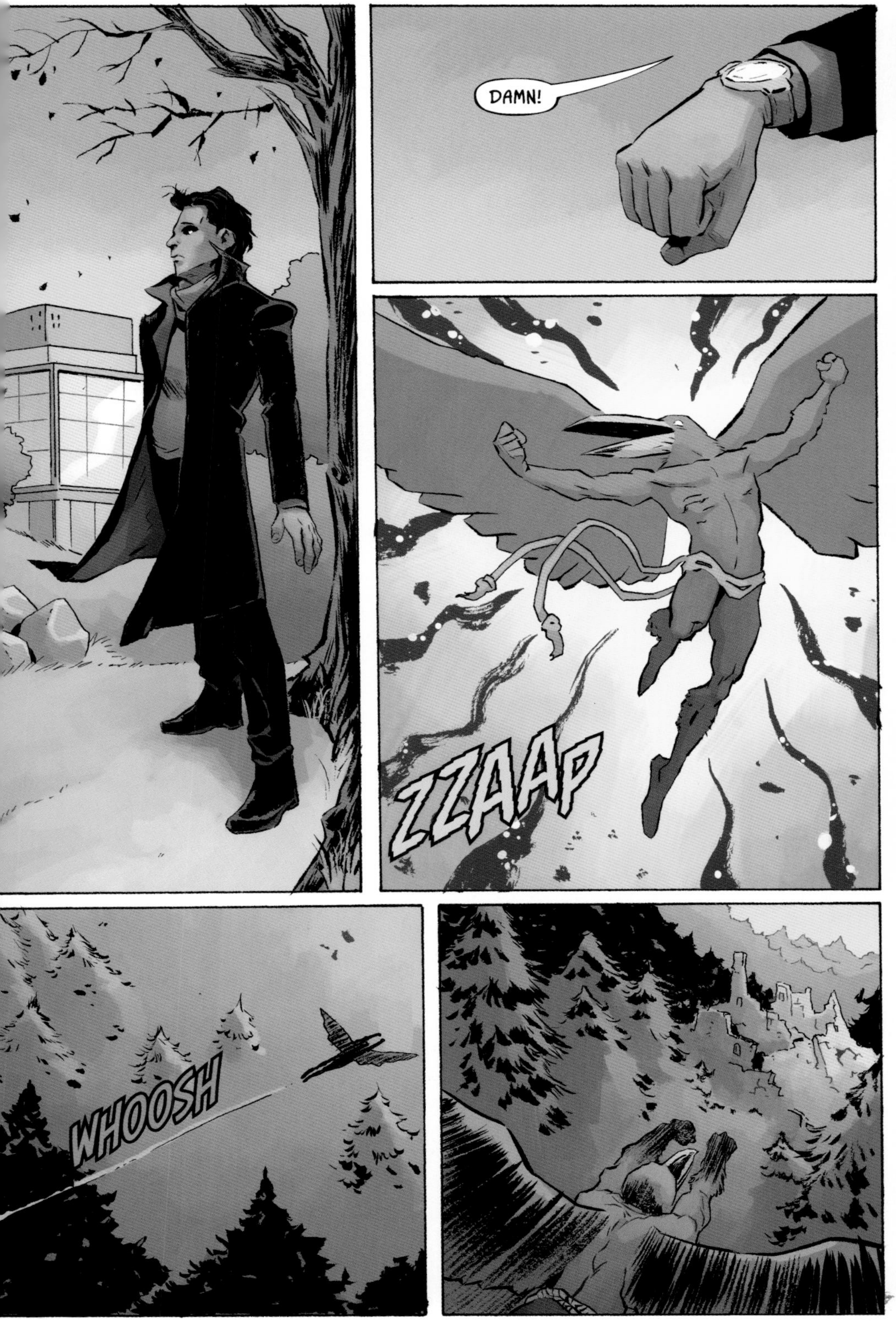
DAMN!
ZZAAP
WHOOSH

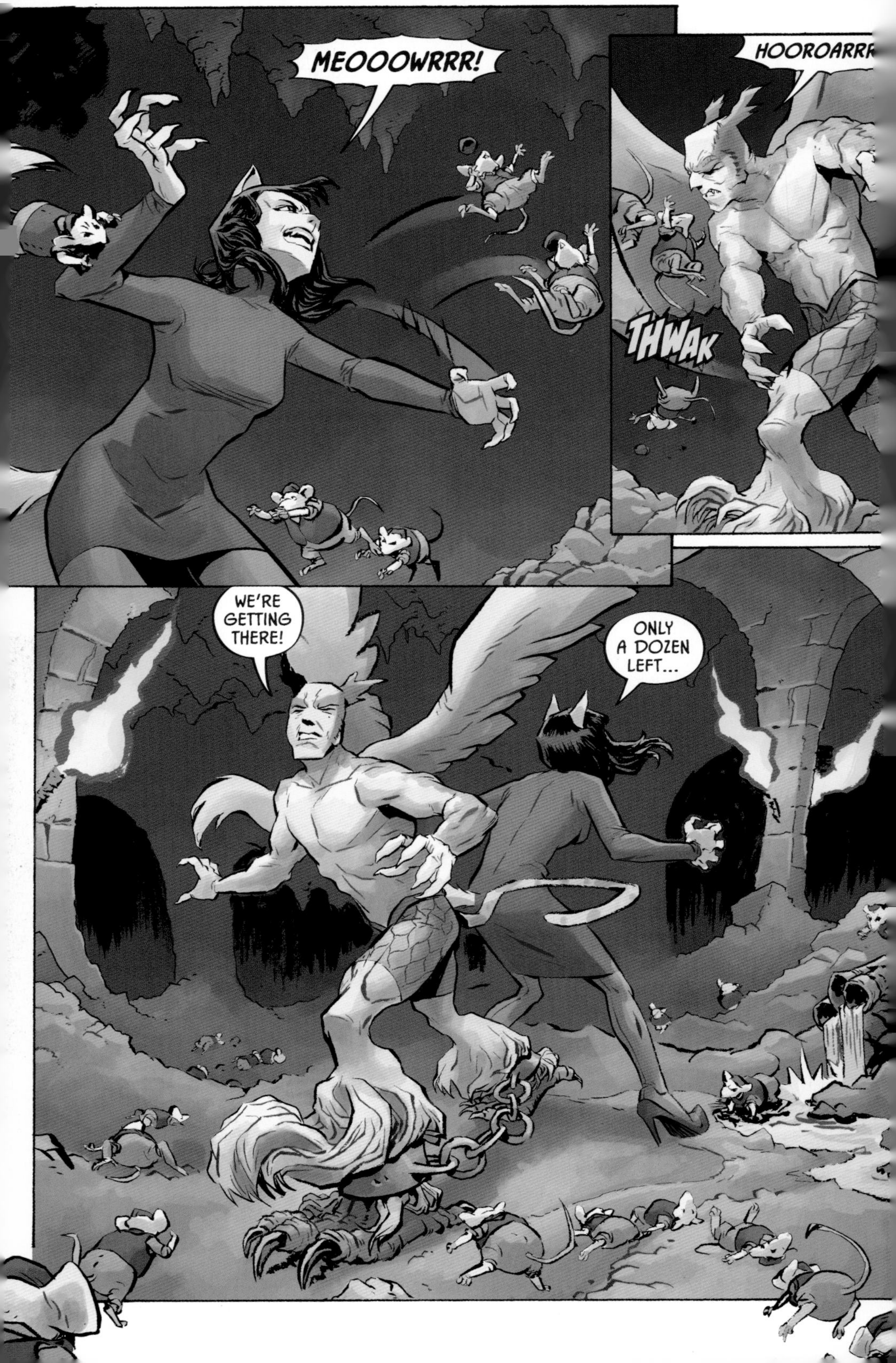
MEOOOWRRR!
HOOROARRR
THWAK
WE'RE GETTING THERE!
ONLY A DOZEN LEFT...

CAT CARNAGE! BUT NOT FOR *LONG!*

RELEASE THE *SPRAY!* ESSENCE OF CATNIP! THEY'LL PASS OUT FROM BLISS! VILE STUFF! *YUCK!* BUT NO EFFECT ON RATS...

SSSSSS

SSSSSS SSSSS

WHAT...

I FEEL...

CLUNK

CATNIP

Catnip is a great way to keep your cat stimulated. You can use it in toys or just sprinkle it around occasionally. Cat grass is another great way to bring a little of the outdoors inside. Read more at www.catsandbirds.ca

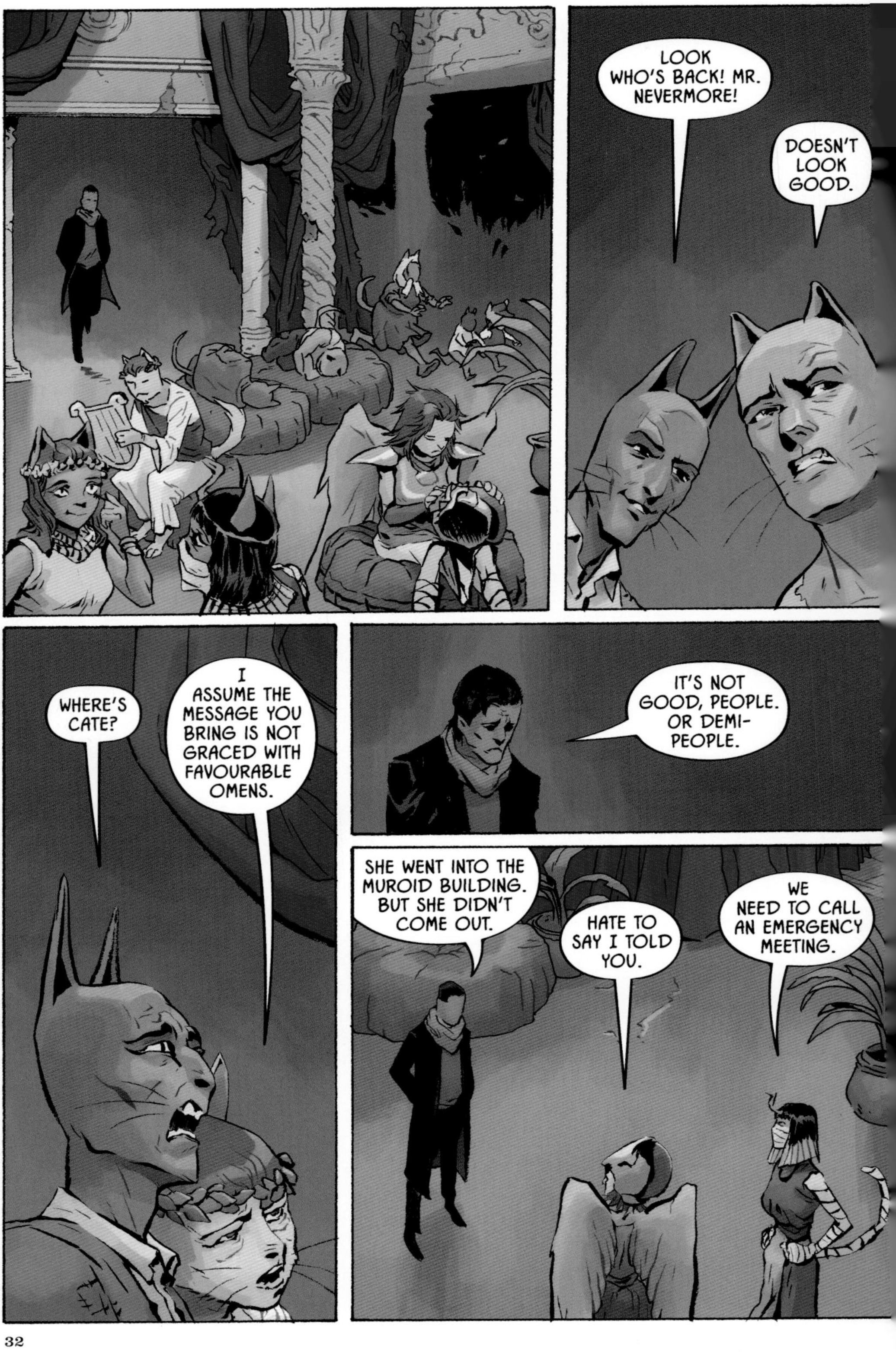
LOOK WHO'S BACK! MR. NEVERMORE!
DOESN'T LOOK GOOD.
WHERE'S CATE?
I ASSUME THE MESSAGE YOU BRING IS NOT GRACED WITH FAVOURABLE OMENS.
IT'S NOT GOOD, PEOPLE. OR DEMI-PEOPLE.
SHE WENT INTO THE MUROID BUILDING. BUT SHE DIDN'T COME OUT.
HATE TO SAY I TOLD YOU.
WE NEED TO CALL AN EMERGENCY MEETING.

CALL THE
STRINGERS!

NTO THE
GES WITH
HEM!"

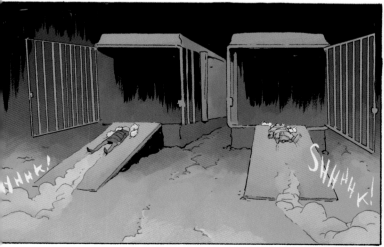

SHHHK!

SHHHHK!

CLANG!

33

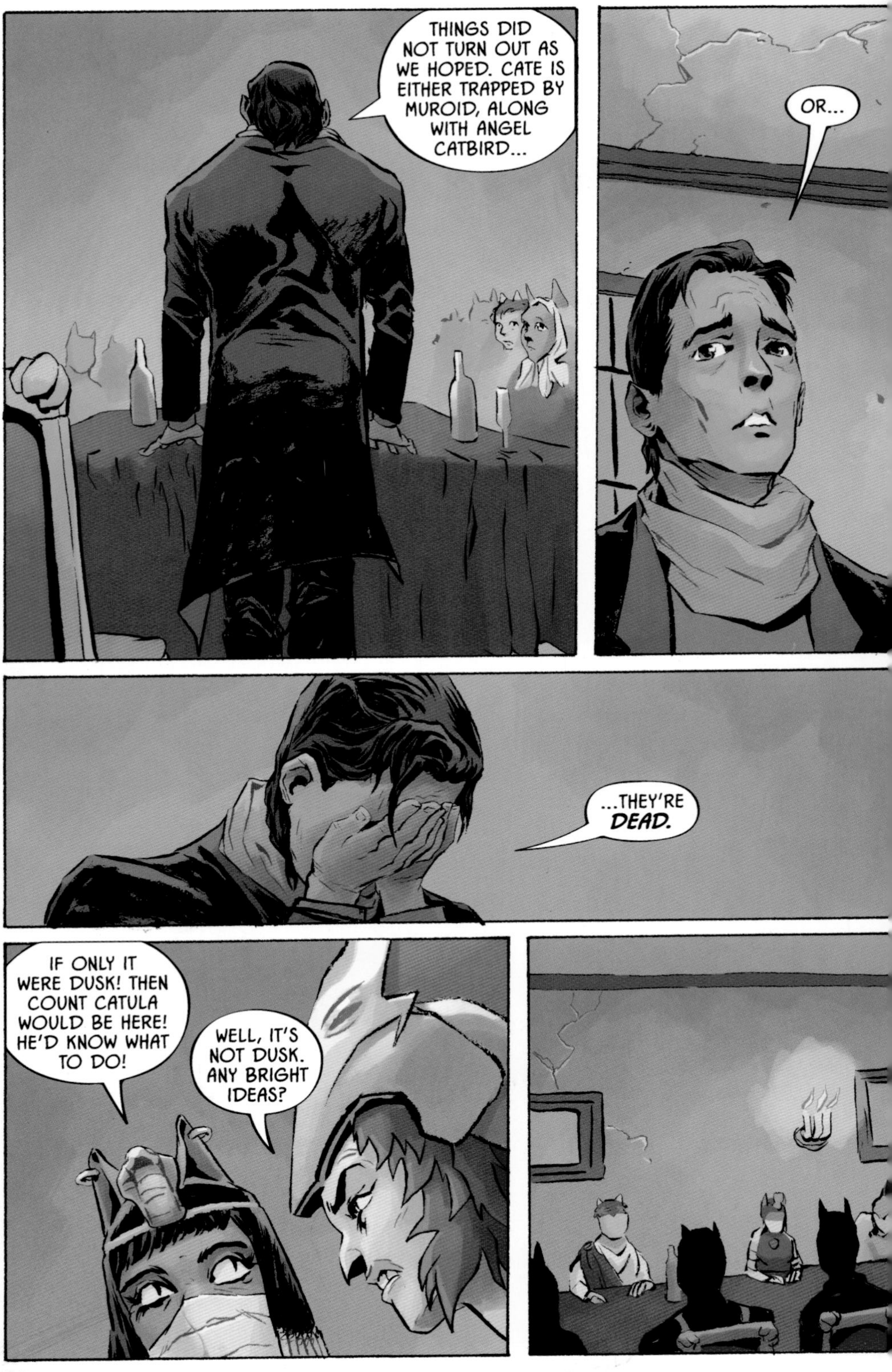
THINGS DID NOT TURN OUT AS WE HOPED. CATE IS EITHER TRAPPED BY MUROID, ALONG WITH ANGEL CATBIRD...
OR...
...THEY'RE *DEAD.*
IF ONLY IT WERE DUSK! THEN COUNT CATULA WOULD BE HERE! HE'D KNOW WHAT TO DO!
WELL, IT'S NOT DUSK. ANY BRIGHT IDEAS?

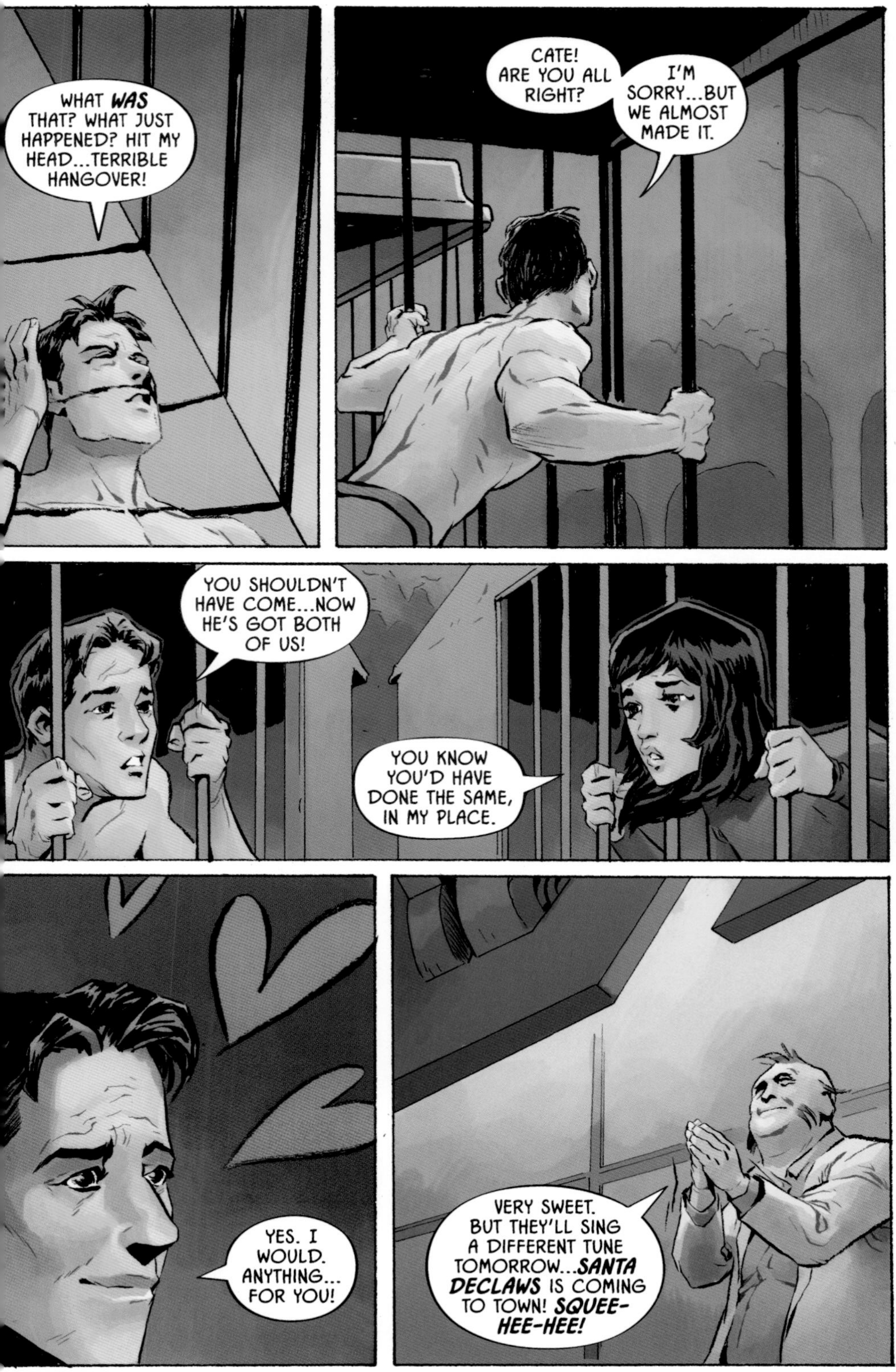
WHAT WAS THAT? WHAT JUST HAPPENED? HIT MY HEAD...TERRIBLE HANGOVER!
CATE! ARE YOU ALL RIGHT?
I'M SORRY...BUT WE ALMOST MADE IT.
YOU SHOULDN'T HAVE COME...NOW HE'S GOT BOTH OF US!
YOU KNOW YOU'D HAVE DONE THE SAME, IN MY PLACE.
YES. I WOULD. ANYTHING... FOR YOU!
VERY SWEET. BUT THEY'LL SING A DIFFERENT TUNE TOMORROW...SANTA DECLAWS IS COMING TO TOWN! SQUEE-HEE-HEE!

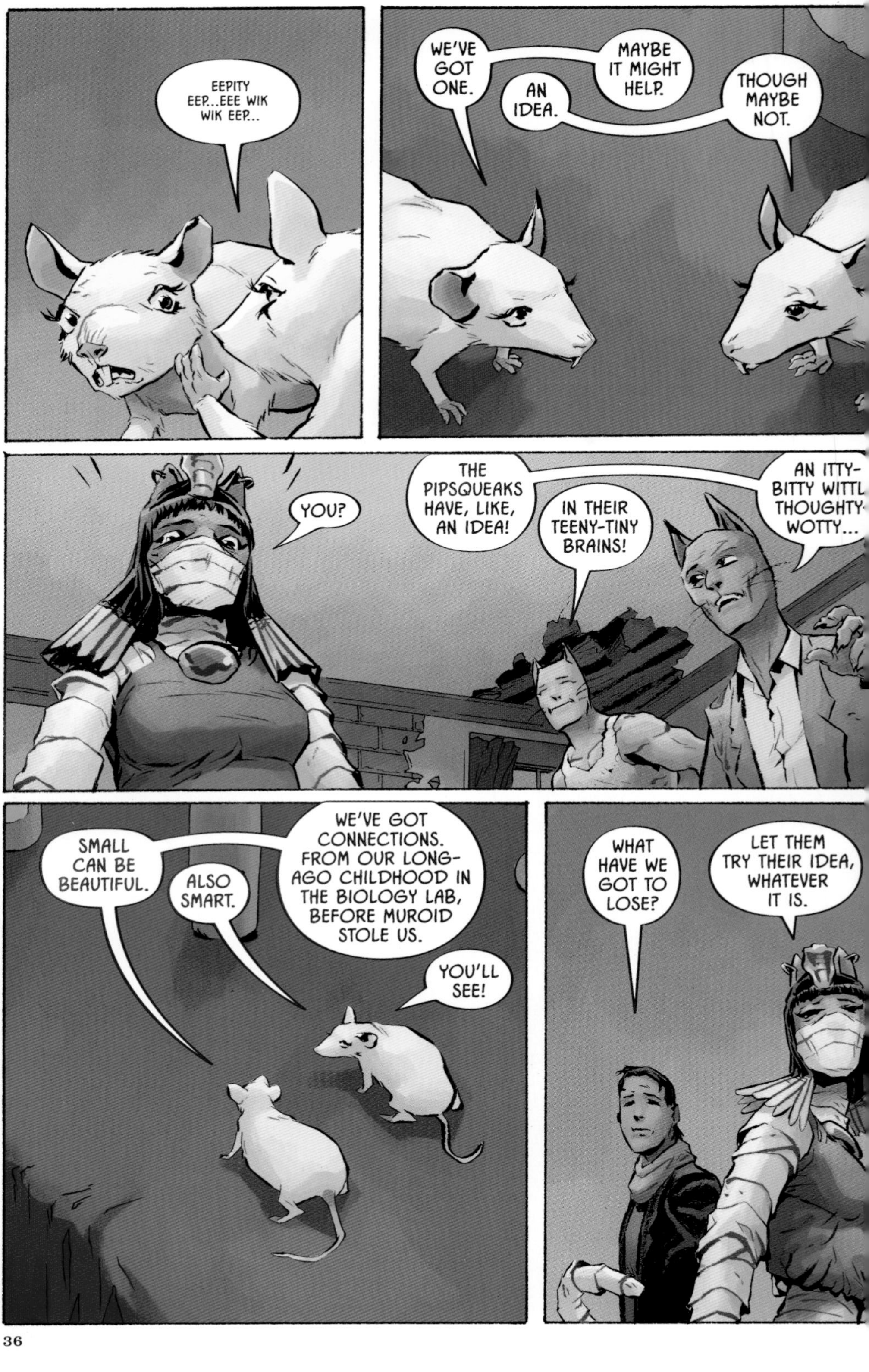
EEPITY EEP...EEE WIK WIK EEP...
WE'VE GOT ONE.
MAYBE IT MIGHT HELP.
AN IDEA.
THOUGH MAYBE NOT.
YOU?
THE PIPSQUEAKS HAVE, LIKE, AN IDEA!
IN THEIR TEENY-TINY BRAINS!
AN ITTY-BITTY WITTL THOUGHTY-WOTTY...
SMALL CAN BE BEAUTIFUL.
ALSO SMART.
WE'VE GOT CONNECTIONS. FROM OUR LONG-AGO CHILDHOOD IN THE BIOLOGY LAB, BEFORE MUROID STOLE US.
YOU'LL SEE!
WHAT HAVE WE GOT TO LOSE?
LET THEM TRY THEIR IDEA, WHATEVER IT IS.

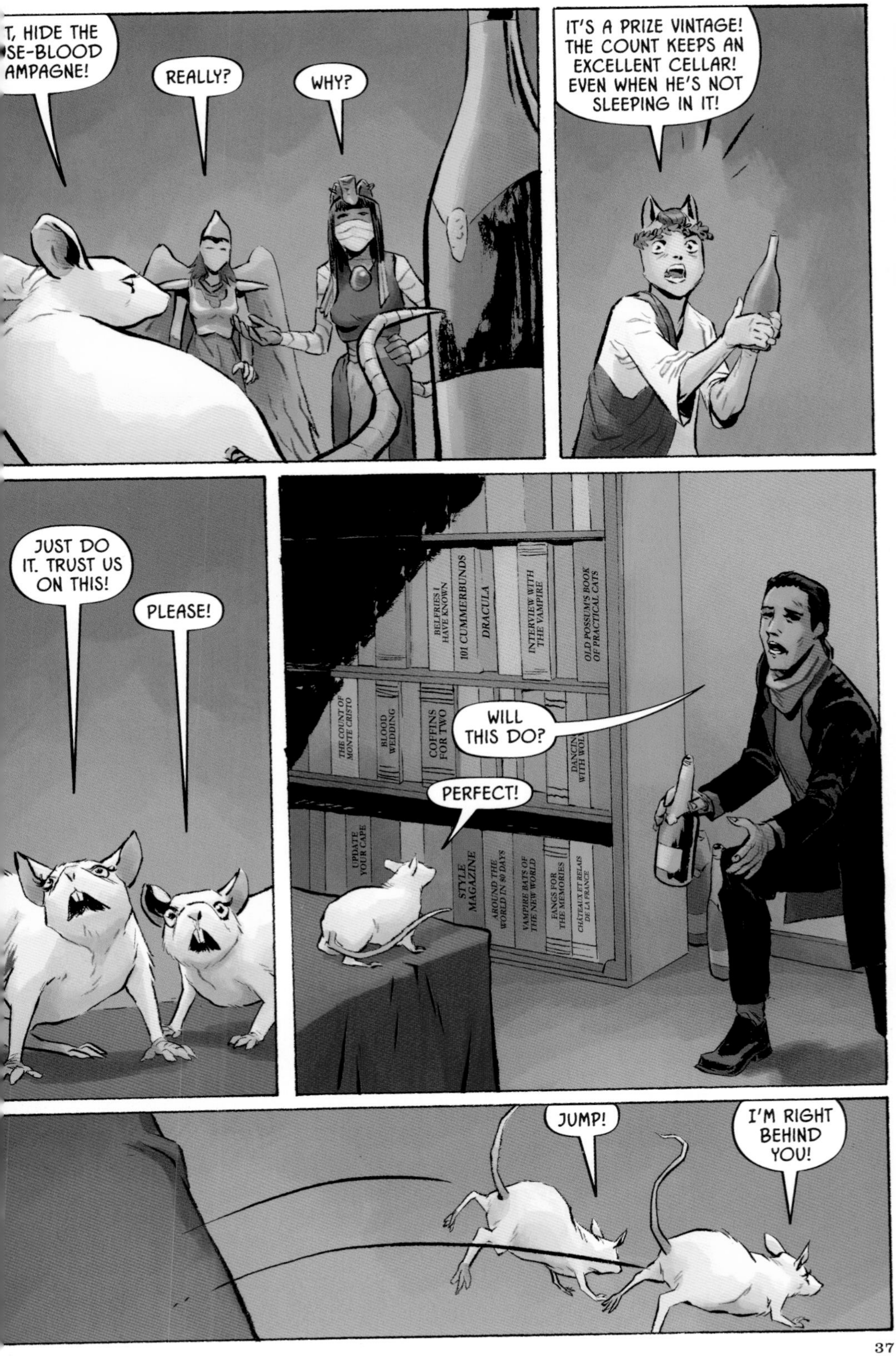
T, HIDE THE SE-BLOOD AMPAGNE!
REALLY?
WHY?
IT'S A PRIZE VINTAGE! THE COUNT KEEPS AN EXCELLENT CELLAR! EVEN WHEN HE'S NOT SLEEPING IN IT!
JUST DO IT. TRUST US ON THIS!
PLEASE!
BELFRIES I HAVE KNOWN
101 CUMMERBUNDS
DRACULA
INTERVIEW WITH THE VAMPIRE
OLD POSSUM'S BOOK OF PRACTICAL CATS
THE COUNT OF MONTE CRISTO
BLOOD WEDDING
COFFINS FOR TWO
UPDATE YOUR CAPE
STYLE MAGAZINE
AROUND THE WORLD IN 80 DAYS
VAMPIRE BATS OF THE NEW WORLD
FANGS FOR THE MEMORIES
CHÂTEAUX ET RELAIS DE LA FRANCE
WILL THIS DO?
PERFECT!
JUMP!
I'M RIGHT BEHIND YOU!

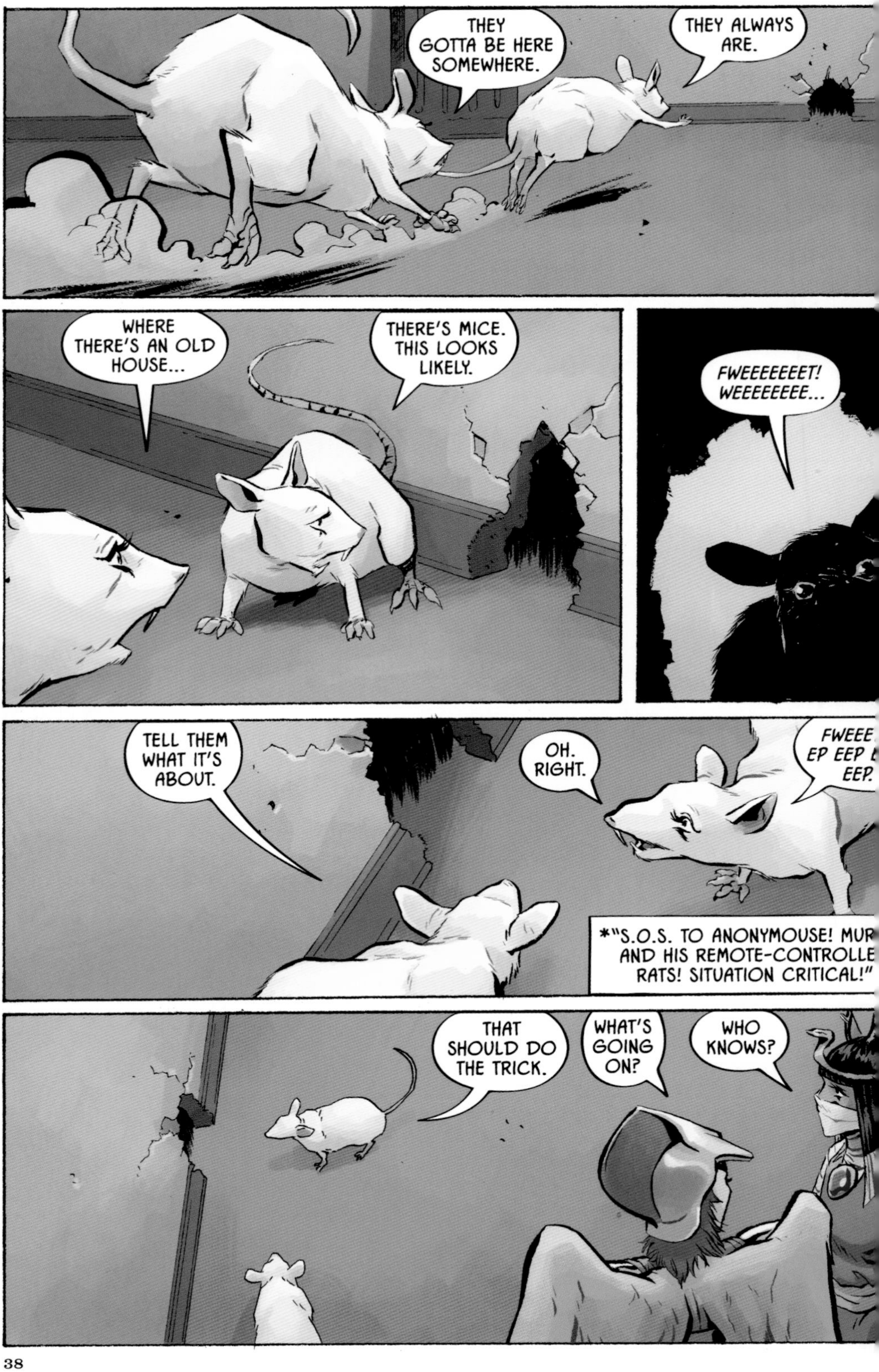
THEY GOTTA BE HERE SOMEWHERE.
THEY ALWAYS ARE.
WHERE THERE'S AN OLD HOUSE...
THERE'S MICE. THIS LOOKS LIKELY.
FWEEEEEEET! WEEEEEEEE...
TELL THEM WHAT IT'S ABOUT.
OH. RIGHT.
*"S.O.S. TO ANONYMOUSE! MUR
AND HIS REMOTE-CONTROLLE
RATS! SITUATION CRITICAL!"
THAT SHOULD DO THE TRICK.
WHAT'S GOING ON?
WHO KNOWS?

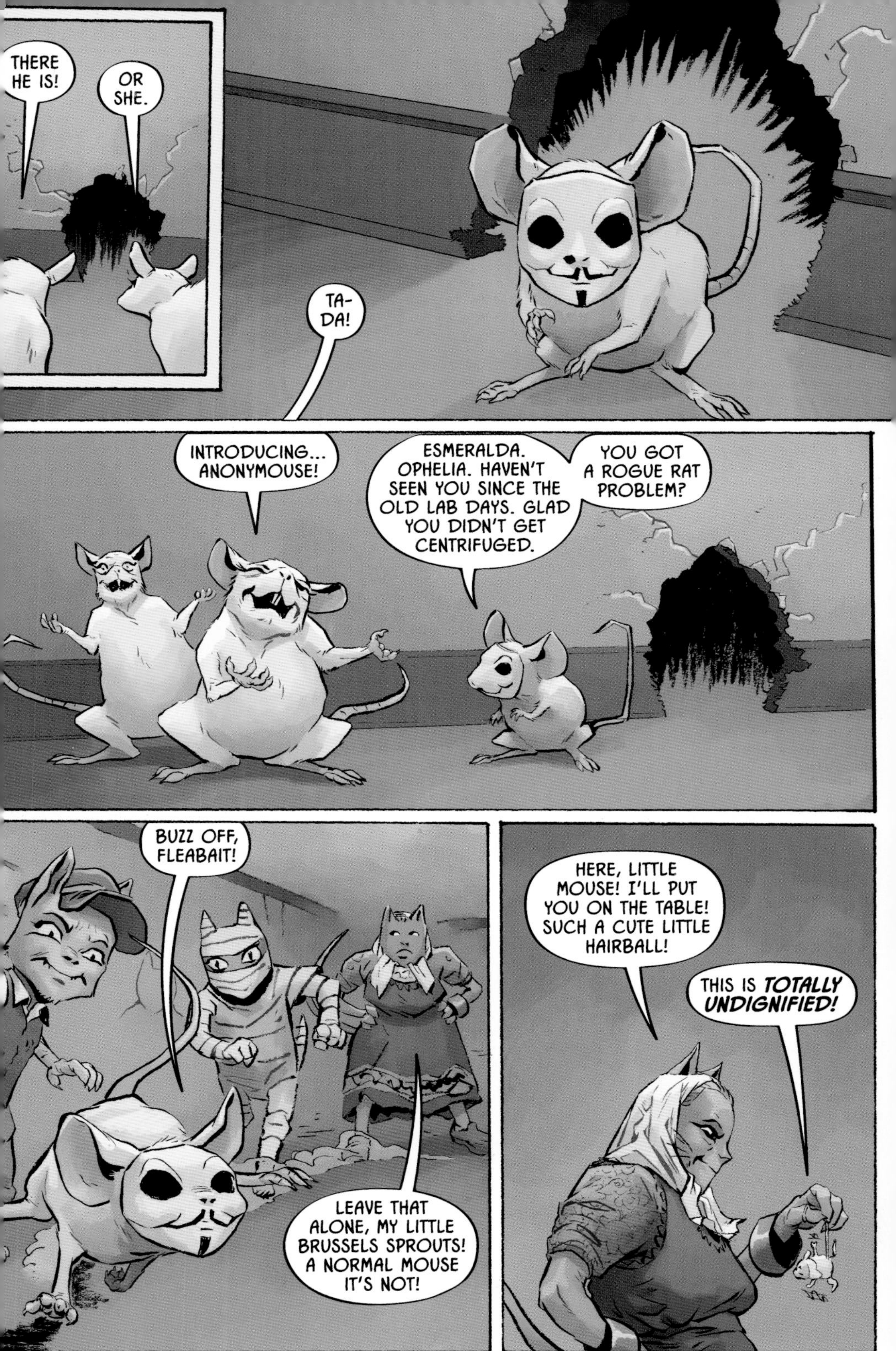
THERE HE IS!
OR SHE.
TA-DA!
INTRODUCING... ANONYMOUSE!
ESMERALDA. OPHELIA. HAVEN'T SEEN YOU SINCE THE OLD LAB DAYS. GLAD YOU DIDN'T GET CENTRIFUGED.
YOU GOT A ROGUE RAT PROBLEM?
BUZZ OFF, FLEABAIT!
LEAVE THAT ALONE, MY LITTLE BRUSSELS SPROUTS! A NORMAL MOUSE IT'S NOT!
HERE, LITTLE MOUSE! I'LL PUT YOU ON THE TABLE! SUCH A CUTE LITTLE HAIRBALL!
THIS IS TOTALLY UNDIGNIFIED!

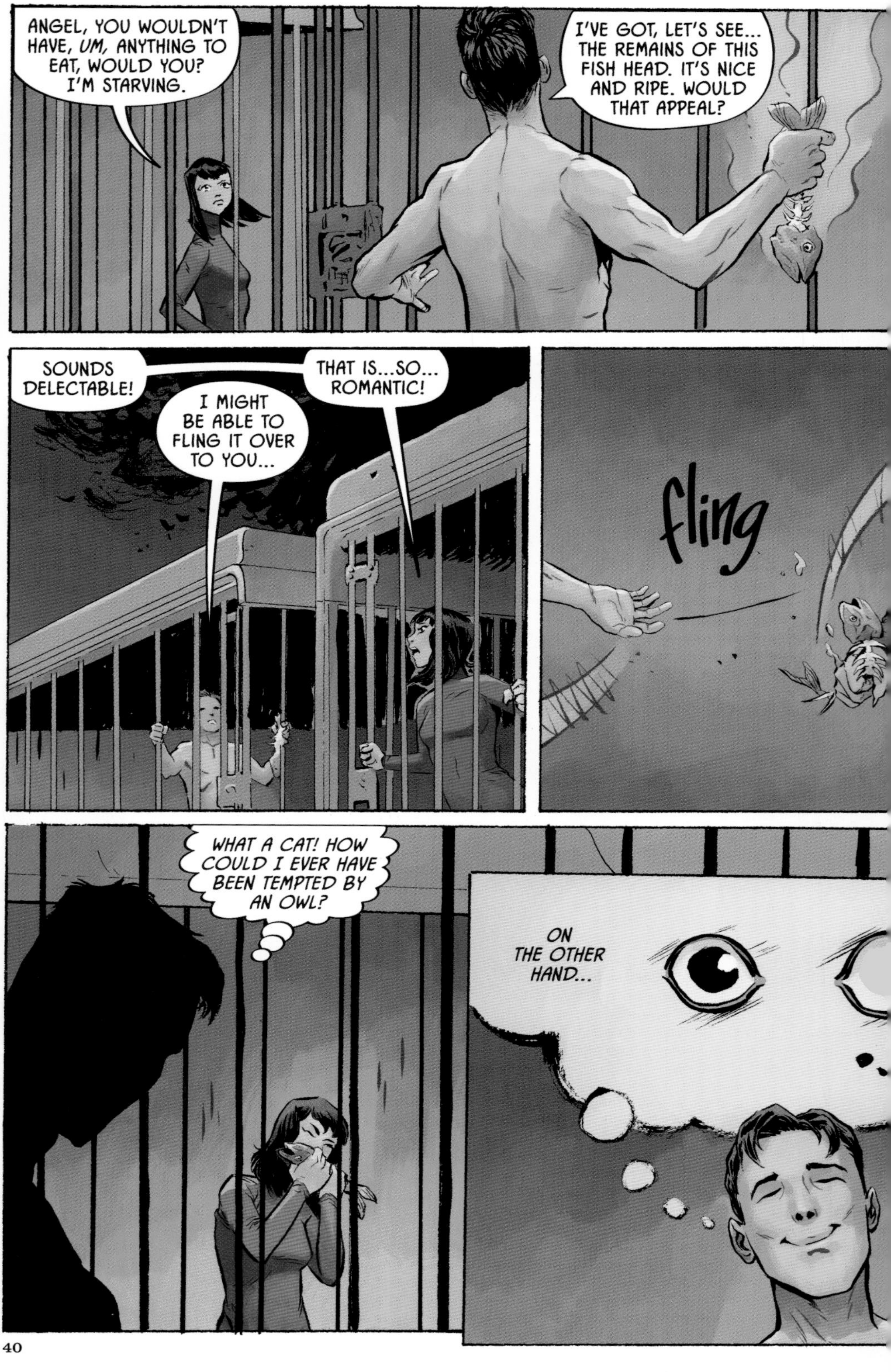

ANGEL, YOU WOULDN'T HAVE, *UM,* ANYTHING TO EAT, WOULD YOU? I'M STARVING.
I'VE GOT, LET'S SEE... THE REMAINS OF THIS FISH HEAD. IT'S NICE AND RIPE. WOULD THAT APPEAL?
SOUNDS DELECTABLE!
THAT IS...SO... ROMANTIC!
I MIGHT BE ABLE TO FLING IT OVER TO YOU...
fling
WHAT A CAT! HOW COULD I EVER HAVE BEEN TEMPTED BY AN OWL?
ON THE OTHER HAND...

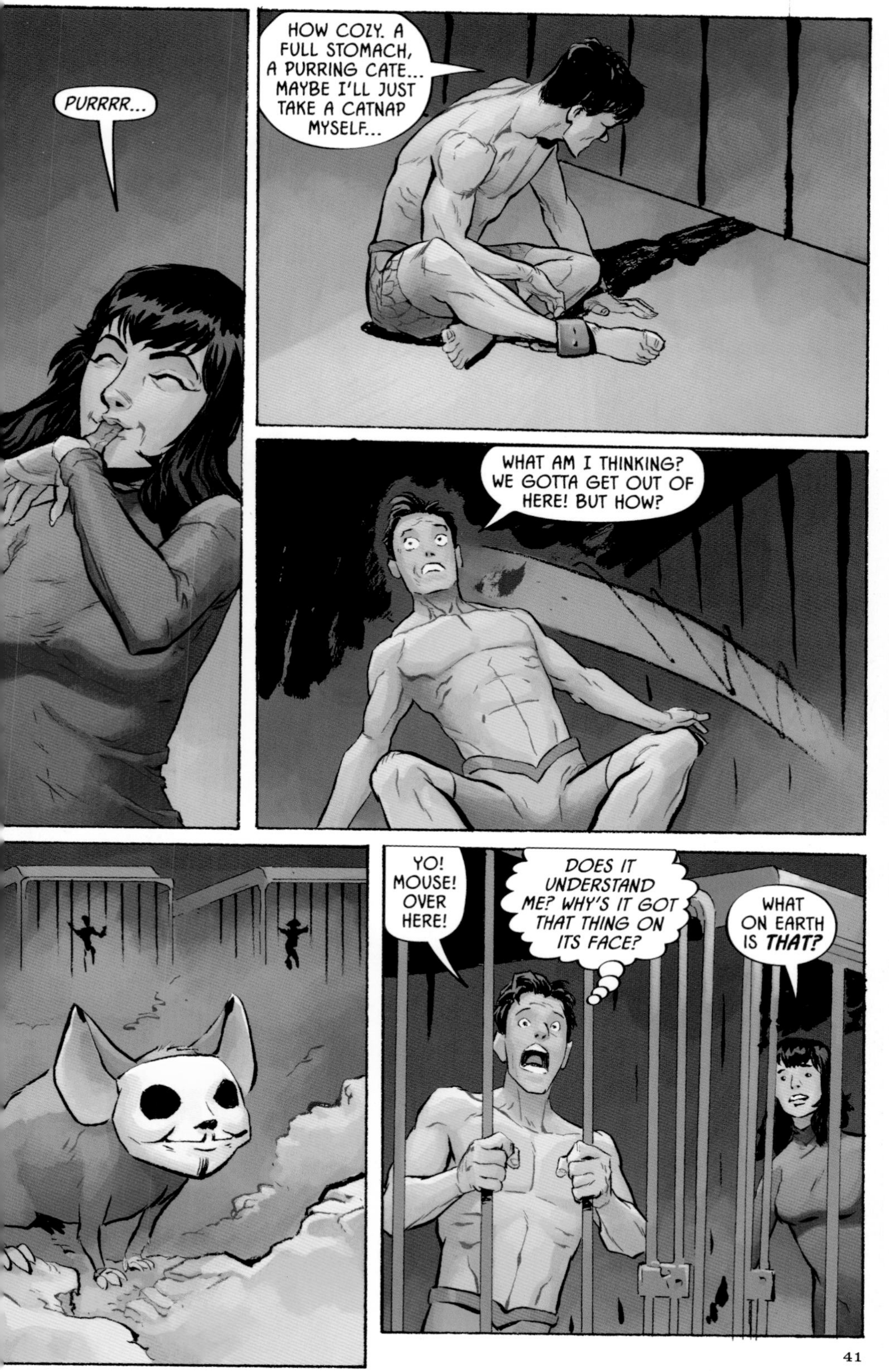
PURRRR...
HOW COZY. A FULL STOMACH, A PURRING CATE... MAYBE I'LL JUST TAKE A CATNAP MYSELF...
WHAT AM I THINKING? WE GOTTA GET OUT OF HERE! BUT HOW?
YO! MOUSE! OVER HERE!
DOES IT UNDERSTAND ME? WHY'S IT GOT THAT THING ON ITS FACE?
WHAT ON EARTH IS **THAT?**

Meanwhile, in Muroid's crypt...

ANONYMOUSE IS A SECRET MOUSE HACKTIVIST GROUP.

AND A FILTHY GOOD ONE, I MUST SAY!

WHY ARE YOU WEARING THAT STUPID MASK? ALL MICE LOOK ALIKE ANYWAY.

THEY ALL LOOK LIKE SNACKS.

MAYBE YOU LOOK A SPECIES- BUT EA OF US MOUSE HIS O HER O RIGHT

OOPS, SORRY!

SINCE WHEN DO YOU HAVE TO APOLOGIZE TO YOUR FOOD?

MiceCream Puffed Mice Mousema

Mice Krispies Chocolate M

YOU WANT OUR HELP, OR NOT?

SHOW SOME RESPECT!

ANONYMOUSE IS VERY FAMILIAR WITH THE CORRIDORS OF POWER!

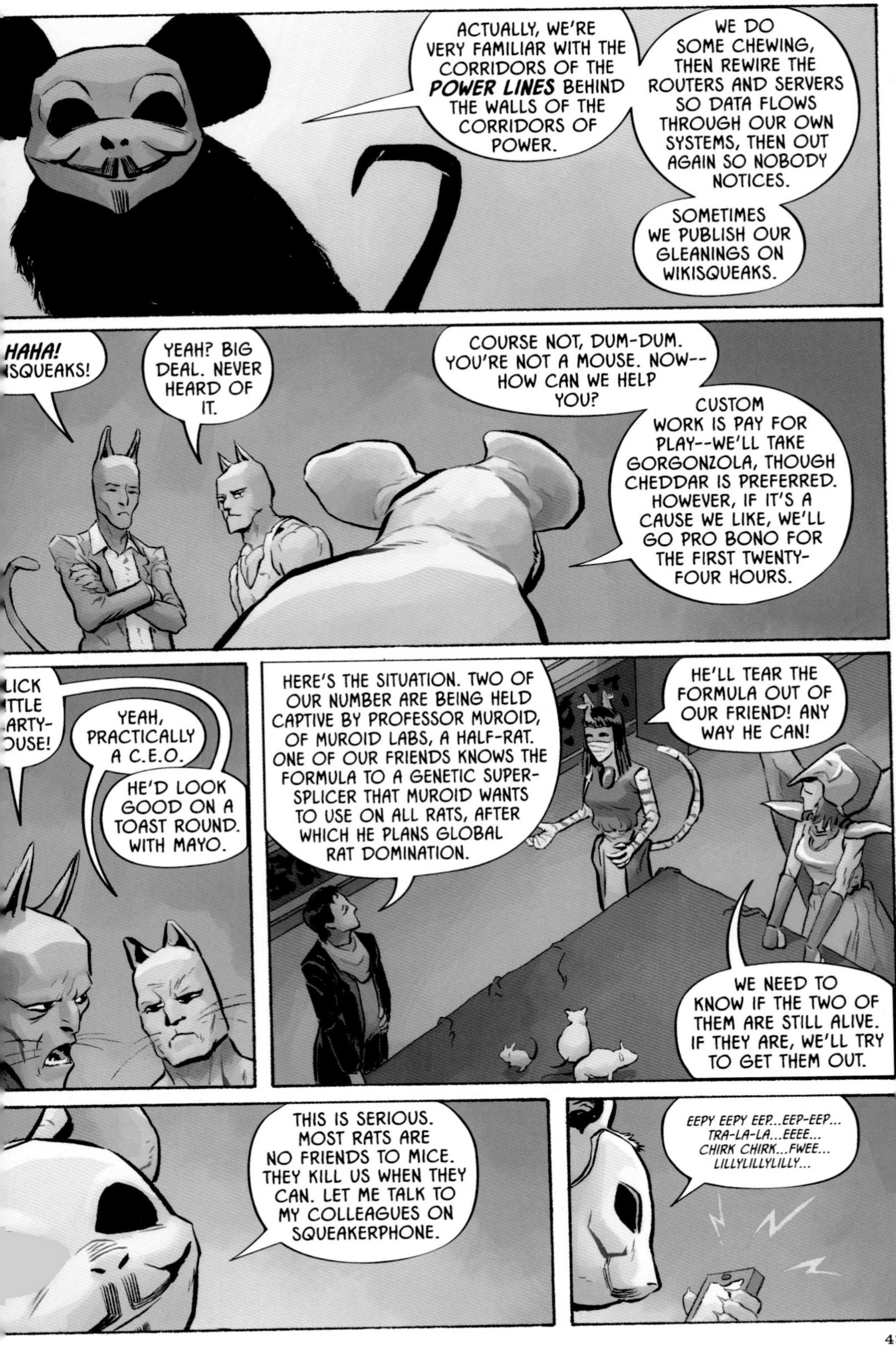
ACTUALLY, WE'RE VERY FAMILIAR WITH THE CORRIDORS OF THE POWER LINES BEHIND THE WALLS OF THE CORRIDORS OF POWER.
WE DO SOME CHEWING, THEN REWIRE THE ROUTERS AND SERVERS SO DATA FLOWS THROUGH OUR OWN SYSTEMS, THEN OUT AGAIN SO NOBODY NOTICES.
SOMETIMES WE PUBLISH OUR GLEANINGS ON WIKISQUEAKS.
HAHA!
YEAH? BIG DEAL. NEVER HEARD OF IT.
COURSE NOT, DUM-DUM. YOU'RE NOT A MOUSE. NOW--HOW CAN WE HELP YOU?
CUSTOM WORK IS PAY FOR PLAY--WE'LL TAKE GORGONZOLA, THOUGH CHEDDAR IS PREFERRED. HOWEVER, IF IT'S A CAUSE WE LIKE, WE'LL GO PRO BONO FOR THE FIRST TWENTY-FOUR HOURS.
YEAH, PRACTICALLY A C.E.O.
HE'D LOOK GOOD ON A TOAST ROUND. WITH MAYO.
HERE'S THE SITUATION. TWO OF OUR NUMBER ARE BEING HELD CAPTIVE BY PROFESSOR MUROID, OF MUROID LABS, A HALF-RAT. ONE OF OUR FRIENDS KNOWS THE FORMULA TO A GENETIC SUPER-SPLICER THAT MUROID WANTS TO USE ON ALL RATS, AFTER WHICH HE PLANS GLOBAL RAT DOMINATION.
HE'LL TEAR THE FORMULA OUT OF OUR FRIEND! ANY WAY HE CAN!
WE NEED TO KNOW IF THE TWO OF THEM ARE STILL ALIVE. IF THEY ARE, WE'LL TRY TO GET THEM OUT.
THIS IS SERIOUS. MOST RATS ARE NO FRIENDS TO MICE. THEY KILL US WHEN THEY CAN. LET ME TALK TO MY COLLEAGUES ON SQUEAKERPHONE.
EEPY EEPY EEP...EEP-EEP... TRA-LA-LA...EEEE... CHIRK CHIRK...FWEE... LILLYLILLYLILLY...

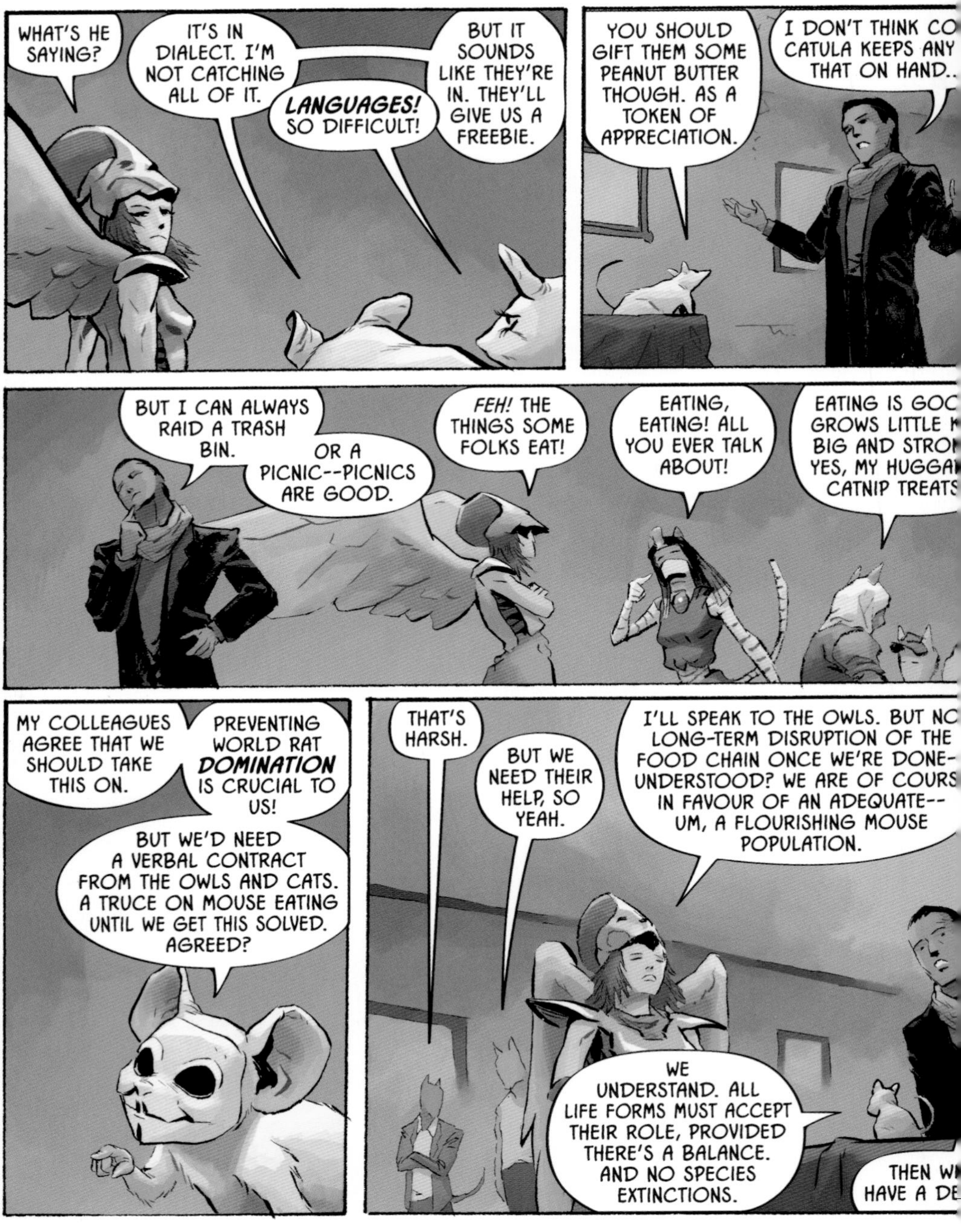
WHAT'S HE SAYING?
IT'S IN DIALECT. I'M NOT CATCHING ALL OF IT.
LANGUAGES! SO DIFFICULT!
BUT IT SOUNDS LIKE THEY'RE IN. THEY'LL GIVE US A FREEBIE.
YOU SHOULD GIFT THEM SOME PEANUT BUTTER THOUGH. AS A TOKEN OF APPRECIATION.
I DON'T THINK CO CATULA KEEPS ANY THAT ON HAND..
BUT I CAN ALWAYS RAID A TRASH BIN.
OR A PICNIC--PICNICS ARE GOOD.
FEH! THE THINGS SOME FOLKS EAT!
EATING, EATING! ALL YOU EVER TALK ABOUT!
EATING IS GOO GROWS LITTLE BIG AND STRO YES, MY HUGGA CATNIP TREATS
MY COLLEAGUES AGREE THAT WE SHOULD TAKE THIS ON.
PREVENTING WORLD RAT DOMINATION IS CRUCIAL TO US!
BUT WE'D NEED A VERBAL CONTRACT FROM THE OWLS AND CATS. A TRUCE ON MOUSE EATING UNTIL WE GET THIS SOLVED. AGREED?
THAT'S HARSH.
BUT WE NEED THEIR HELP, SO YEAH.
I'LL SPEAK TO THE OWLS. BUT NO LONG-TERM DISRUPTION OF THE FOOD CHAIN ONCE WE'RE DONE-- UNDERSTOOD? WE ARE OF COURS IN FAVOUR OF AN ADEQUATE-- UM, A FLOURISHING MOUSE POPULATION.
WE UNDERSTAND. ALL LIFE FORMS MUST ACCEPT THEIR ROLE, PROVIDED THERE'S A BALANCE. AND NO SPECIES EXTINCTIONS.
THEN W HAVE A DE

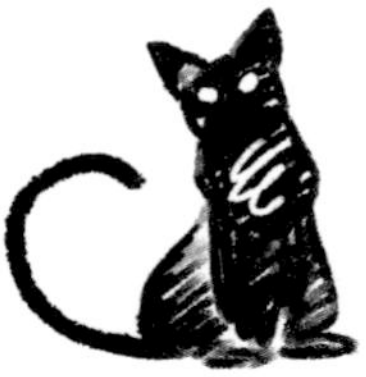

THE NATURE BALANCING ACT

It's natural for cats to hunt birds and wildlife, but letting our cats hunt disrupts the balance of nature. That's because cats aren't native animals, we keep very large numbers of them as pets, and so many are allowed outdoors unsupervised. Keep cats safe and save bird lives! Read more at www.catsandbirds.ca

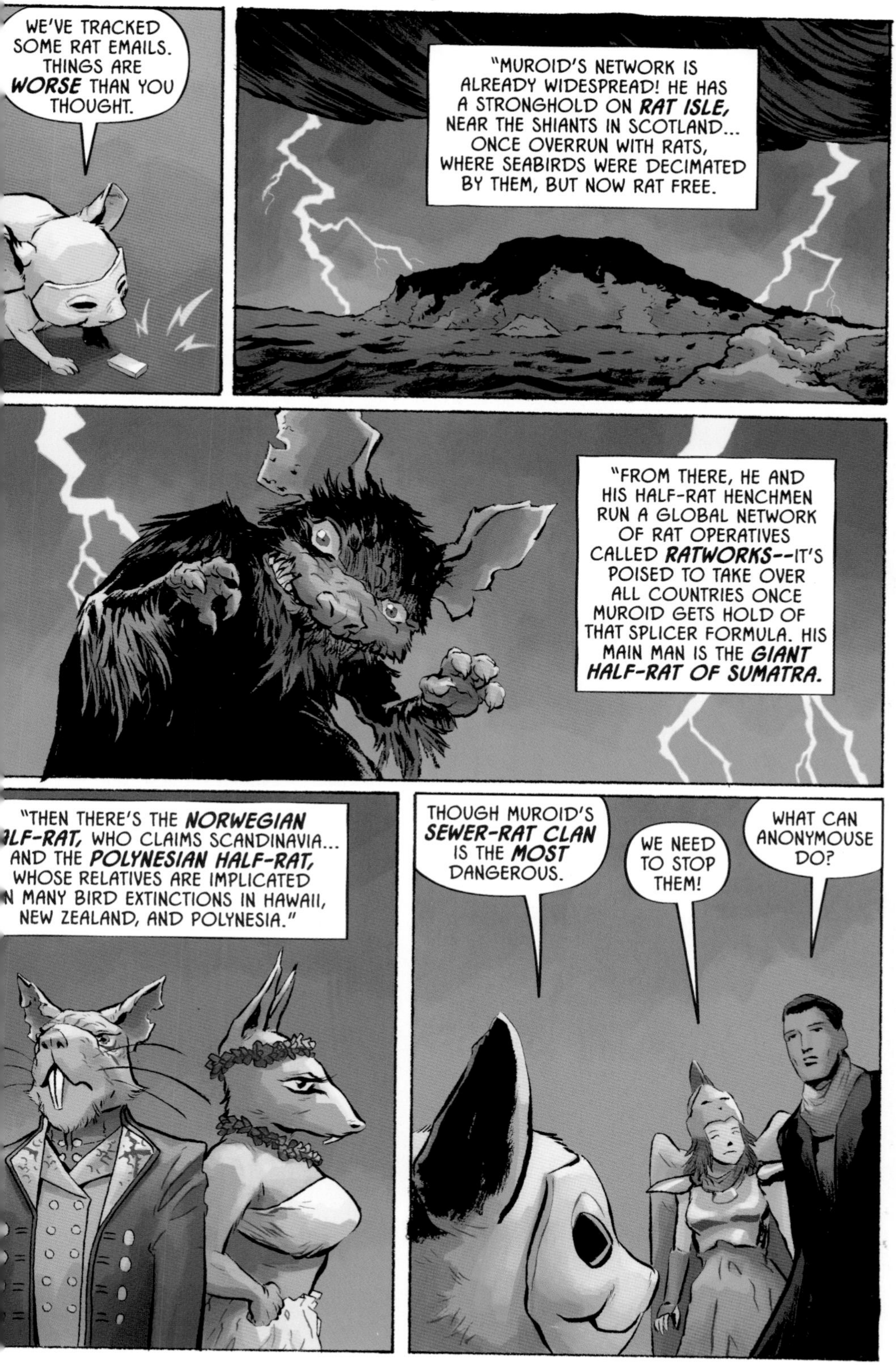
WE'VE TRACKED SOME RAT EMAILS. THINGS ARE **WORSE** THAN YOU THOUGHT.
"MUROID'S NETWORK IS ALREADY WIDESPREAD! HE HAS A STRONGHOLD ON **RAT ISLE,** NEAR THE SHIANTS IN SCOTLAND... ONCE OVERRUN WITH RATS, WHERE SEABIRDS WERE DECIMATED BY THEM, BUT NOW RAT FREE.
"FROM THERE, HE AND HIS HALF-RAT HENCHMEN RUN A GLOBAL NETWORK OF RAT OPERATIVES CALLED **RATWORKS**--IT'S POISED TO TAKE OVER ALL COUNTRIES ONCE MUROID GETS HOLD OF THAT SPLICER FORMULA. HIS MAIN MAN IS THE **GIANT HALF-RAT OF SUMATRA.**
"THEN THERE'S THE **NORWEGIAN HALF-RAT,** WHO CLAIMS SCANDINAVIA... AND THE **POLYNESIAN HALF-RAT,** WHOSE RELATIVES ARE IMPLICATED IN MANY BIRD EXTINCTIONS IN HAWAII, NEW ZEALAND, AND POLYNESIA."
THOUGH MUROID'S **SEWER-RAT CLAN** IS THE **MOST** DANGEROUS.
WE NEED TO STOP THEM!
WHAT CAN ANONYMOUSE DO?

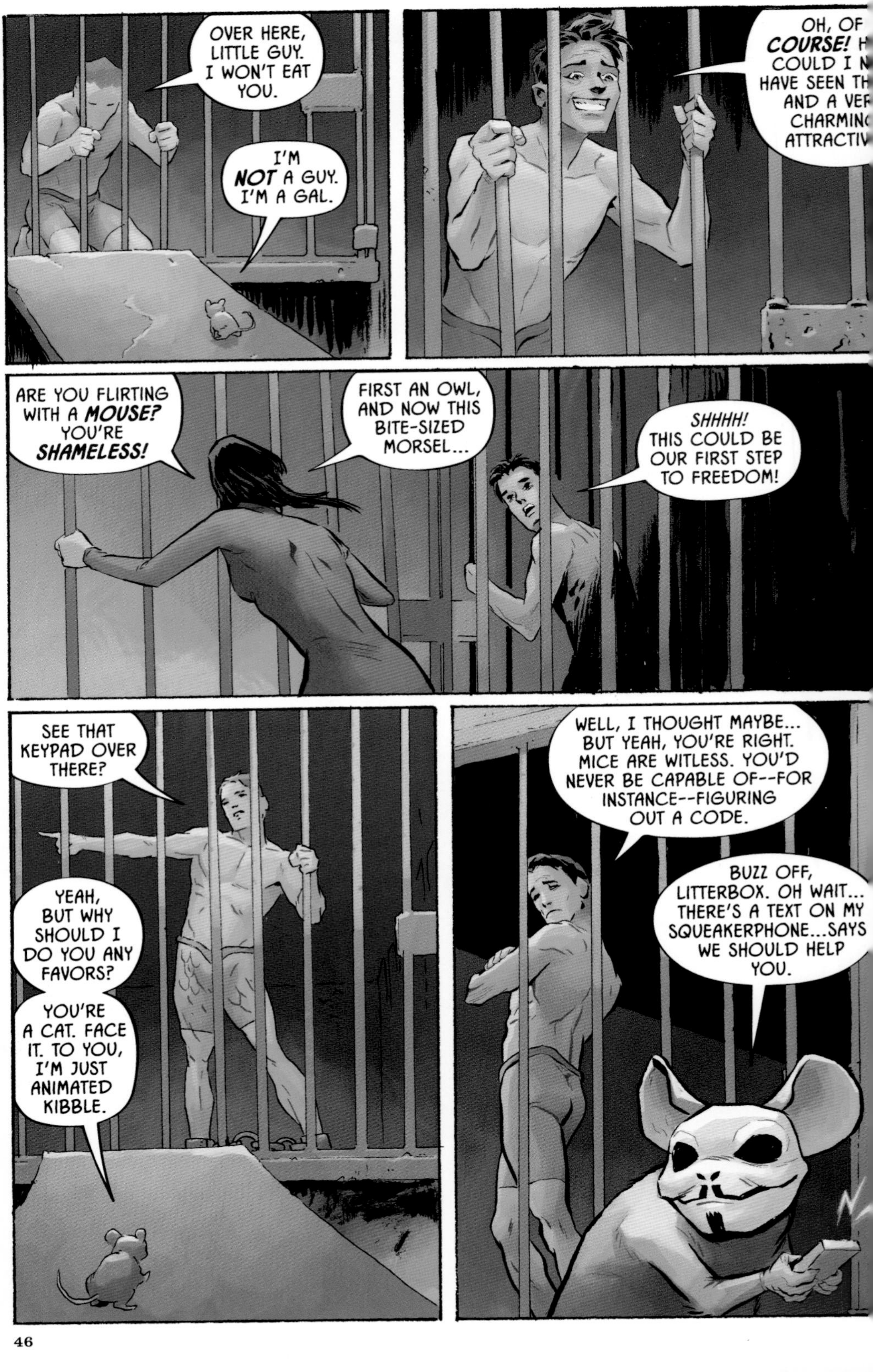

OVER HERE, LITTLE GUY. I WON'T EAT YOU.
I'M NOT A GUY. I'M A GAL.
OH, OF COURSE! H COULD I N HAVE SEEN TH AND A VER CHARMING ATTRACTIV
ARE YOU FLIRTING WITH A MOUSE? YOU'RE SHAMELESS!
FIRST AN OWL, AND NOW THIS BITE-SIZED MORSEL...
SHHHH! THIS COULD BE OUR FIRST STEP TO FREEDOM!
SEE THAT KEYPAD OVER THERE?
YEAH, BUT WHY SHOULD I DO YOU ANY FAVORS?
YOU'RE A CAT. FACE IT. TO YOU, I'M JUST ANIMATED KIBBLE.
WELL, I THOUGHT MAYBE... BUT YEAH, YOU'RE RIGHT. MICE ARE WITLESS. YOU'D NEVER BE CAPABLE OF--FOR INSTANCE--FIGURING OUT A CODE.
BUZZ OFF, LITTERBOX. OH WAIT... THERE'S A TEXT ON MY SQUEAKERPHONE...SAYS WE SHOULD HELP YOU.

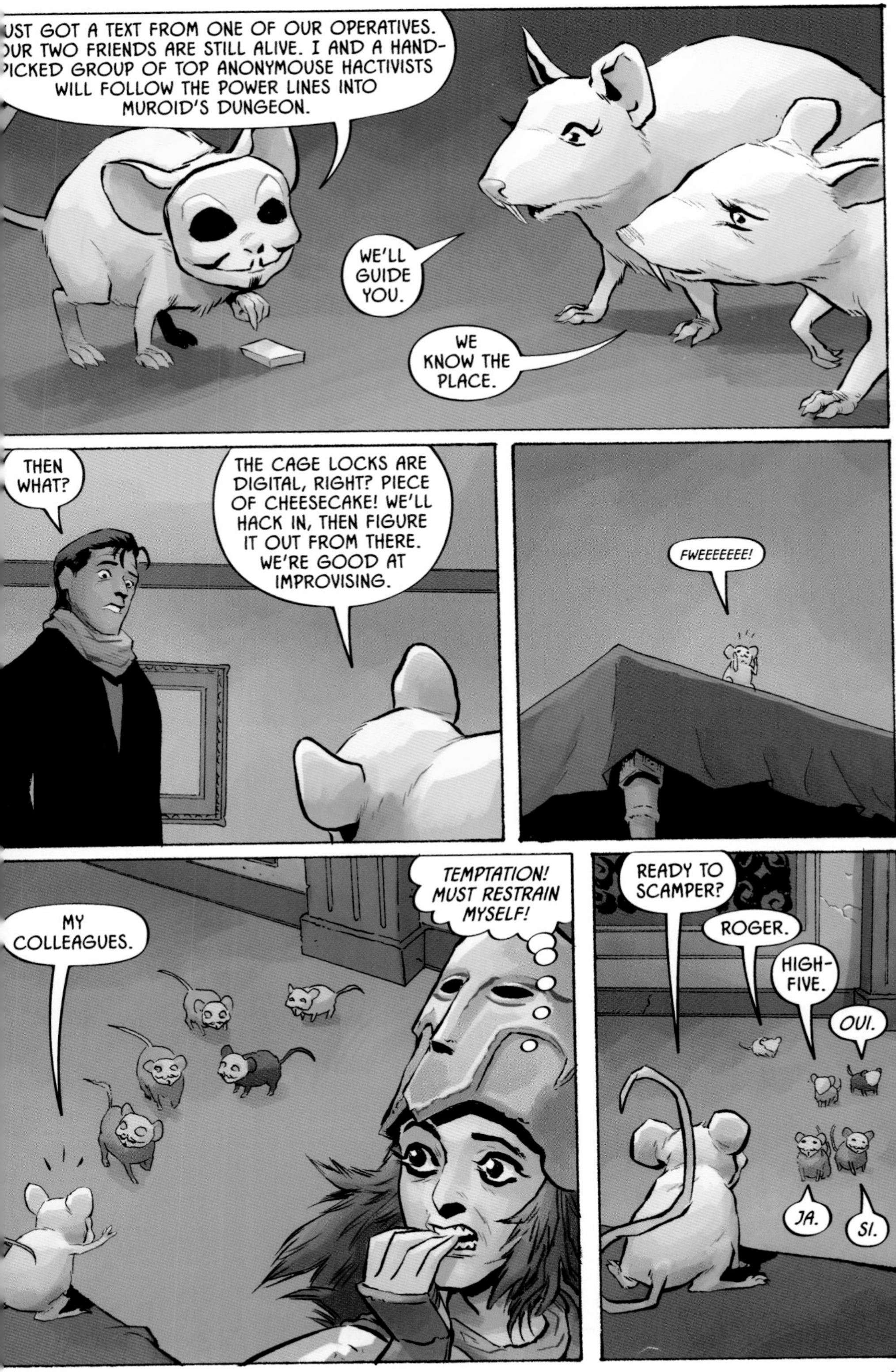
UST GOT A TEXT FROM ONE OF OUR OPERATIVES. OUR TWO FRIENDS ARE STILL ALIVE. I AND A HAND-PICKED GROUP OF TOP ANONYMOUSE HACTIVISTS WILL FOLLOW THE POWER LINES INTO MUROID'S DUNGEON.
WE'LL GUIDE YOU.
WE KNOW THE PLACE.
THEN WHAT?
THE CAGE LOCKS ARE DIGITAL, RIGHT? PIECE OF CHEESECAKE! WE'LL HACK IN, THEN FIGURE IT OUT FROM THERE. WE'RE GOOD AT IMPROVISING.
FWEEEEEEE!
MY COLLEAGUES.
TEMPTATION! MUST RESTRAIN MYSELF!
READY TO SCAMPER?
ROGER.
HIGH-FIVE.
OUI.
JA.
SI.

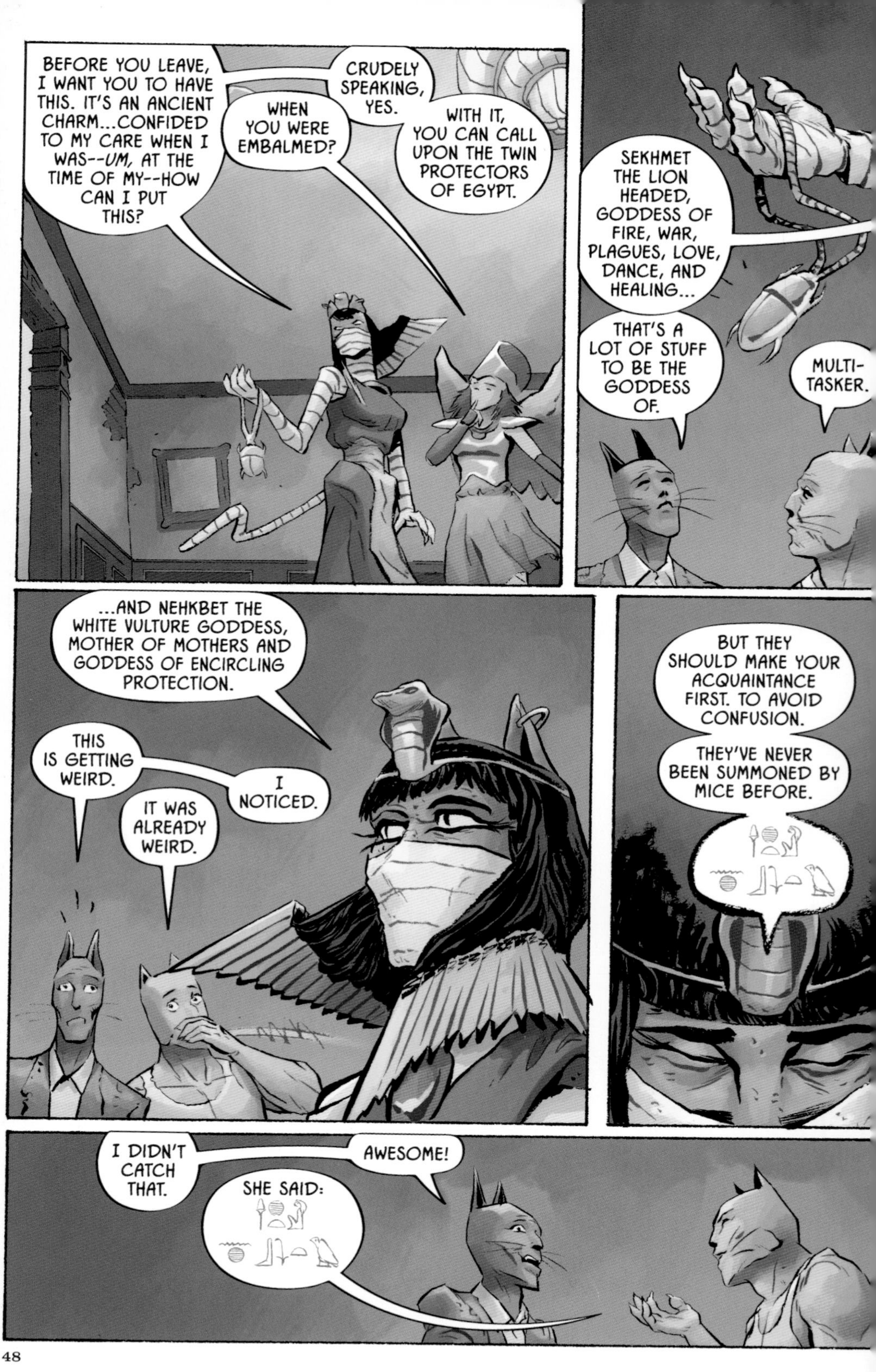
BEFORE YOU LEAVE, I WANT YOU TO HAVE THIS. IT'S AN ANCIENT CHARM...CONFIDED TO MY CARE WHEN I WAS--*UM,* AT THE TIME OF MY--HOW CAN I PUT THIS?
WHEN YOU WERE EMBALMED?
CRUDELY SPEAKING, YES.
WITH IT, YOU CAN CALL UPON THE TWIN PROTECTORS OF EGYPT.
SEKHMET THE LION HEADED, GODDESS OF FIRE, WAR, PLAGUES, LOVE, DANCE, AND HEALING...
THAT'S A LOT OF STUFF TO BE THE GODDESS OF.
MULTI-TASKER.
...AND NEHKBET THE WHITE VULTURE GODDESS, MOTHER OF MOTHERS AND GODDESS OF ENCIRCLING PROTECTION.
THIS IS GETTING WEIRD.
I NOTICED.
IT WAS ALREADY WEIRD.
BUT THEY SHOULD MAKE YOUR ACQUAINTANCE FIRST. TO AVOID CONFUSION.
THEY'VE NEVER BEEN SUMMONED BY MICE BEFORE.
I DIDN'T CATCH THAT.
AWESOME!
SHE SAID:

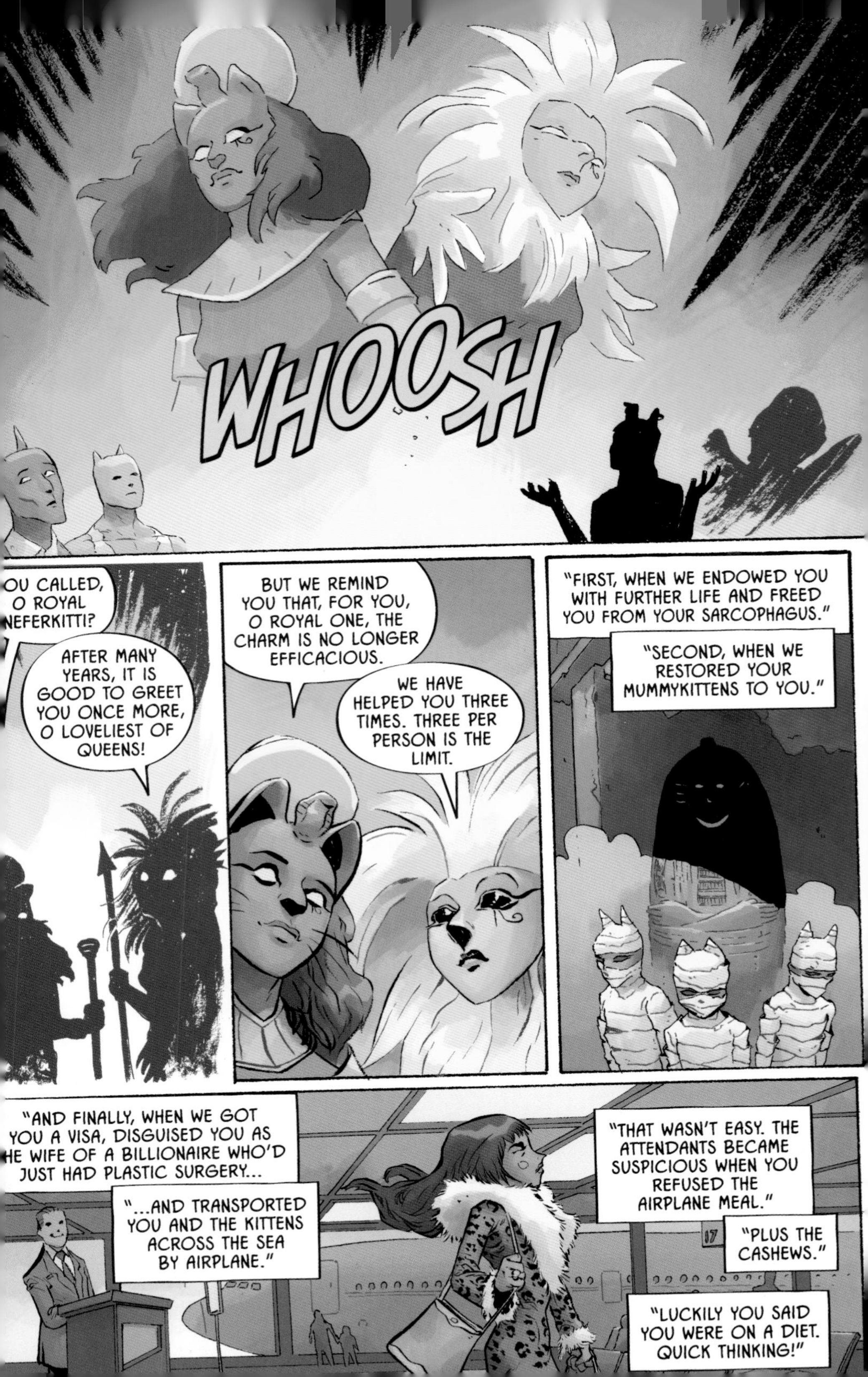
WHOOSH
OU CALLED, O ROYAL NEFERKITTI?
AFTER MANY YEARS, IT IS GOOD TO GREET YOU ONCE MORE, O LOVELIEST OF QUEENS!
BUT WE REMIND YOU THAT, FOR YOU, O ROYAL ONE, THE CHARM IS NO LONGER EFFICACIOUS.
WE HAVE HELPED YOU THREE TIMES. THREE PER PERSON IS THE LIMIT.
"FIRST, WHEN WE ENDOWED YOU WITH FURTHER LIFE AND FREED YOU FROM YOUR SARCOPHAGUS."
"SECOND, WHEN WE RESTORED YOUR MUMMYKITTENS TO YOU."
"AND FINALLY, WHEN WE GOT YOU A VISA, DISGUISED YOU AS HE WIFE OF A BILLIONAIRE WHO'D JUST HAD PLASTIC SURGERY...
"...AND TRANSPORTED YOU AND THE KITTENS ACROSS THE SEA BY AIRPLANE."
"THAT WASN'T EASY. THE ATTENDANTS BECAME SUSPICIOUS WHEN YOU REFUSED THE AIRPLANE MEAL."
"PLUS THE CASHEWS."
"LUCKILY YOU SAID YOU WERE ON A DIET. QUICK THINKING!"

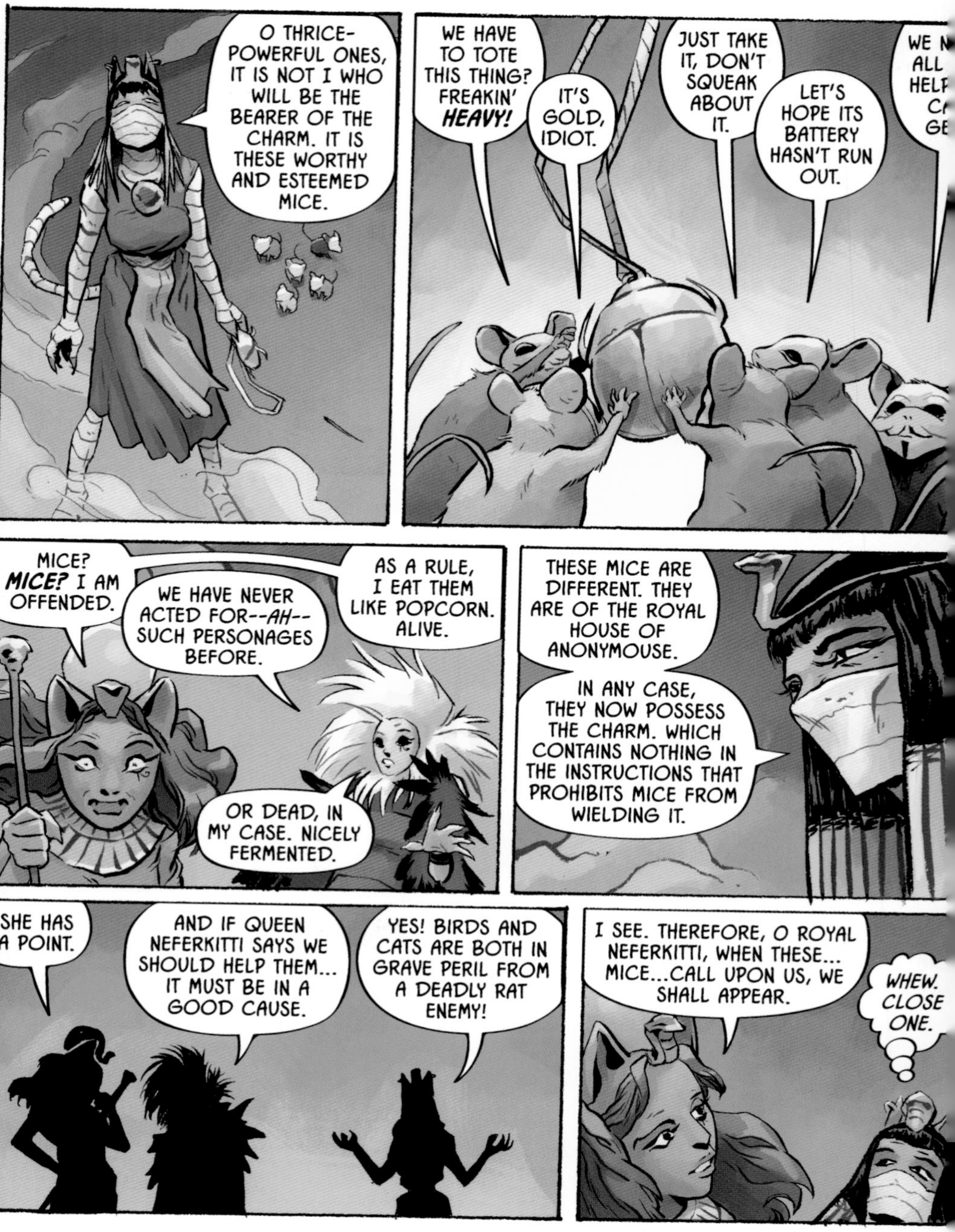
O THRICE-POWERFUL ONES, IT IS NOT I WHO WILL BE THE BEARER OF THE CHARM. IT IS THESE WORTHY AND ESTEEMED MICE.
WE HAVE TO TOTE THIS THING? FREAKIN' HEAVY!
IT'S GOLD, IDIOT.
JUST TAKE IT, DON'T SQUEAK ABOUT IT.
LET'S HOPE ITS BATTERY HASN'T RUN OUT.
MICE? MICE? I AM OFFENDED.
WE HAVE NEVER ACTED FOR--AH--SUCH PERSONAGES BEFORE.
AS A RULE, I EAT THEM LIKE POPCORN. ALIVE.
OR DEAD, IN MY CASE. NICELY FERMENTED.
THESE MICE ARE DIFFERENT. THEY ARE OF THE ROYAL HOUSE OF ANONYMOUSE.
IN ANY CASE, THEY NOW POSSESS THE CHARM. WHICH CONTAINS NOTHING IN THE INSTRUCTIONS THAT PROHIBITS MICE FROM WIELDING IT.
SHE HAS A POINT.
AND IF QUEEN NEFERKITTI SAYS WE SHOULD HELP THEM... IT MUST BE IN A GOOD CAUSE.
YES! BIRDS AND CATS ARE BOTH IN GRAVE PERIL FROM A DEADLY RAT ENEMY!
I SEE. THEREFORE, O ROYAL NEFERKITTI, WHEN THESE... MICE...CALL UPON US, WE SHALL APPEAR.
WHEW. CLOSE ONE.

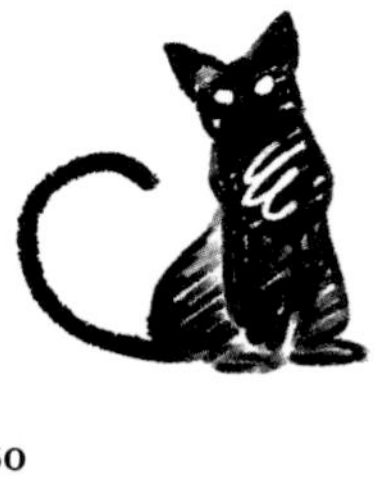

RATS

Rats are a danger to birds—they eat their eggs and young—and they're also a danger to cats. Rat bites and scratches carry a high risk of infection, and if your cat eats a rat that's eaten poison, they can be poisoned too. Keeping cats from roaming unsupervised is a great way to protect your cat from rats, not to mention other wildlife, like raccoons and coyotes. Read more at www.catsandbirds.ca

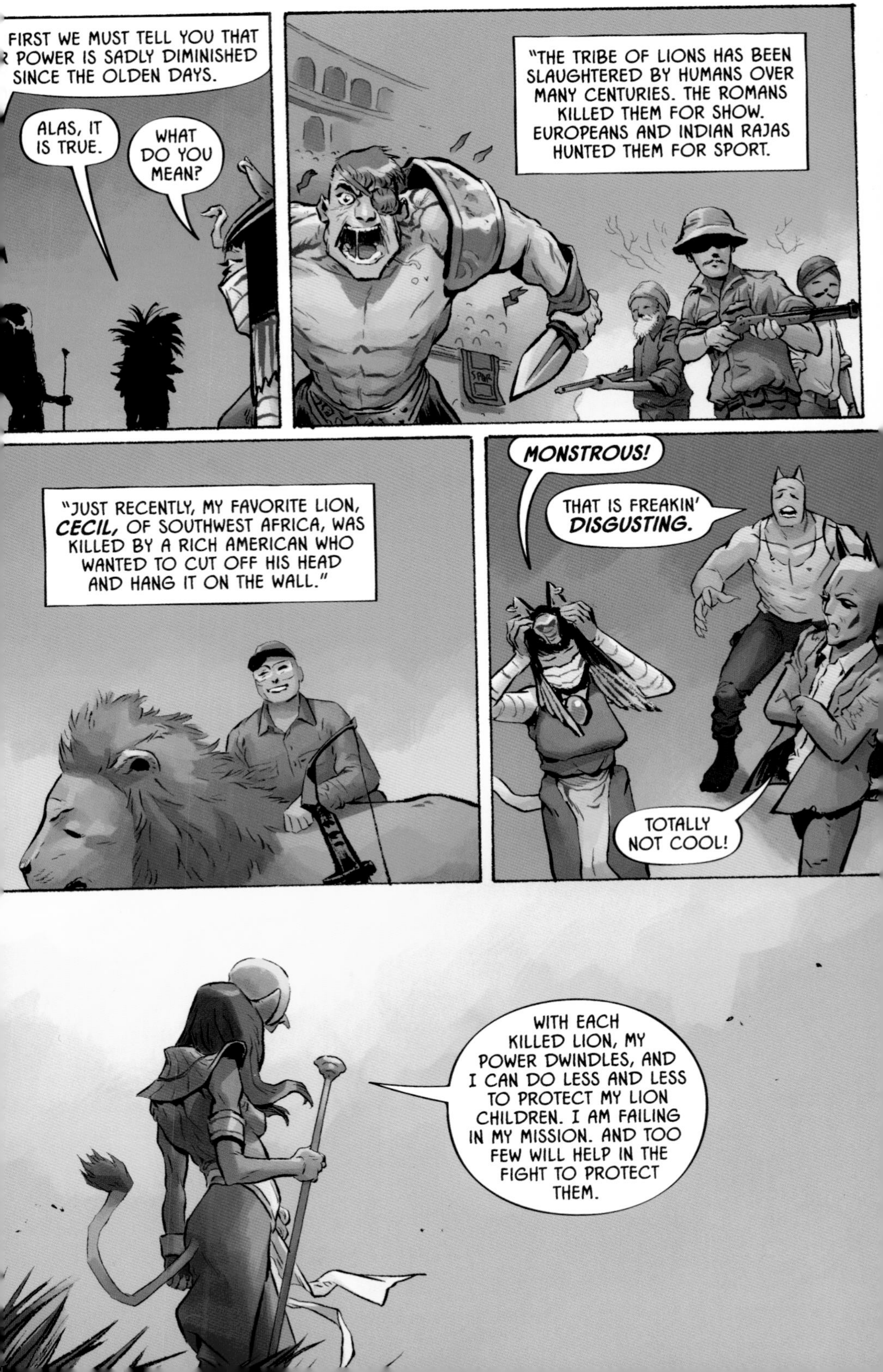

FIRST WE MUST TELL YOU THAT POWER IS SADLY DIMINISHED SINCE THE OLDEN DAYS.
ALAS, IT IS TRUE.
WHAT DO YOU MEAN?
"THE TRIBE OF LIONS HAS BEEN SLAUGHTERED BY HUMANS OVER MANY CENTURIES. THE ROMANS KILLED THEM FOR SHOW. EUROPEANS AND INDIAN RAJAS HUNTED THEM FOR SPORT.
"JUST RECENTLY, MY FAVORITE LION, **CECIL,** OF SOUTHWEST AFRICA, WAS KILLED BY A RICH AMERICAN WHO WANTED TO CUT OFF HIS HEAD AND HANG IT ON THE WALL."
MONSTROUS!
THAT IS FREAKIN' ***DISGUSTING.***
TOTALLY NOT COOL!
WITH EACH KILLED LION, MY POWER DWINDLES, AND I CAN DO LESS AND LESS TO PROTECT MY LION CHILDREN. I AM FAILING IN MY MISSION. AND TOO FEW WILL HELP IN THE FIGHT TO PROTECT THEM.

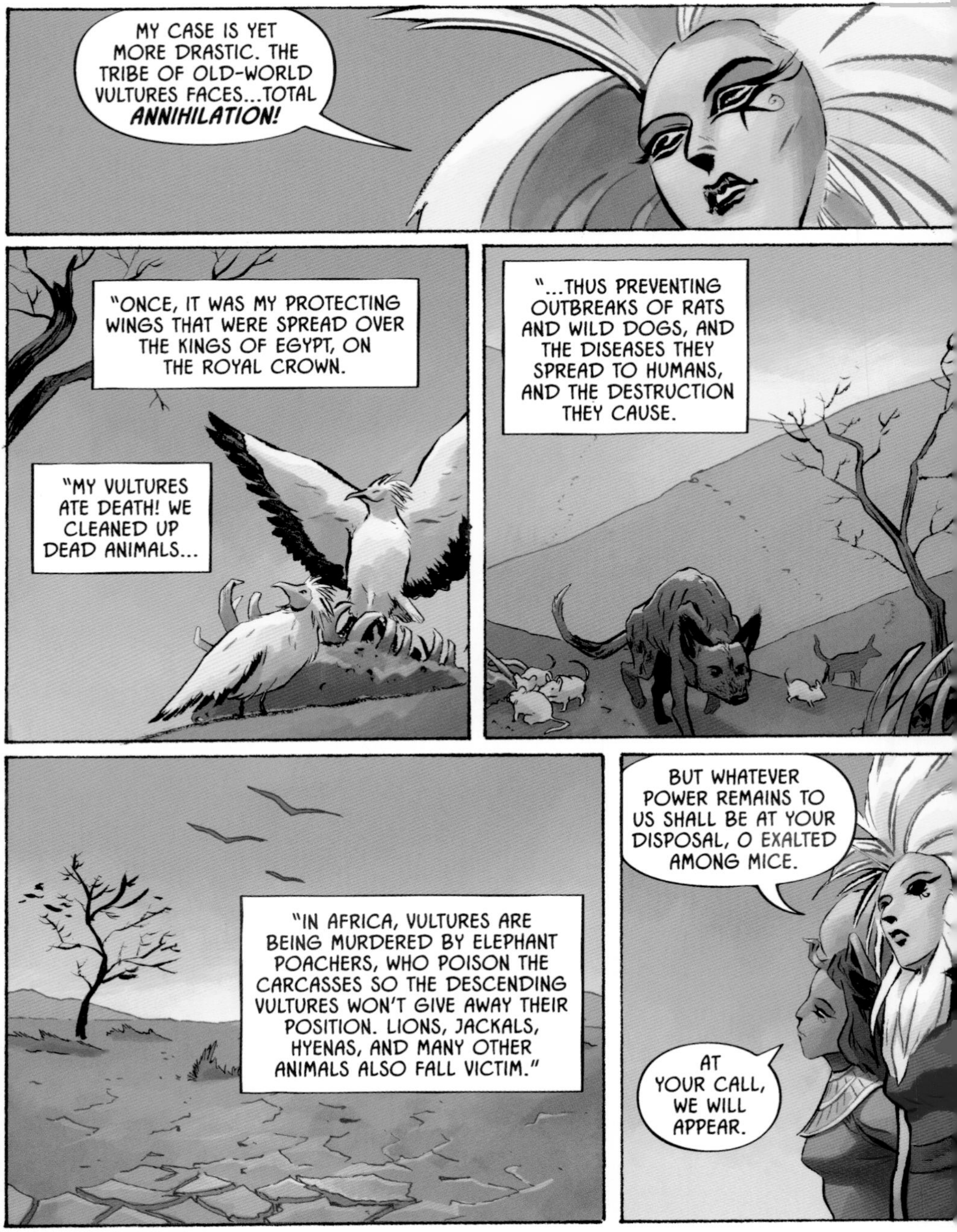
MY CASE IS YET MORE DRASTIC. THE TRIBE OF OLD-WORLD VULTURES FACES...TOTAL ***ANNIHILATION!***
"ONCE, IT WAS MY PROTECTING WINGS THAT WERE SPREAD OVER THE KINGS OF EGYPT, ON THE ROYAL CROWN.
"MY VULTURES ATE DEATH! WE CLEANED UP DEAD ANIMALS...
"...THUS PREVENTING OUTBREAKS OF RATS AND WILD DOGS, AND THE DISEASES THEY SPREAD TO HUMANS, AND THE DESTRUCTION THEY CAUSE.
"IN AFRICA, VULTURES ARE BEING MURDERED BY ELEPHANT POACHERS, WHO POISON THE CARCASSES SO THE DESCENDING VULTURES WON'T GIVE AWAY THEIR POSITION. LIONS, JACKALS, HYENAS, AND MANY OTHER ANIMALS ALSO FALL VICTIM."
BUT WHATEVER POWER REMAINS TO US SHALL BE AT YOUR DISPOSAL, O EXALTED AMONG MICE.
AT YOUR CALL, WE WILL APPEAR.

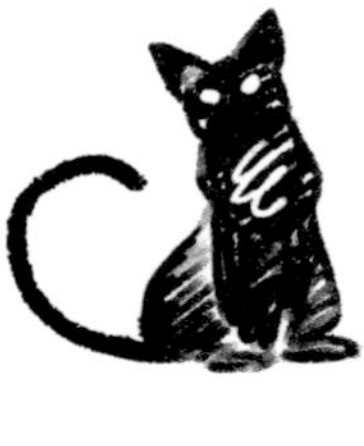

VULTURES

Six of ten African vulture species are on the edge of extinction, and Indian vulture populations have dropped by 97%–99% since the nineties. The costs of this decline are estimated in the billions of dollars, since vultures provide vital ecological servic
Read more at www.catsandbirds.ca

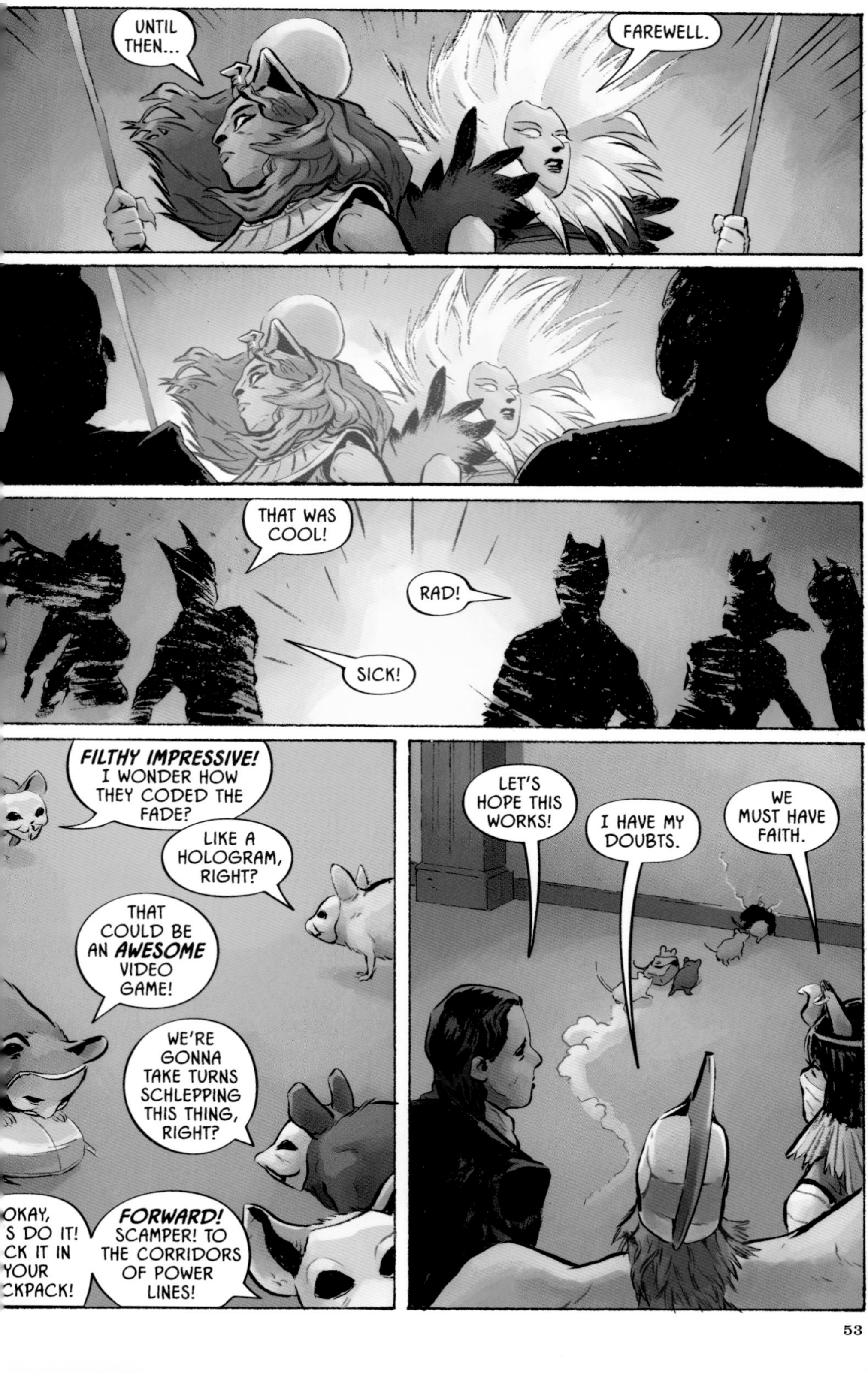
UNTIL THEN...
FAREWELL.
THAT WAS COOL!
RAD!
SICK!
FILTHY IMPRESSIVE! I WONDER HOW THEY CODED THE FADE?
LIKE A HOLOGRAM, RIGHT?
THAT COULD BE AN AWESOME VIDEO GAME!
WE'RE GONNA TAKE TURNS SCHLEPPING THIS THING, RIGHT?
OKAY, S DO IT! CK IT IN YOUR CKPACK!
FORWARD! SCAMPER! TO THE CORRIDORS OF POWER LINES!
LET'S HOPE THIS WORKS!
I HAVE MY DOUBTS.
WE MUST HAVE FAITH.

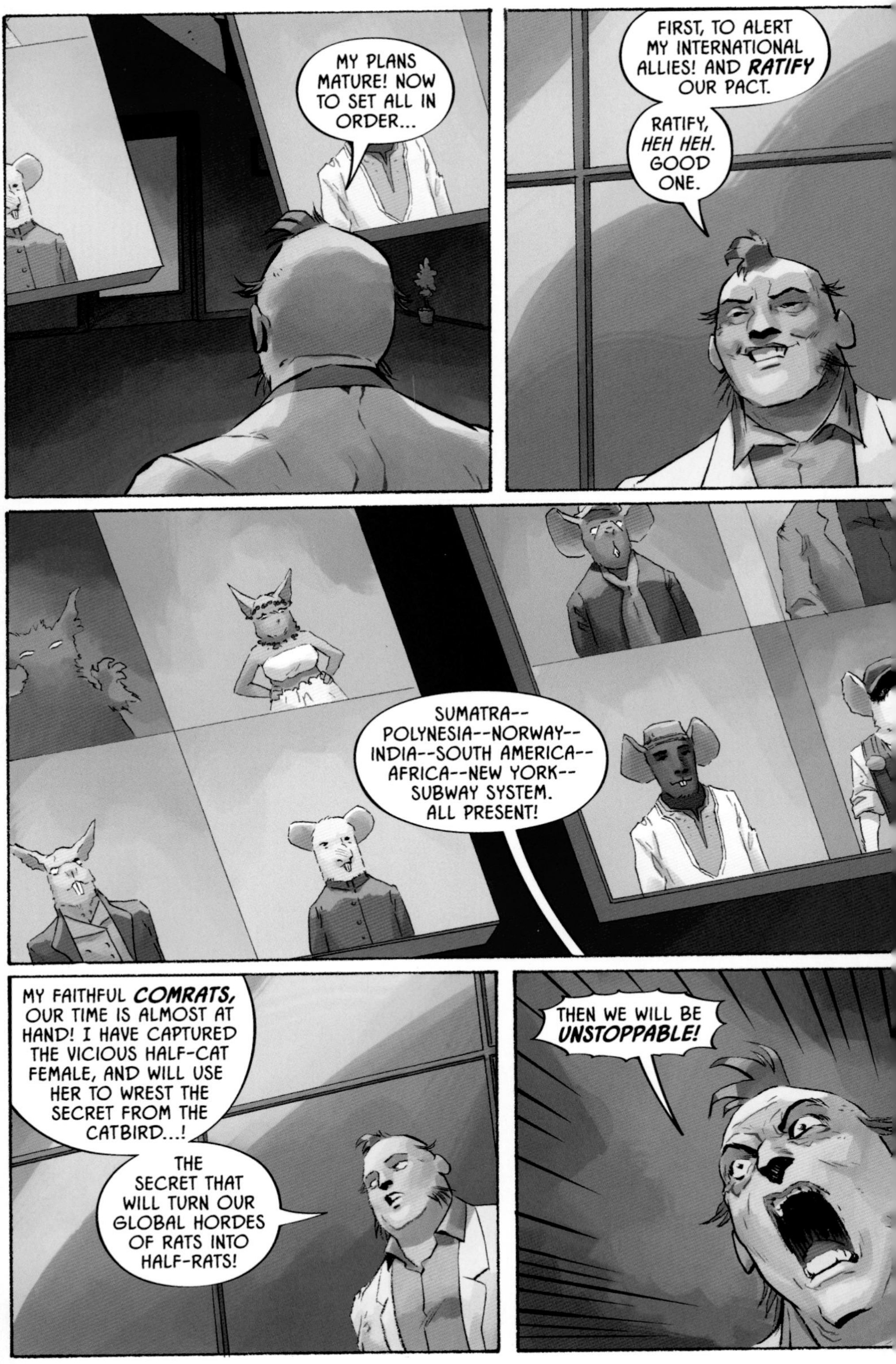
MY PLANS MATURE! NOW TO SET ALL IN ORDER...
FIRST, TO ALERT MY INTERNATIONAL ALLIES! AND RATIFY OUR PACT.
RATIFY, HEH HEH. GOOD ONE.
SUMATRA--POLYNESIA--NORWAY--INDIA--SOUTH AMERICA--AFRICA--NEW YORK--SUBWAY SYSTEM. ALL PRESENT!
MY FAITHFUL COMRATS, OUR TIME IS ALMOST AT HAND! I HAVE CAPTURED THE VICIOUS HALF-CAT FEMALE, AND WILL USE HER TO WREST THE SECRET FROM THE CATBIRD...!
THE SECRET THAT WILL TURN OUR GLOBAL HORDES OF RATS INTO HALF-RATS!
THEN WE WILL BE UNSTOPPABLE!

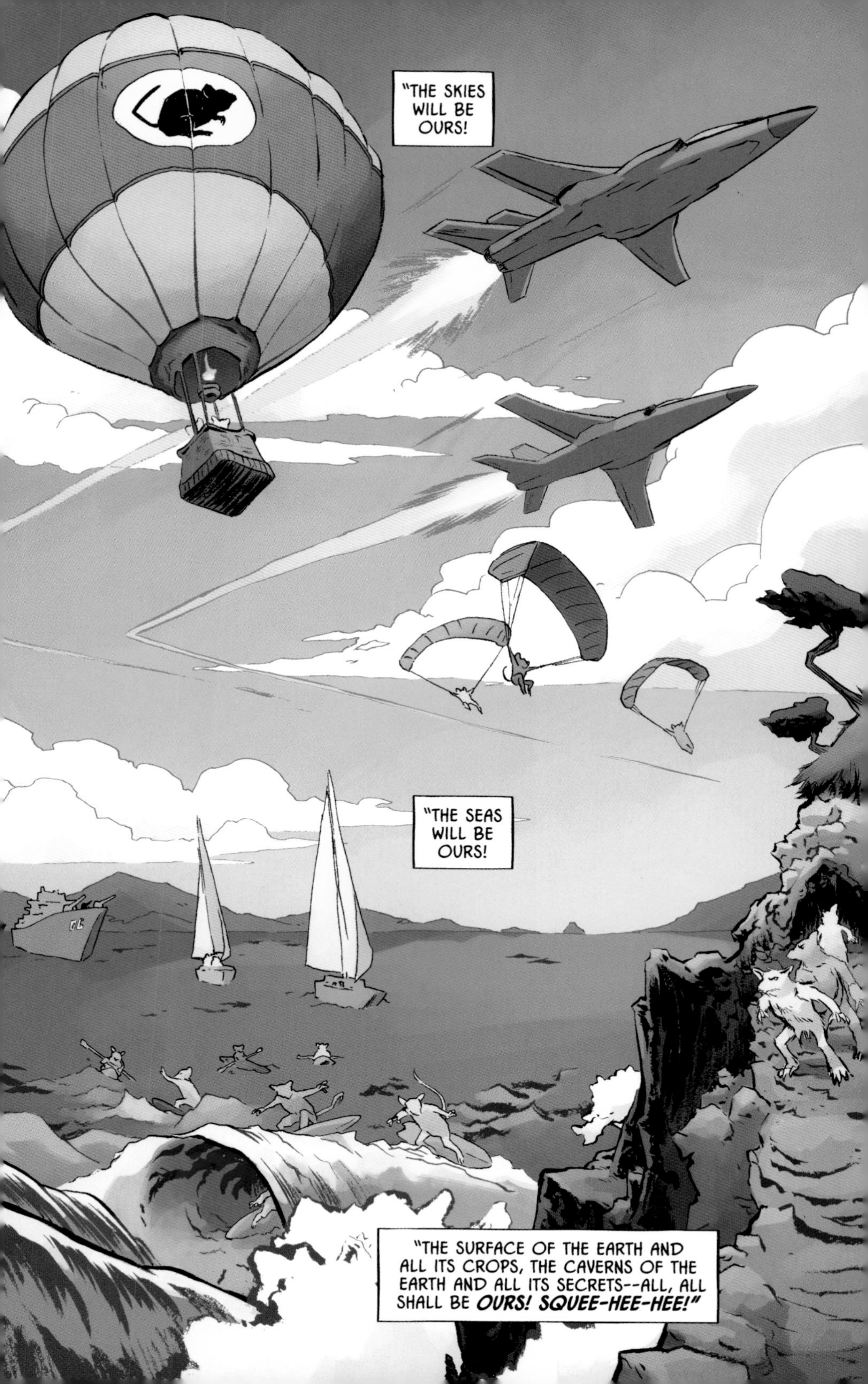
"THE SKIES WILL BE OURS!
"THE SEAS WILL BE OURS!
"THE SURFACE OF THE EARTH AND ALL ITS CROPS, THE CAVERNS OF THE EARTH AND ALL ITS SECRETS--ALL, ALL SHALL BE ***OURS! SQUEE-HEE-HEE!"***

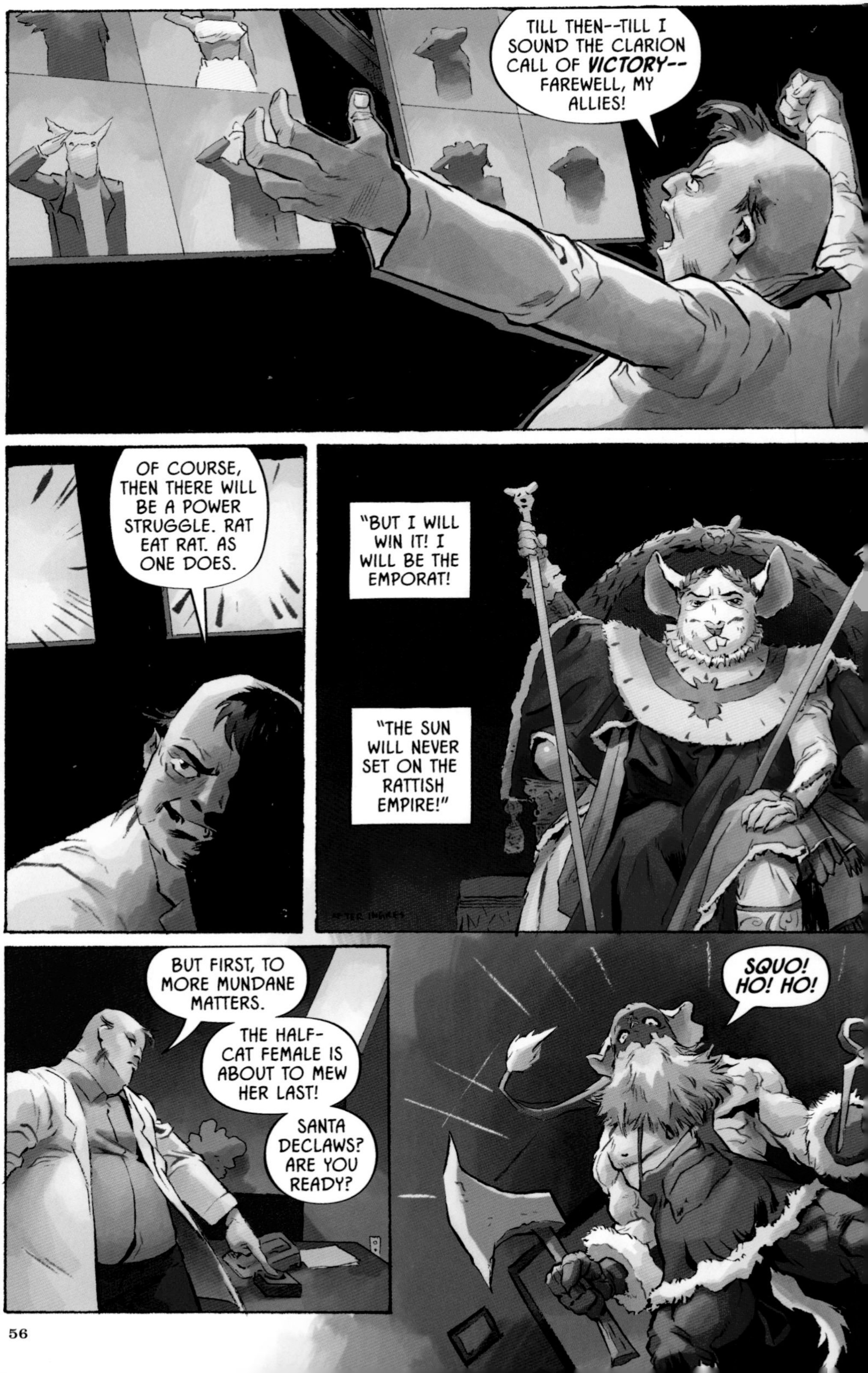
TILL THEN--TILL I SOUND THE CLARION CALL OF *VICTORY*-- FAREWELL, MY ALLIES!
OF COURSE, THEN THERE WILL BE A POWER STRUGGLE. RAT EAT RAT. AS ONE DOES.
"BUT I WILL WIN IT! I WILL BE THE EMPORAT!
"THE SUN WILL NEVER SET ON THE RATTISH EMPIRE!"
AFTER INGRES
BUT FIRST, TO MORE MUNDANE MATTERS.
THE HALF-CAT FEMALE IS ABOUT TO MEW HER LAST!
SANTA DECLAWS? ARE YOU READY?
SQUO! HO! HO!

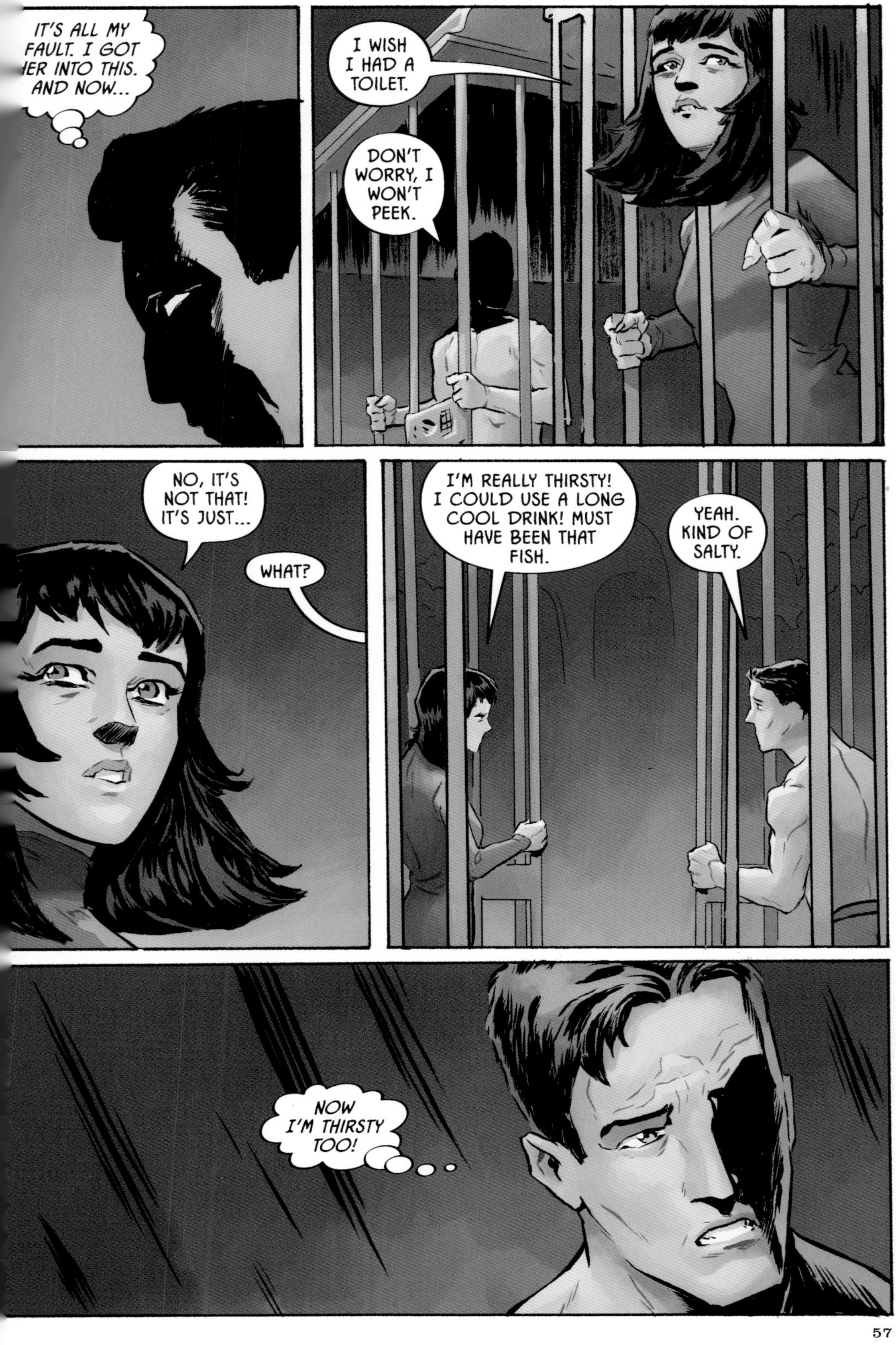
IT'S ALL MY FAULT. I GOT HER INTO THIS. AND NOW...
I WISH I HAD A TOILET.
DON'T WORRY, I WON'T PEEK.
NO, IT'S NOT THAT! IT'S JUST...
WHAT?
I'M REALLY THIRSTY! I COULD USE A LONG COOL DRINK! MUST HAVE BEEN THAT FISH.
YEAH. KIND OF SALTY.
NOW I'M THIRSTY TOO!

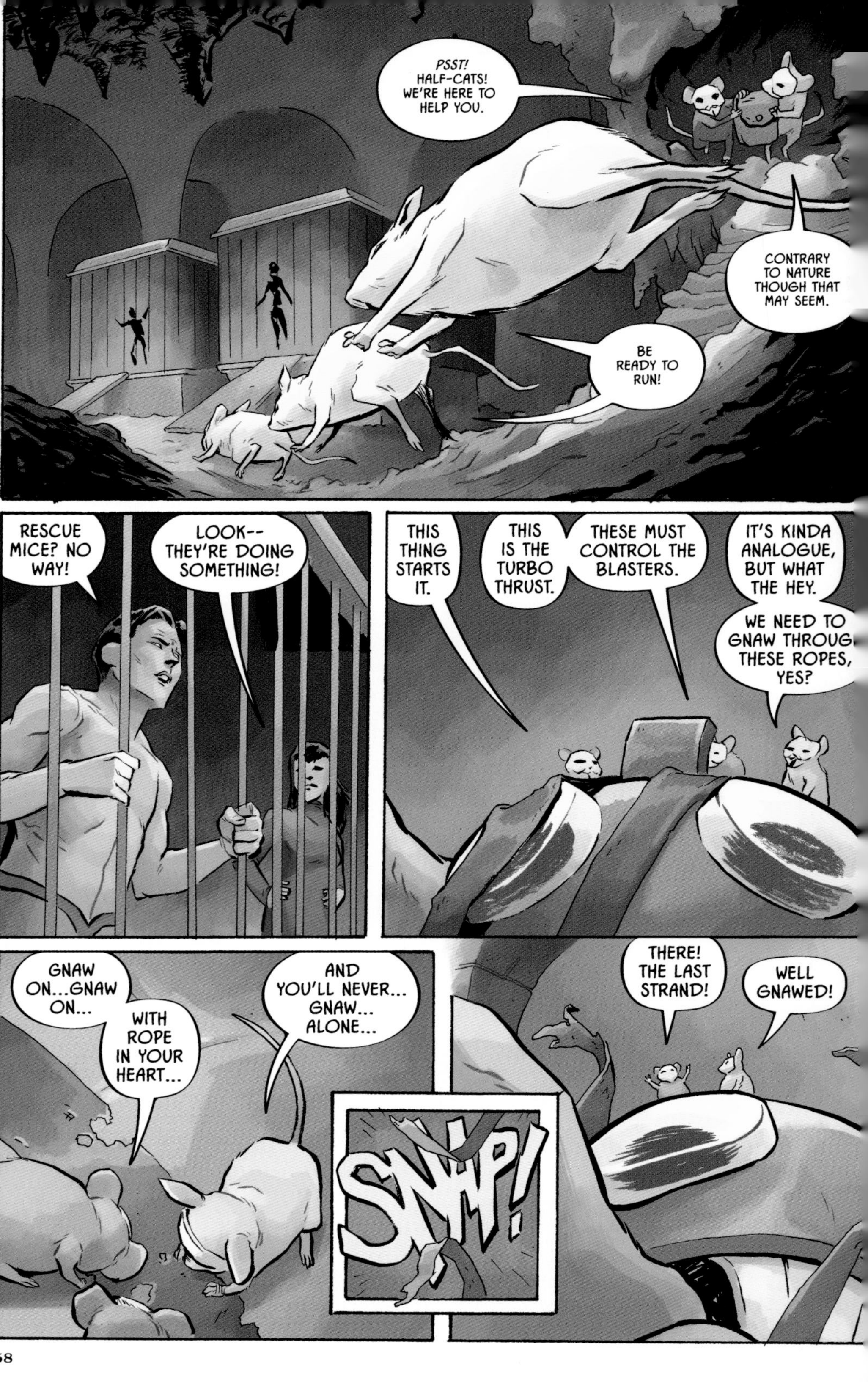
PSST! HALF-CATS! WE'RE HERE TO HELP YOU.
CONTRARY TO NATURE THOUGH THAT MAY SEEM.
BE READY TO RUN!
RESCUE MICE? NO WAY!
LOOK-- THEY'RE DOING SOMETHING!
THIS THING STARTS IT.
THIS IS THE TURBO THRUST.
THESE MUST CONTROL THE BLASTERS.
IT'S KINDA ANALOGUE, BUT WHAT THE HEY.
WE NEED TO GNAW THROUG THESE ROPES, YES?
GNAW ON...GNAW ON...
WITH ROPE IN YOUR HEART...
AND YOU'LL NEVER... GNAW... ALONE...
SNAP!
THERE! THE LAST STRAND!
WELL GNAWED!

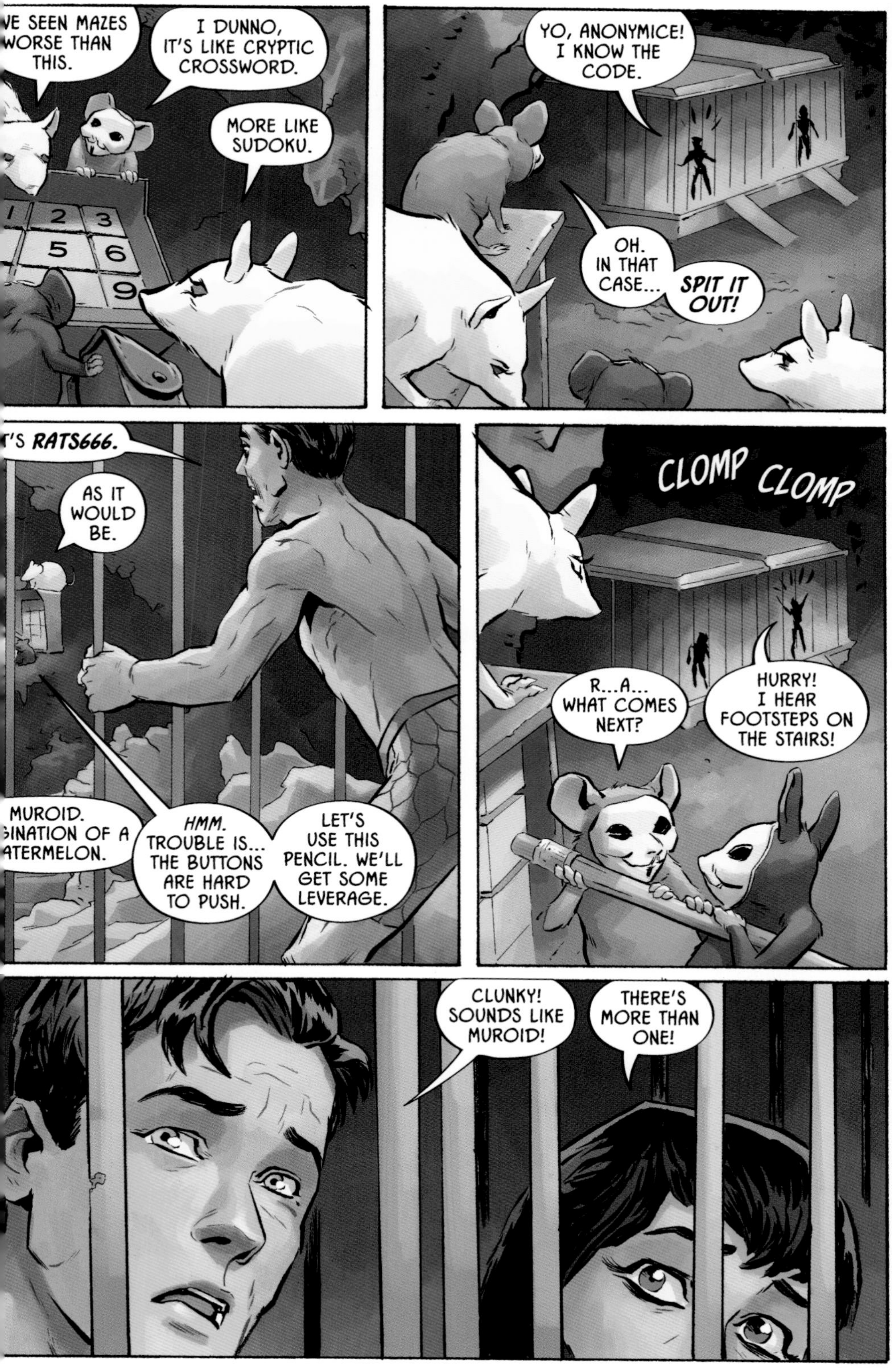
VE SEEN MAZES WORSE THAN THIS.
I DUNNO, IT'S LIKE CRYPTIC CROSSWORD.
MORE LIKE SUDOKU.
1 2 3 5 6 9
YO, ANONYMICE! I KNOW THE CODE.
OH. IN THAT CASE...
SPIT IT OUT!
T'S RATS666.
AS IT WOULD BE.
MUROID. GINATION OF A ATERMELON.
HMM. TROUBLE IS... THE BUTTONS ARE HARD TO PUSH.
LET'S USE THIS PENCIL. WE'LL GET SOME LEVERAGE.
CLOMP CLOMP
R...A... WHAT COMES NEXT?
HURRY! I HEAR FOOTSTEPS ON THE STAIRS!
CLUNKY! SOUNDS LIKE MUROID!
THERE'S MORE THAN ONE!

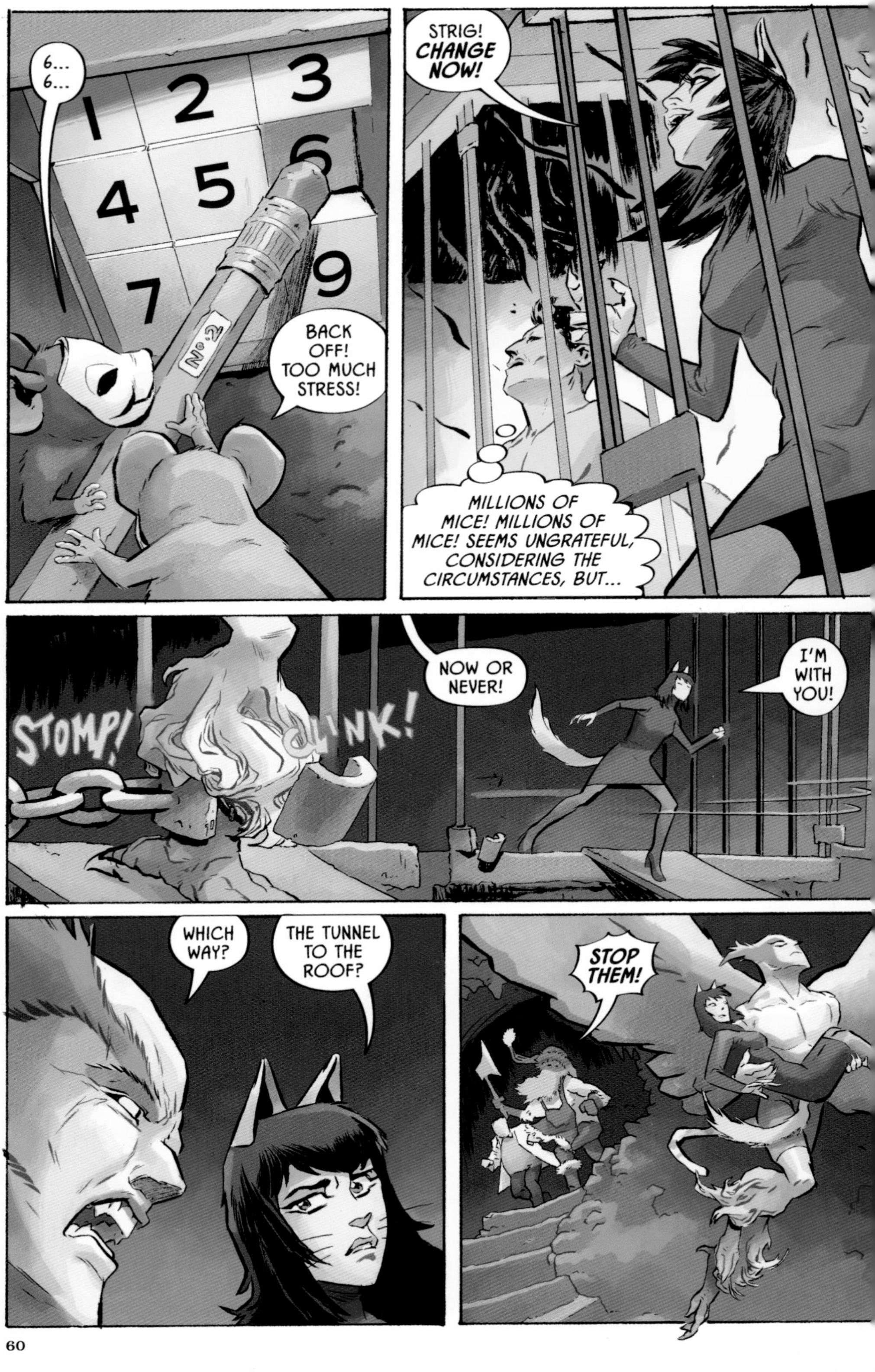
6...
6...
1 2 3
4 5 6
7 9
No 2
BACK OFF! TOO MUCH STRESS!
STRIG! CHANGE NOW!
MILLIONS OF MICE! MILLIONS OF MICE! SEEMS UNGRATEFUL, CONSIDERING THE CIRCUMSTANCES, BUT...
STOMP!
CLINK!
NOW OR NEVER!
I'M WITH YOU!
WHICH WAY?
THE TUNNEL TO THE ROOF?
STOP THEM!

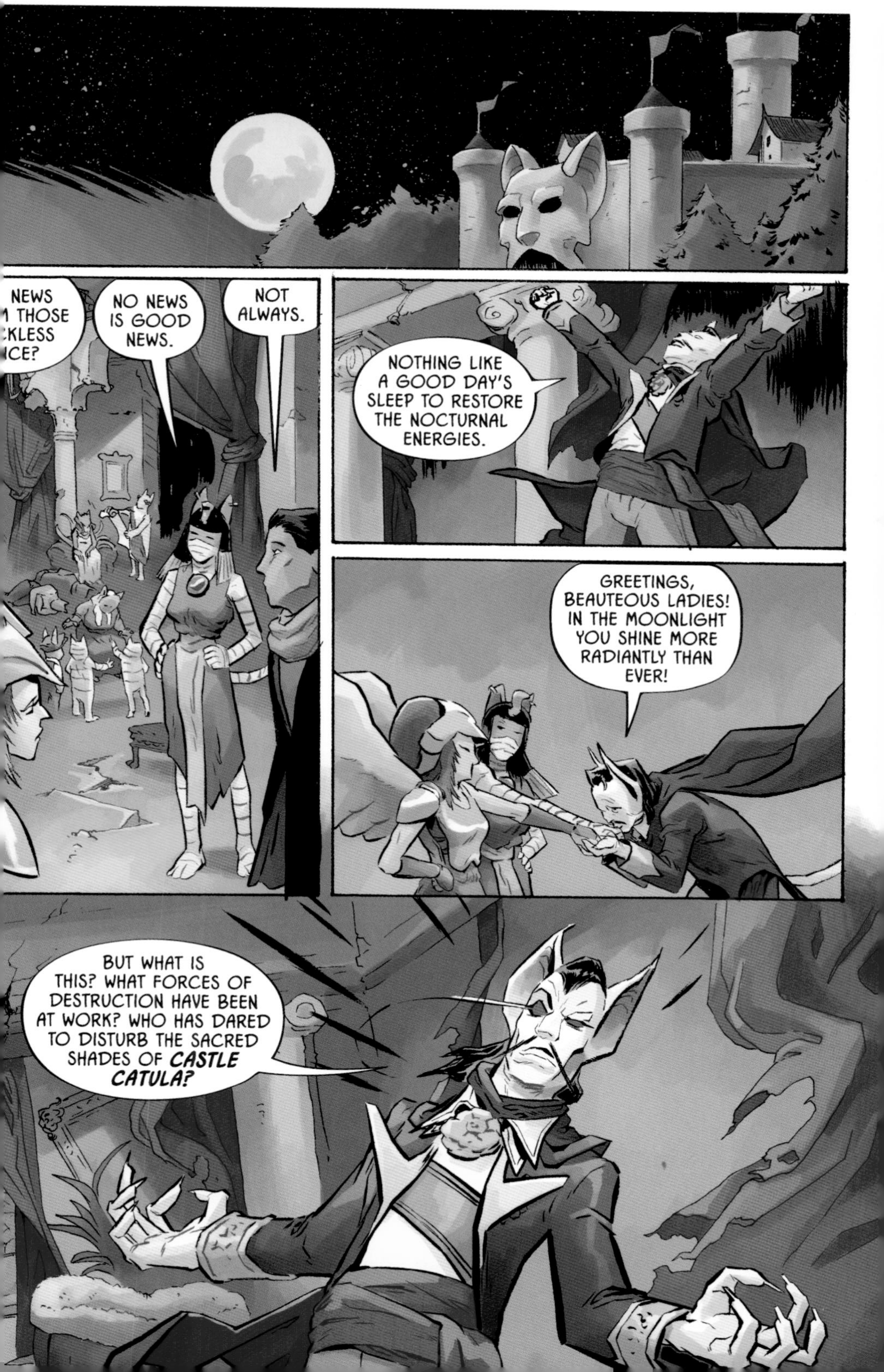
NEWS
1 THOSE
KLESS
ICE?
NO NEWS IS GOOD NEWS.
NOT ALWAYS.
NOTHING LIKE A GOOD DAY'S SLEEP TO RESTORE THE NOCTURNAL ENERGIES.
GREETINGS, BEAUTEOUS LADIES! IN THE MOONLIGHT YOU SHINE MORE RADIANTLY THAN EVER!
BUT WHAT IS THIS? WHAT FORCES OF DESTRUCTION HAVE BEEN AT WORK? WHO HAS DARED TO DISTURB THE SACRED SHADES OF ***CASTLE CATULA?***

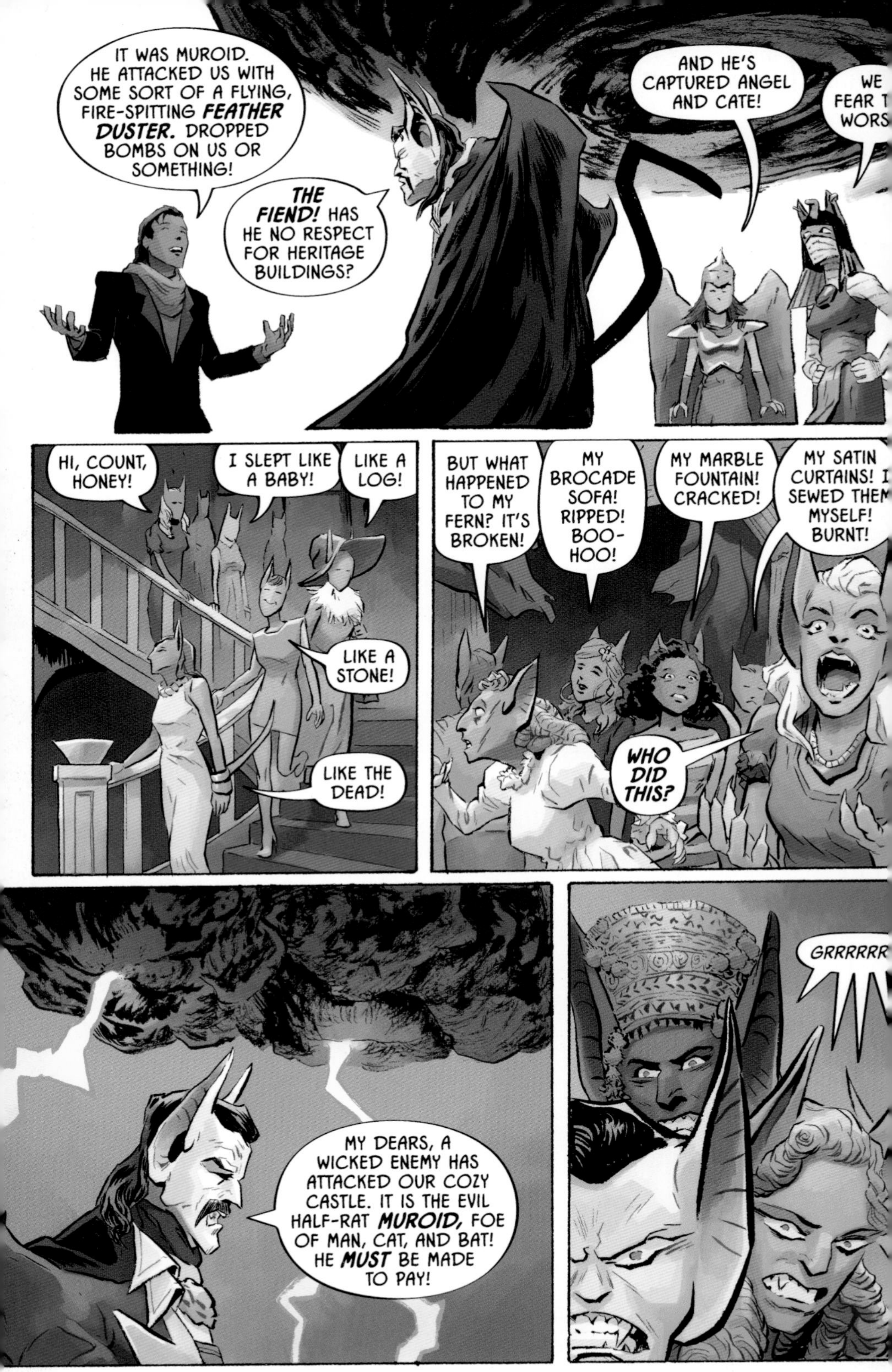
IT WAS MUROID. HE ATTACKED US WITH SOME SORT OF A FLYING, FIRE-SPITTING **FEATHER DUSTER.** DROPPED BOMBS ON US OR SOMETHING!
THE FIEND! HAS HE NO RESPECT FOR HERITAGE BUILDINGS?
AND HE'S CAPTURED ANGEL AND CATE!
WE FEAR T WORS
HI, COUNT, HONEY!
I SLEPT LIKE A BABY!
LIKE A LOG!
LIKE A STONE!
LIKE THE DEAD!
BUT WHAT HAPPENED TO MY FERN? IT'S BROKEN!
MY BROCADE SOFA! RIPPED! BOO-HOO!
MY MARBLE FOUNTAIN! CRACKED!
MY SATIN CURTAINS! I SEWED THEM MYSELF! BURNT!
WHO DID THIS?
MY DEARS, A WICKED ENEMY HAS ATTACKED OUR COZY CASTLE. IT IS THE EVIL HALF-RAT ***MUROID,*** FOE OF MAN, CAT, AND BAT! HE ***MUST*** BE MADE TO PAY!
GRRRRRR

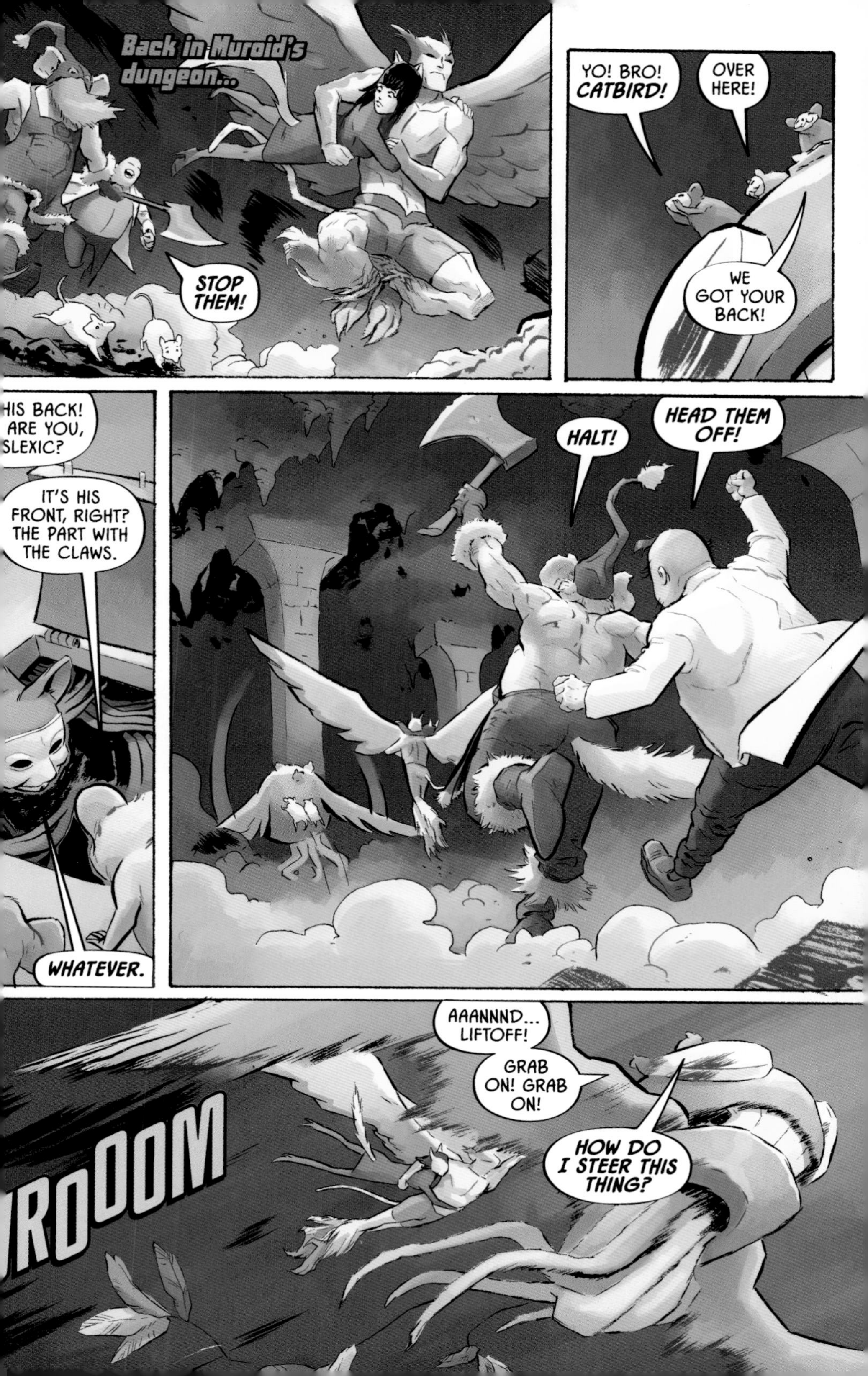

Back in Muroid's dungeon...
STOP THEM!
YO! BRO! CATBIRD!
OVER HERE!
WE GOT YOUR BACK!
HIS BACK! ARE YOU, SLEXIC?
IT'S HIS FRONT, RIGHT? THE PART WITH THE CLAWS.
WHATEVER.
HALT!
HEAD THEM OFF!
VROOOM
AAANNND... LIFTOFF!
GRAB ON! GRAB ON!
HOW DO I STEER THIS THING?

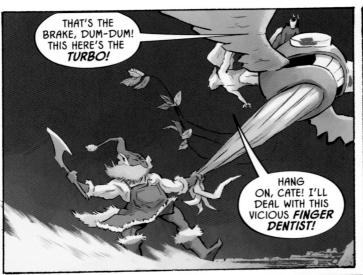

THAT'S THE BRAKE, DUM-DUM! THIS HERE'S THE *TURBO!*

HANG ON, CATE! I'LL DEAL WITH THIS VICIOUS *FINGER DENTIST!*

RED ALERT! RED ALERT! ROOFTOP MURINE TO THE CELLAR, NOW!

WHOOSH

COME NEAR ME, *FLUFF BOY,* AND YOU'LL BE MINUTE STEAK!

DECLAWS!

SLASH

SQUEEE-OOOOW!

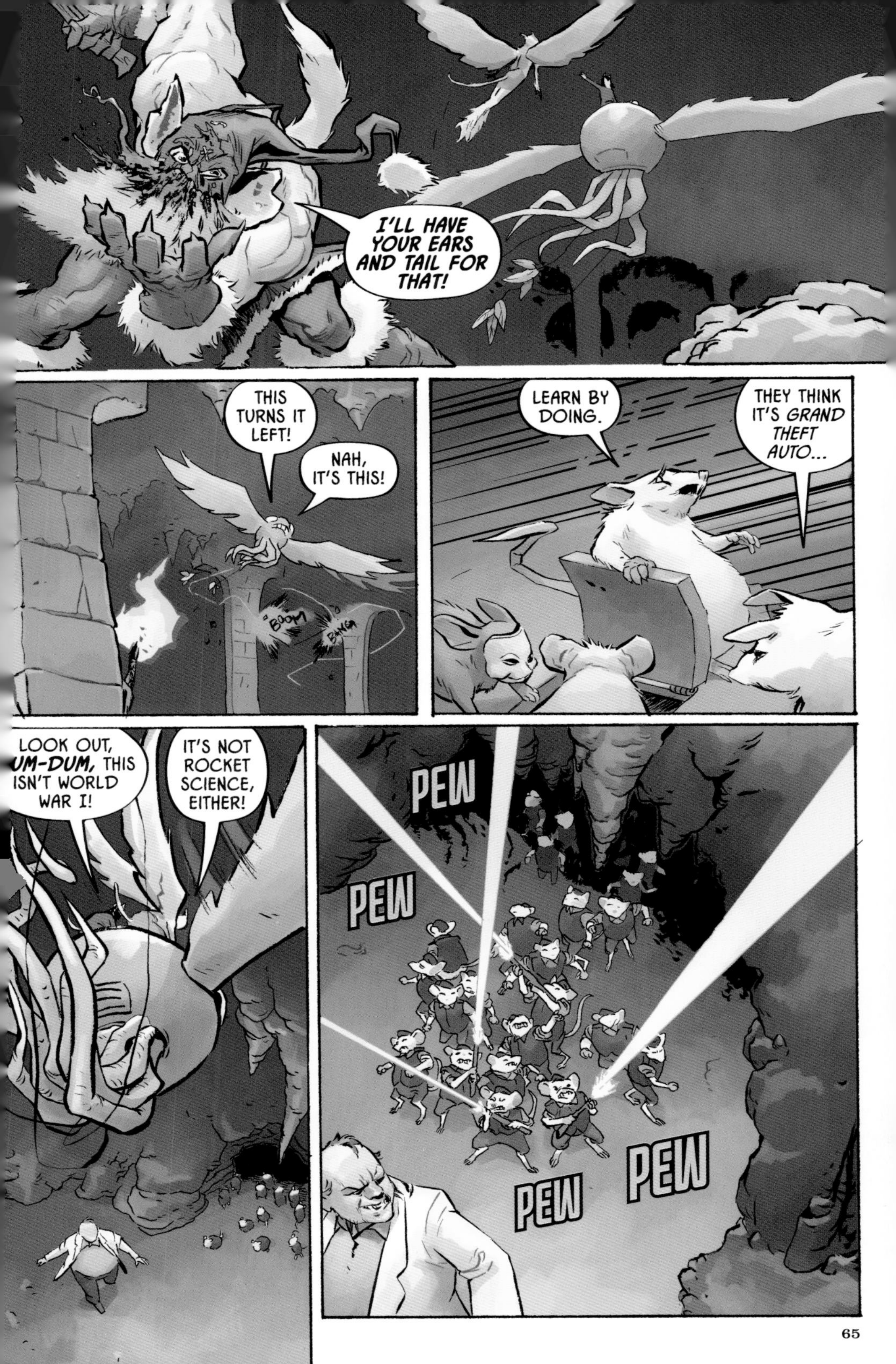
I'LL HAVE YOUR EARS AND TAIL FOR THAT!
THIS TURNS IT LEFT!
NAH, IT'S THIS!
BOOM
BANG
LEARN BY DOING.
THEY THINK IT'S *GRAND THEFT AUTO*...
LOOK OUT, **UM-DUM,** THIS ISN'T WORLD WAR I!
IT'S NOT ROCKET SCIENCE, EITHER!
PEW
PEW
PEW
PEW

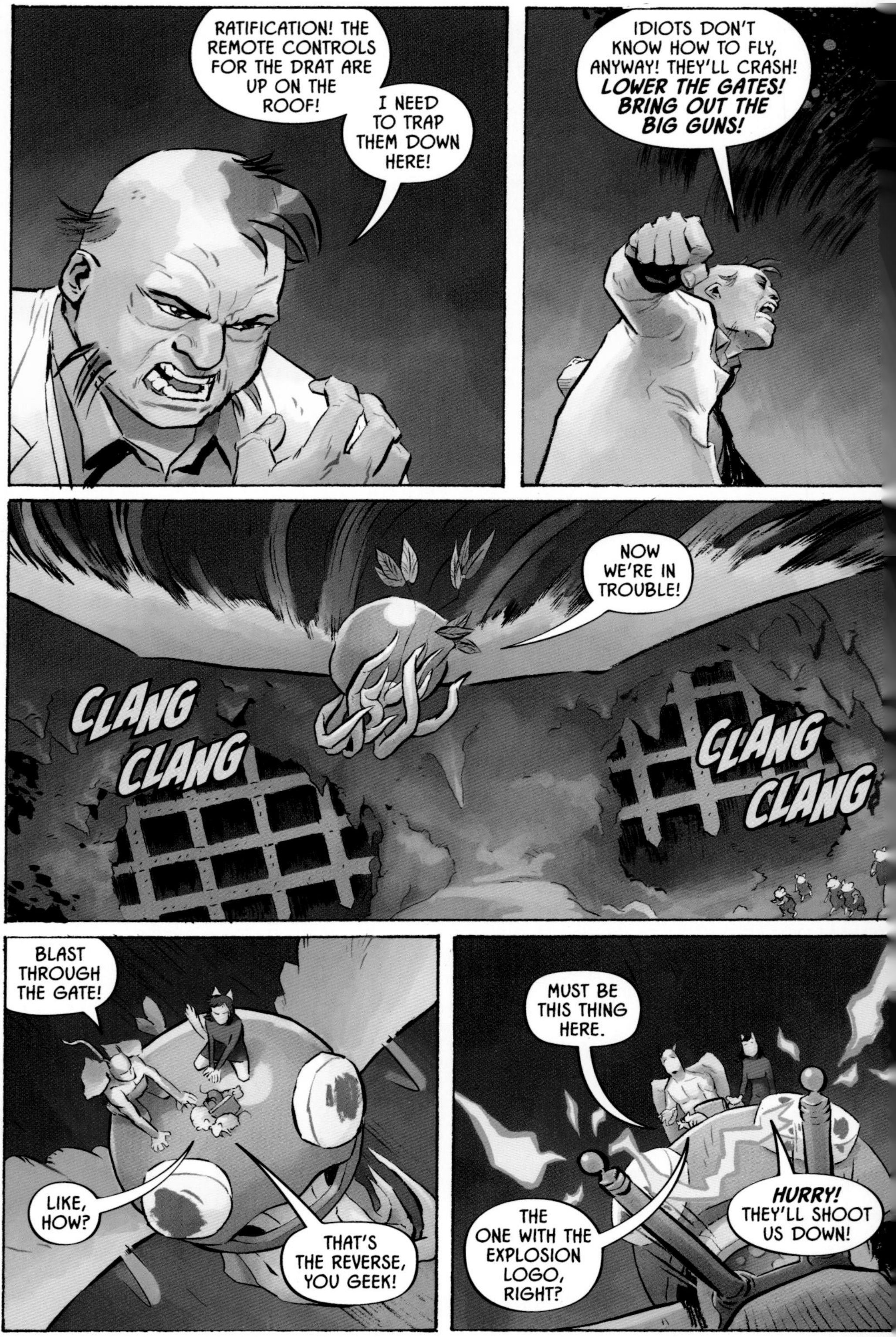
RATIFICATION! THE REMOTE CONTROLS FOR THE DRAT ARE UP ON THE ROOF!
I NEED TO TRAP THEM DOWN HERE!
IDIOTS DON'T KNOW HOW TO FLY, ANYWAY! THEY'LL CRASH! LOWER THE GATES! BRING OUT THE BIG GUNS!
NOW WE'RE IN TROUBLE!
CLANG CLANG
CLANG CLANG
BLAST THROUGH THE GATE!
LIKE, HOW?
THAT'S THE REVERSE, YOU GEEK!
MUST BE THIS THING HERE.
THE ONE WITH THE EXPLOSION LOGO, RIGHT?
HURRY! THEY'LL SHOOT US DOWN!

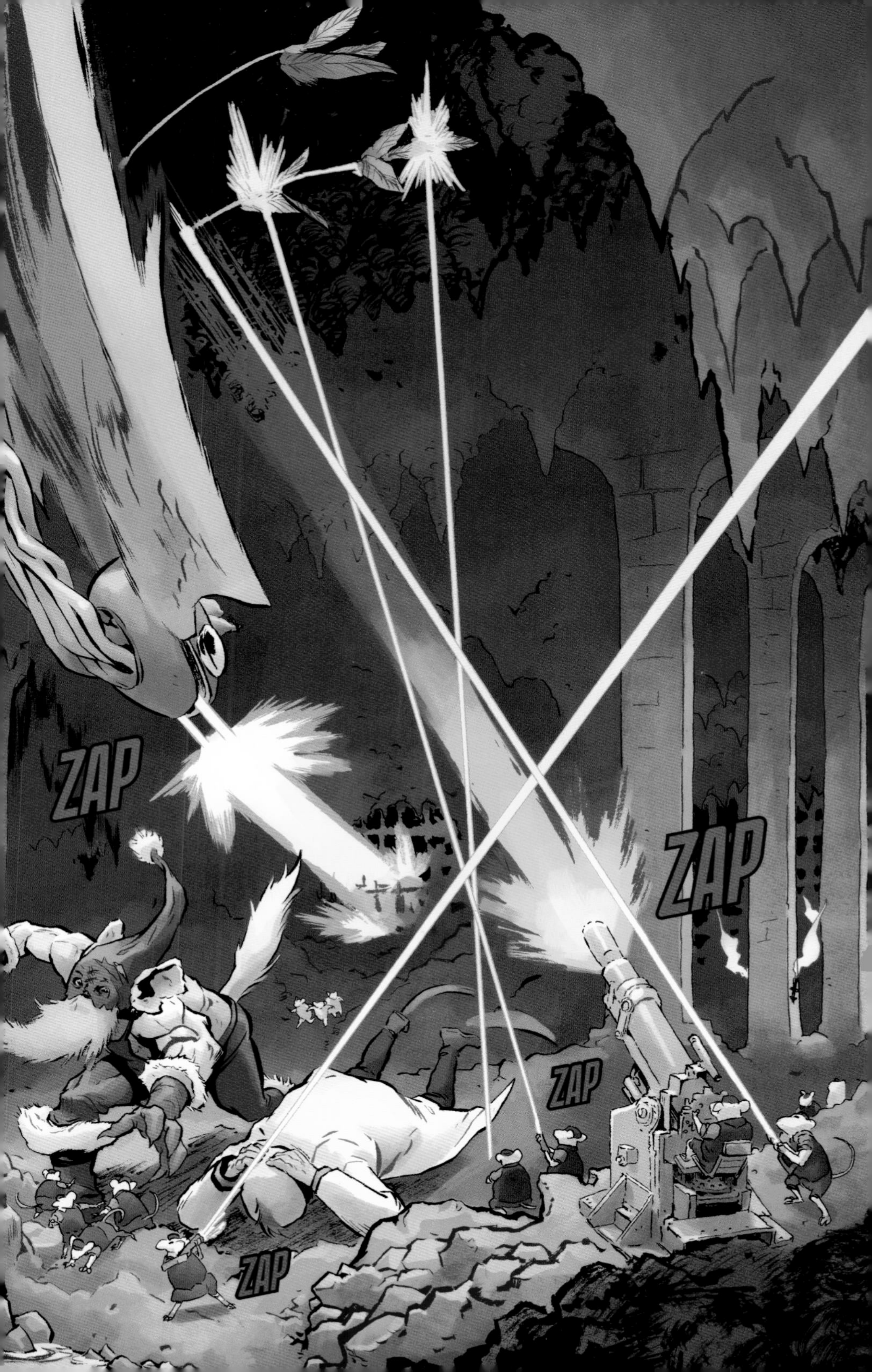
ZAP
ZAP
ZAP
ZAP

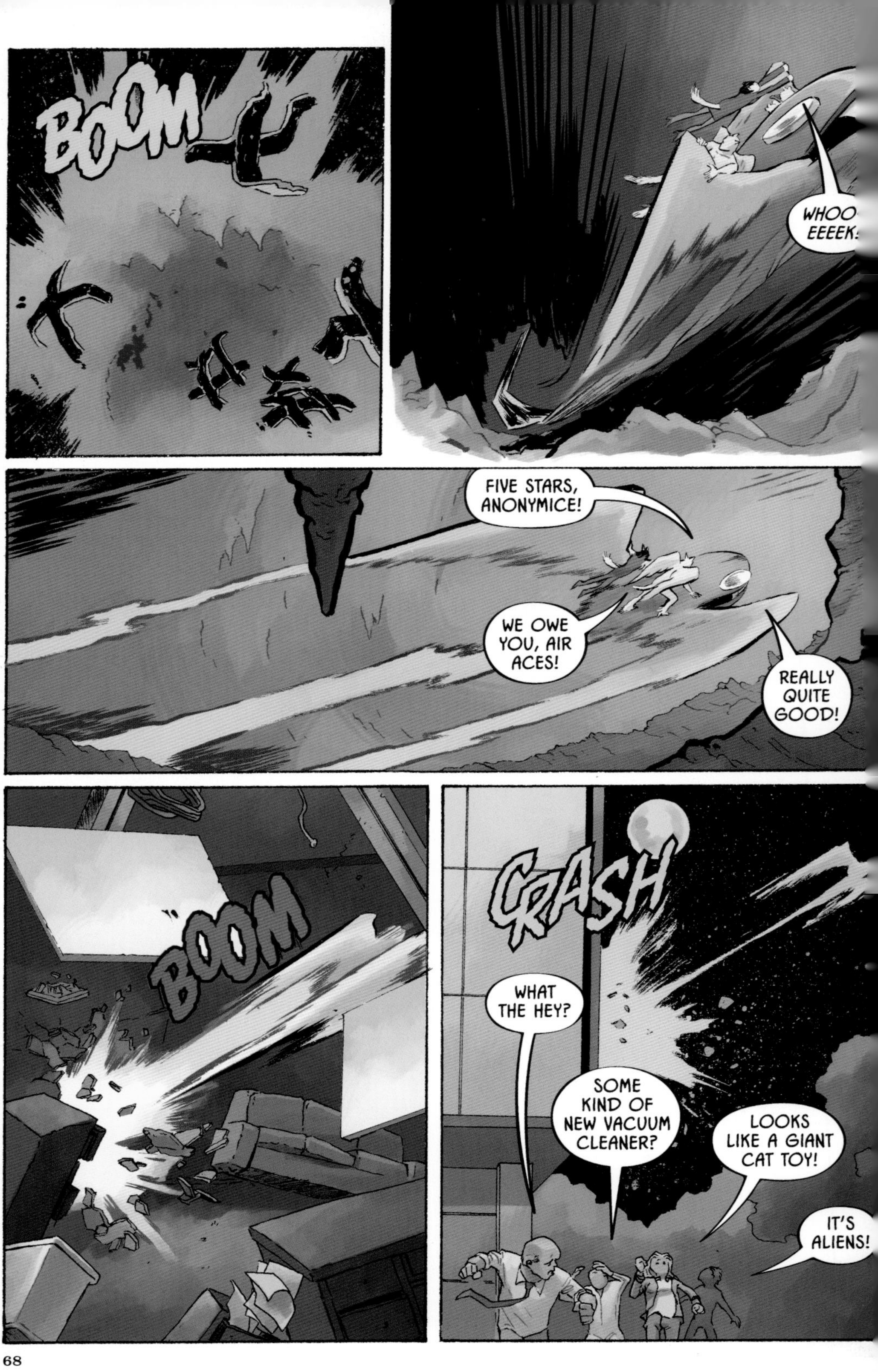
BOOM
WHOO EEEEK!
FIVE STARS, ANONYMICE!
WE OWE YOU, AIR ACES!
REALLY QUITE GOOD!
BOOM
CRASH
WHAT THE HEY?
SOME KIND OF NEW VACUUM CLEANER?
LOOKS LIKE A GIANT CAT TOY!
IT'S ALIENS!

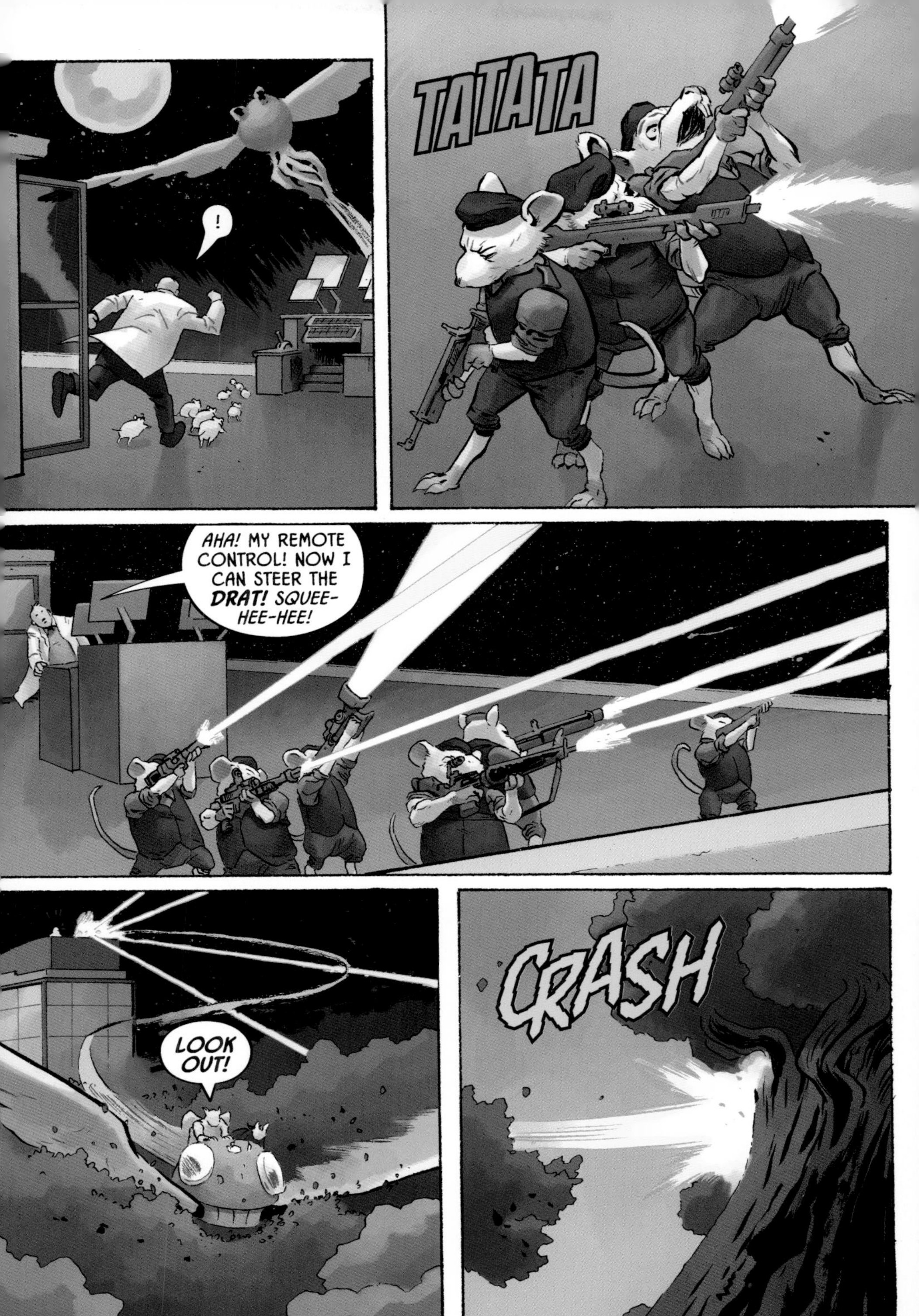
!
TATATA
AHA! MY REMOTE CONTROL! NOW I CAN STEER THE DRAT! SQUEE-HEE-HEE!
LOOK OUT!
CRASH

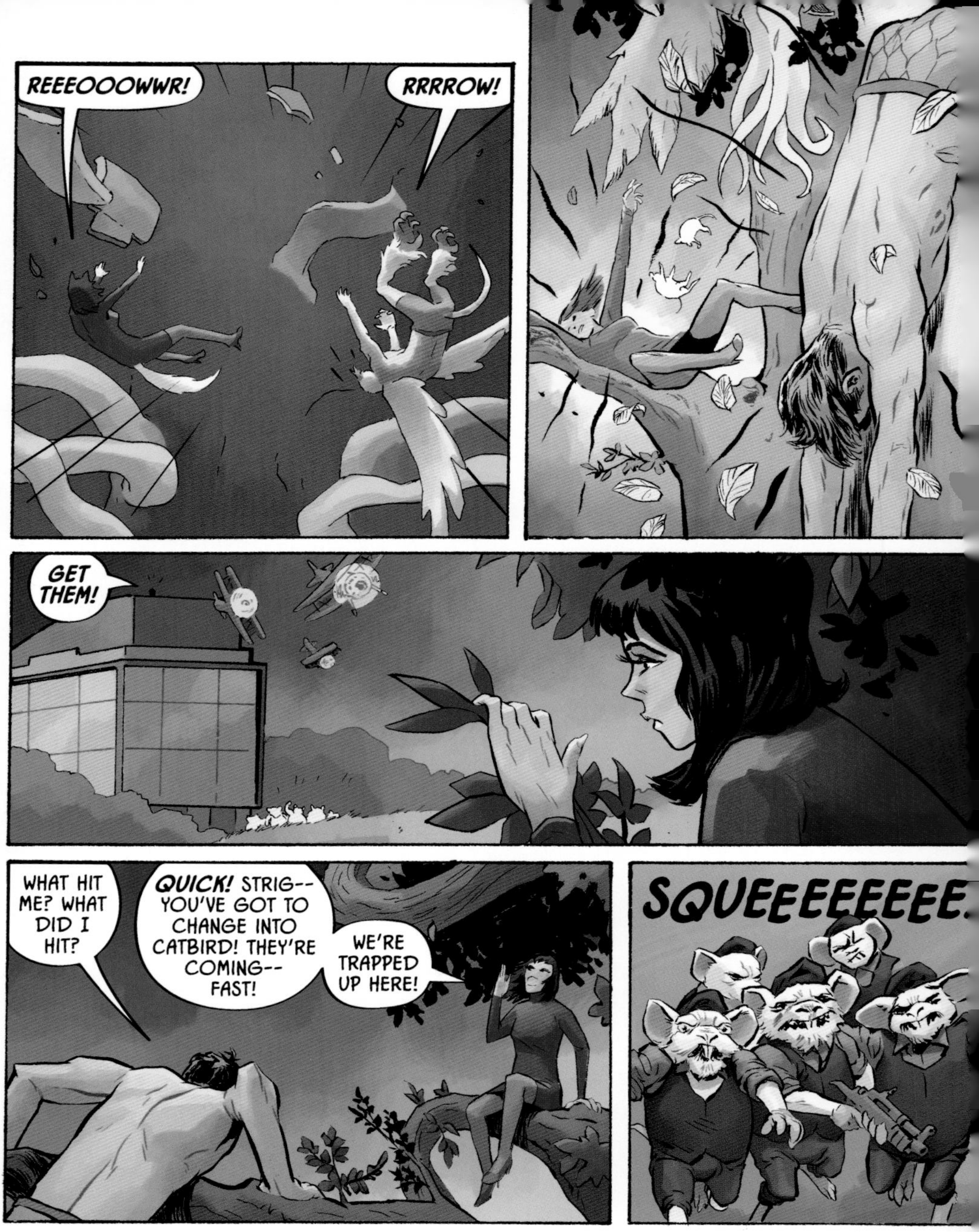
REEEOOOWWR!
RRRROW!
GET THEM!
WHAT HIT ME? WHAT DID I HIT?
QUICK! STRIG-- YOU'VE GOT TO CHANGE INTO CATBIRD! THEY'RE COMING-- FAST!
WE'RE TRAPPED UP HERE!
SQUEEEEEEEEE.

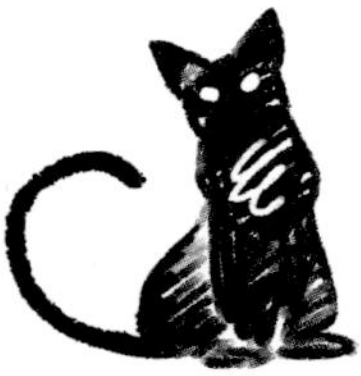

TREE CLIMBERS

Outdoor cats often climb trees, and sometimes they get stuck and can't get down. The best way to avoid having to call the fire department to rescue your cat is not to let them outside unsupervised in the first place!
Read more at www.catsandbirds.ca

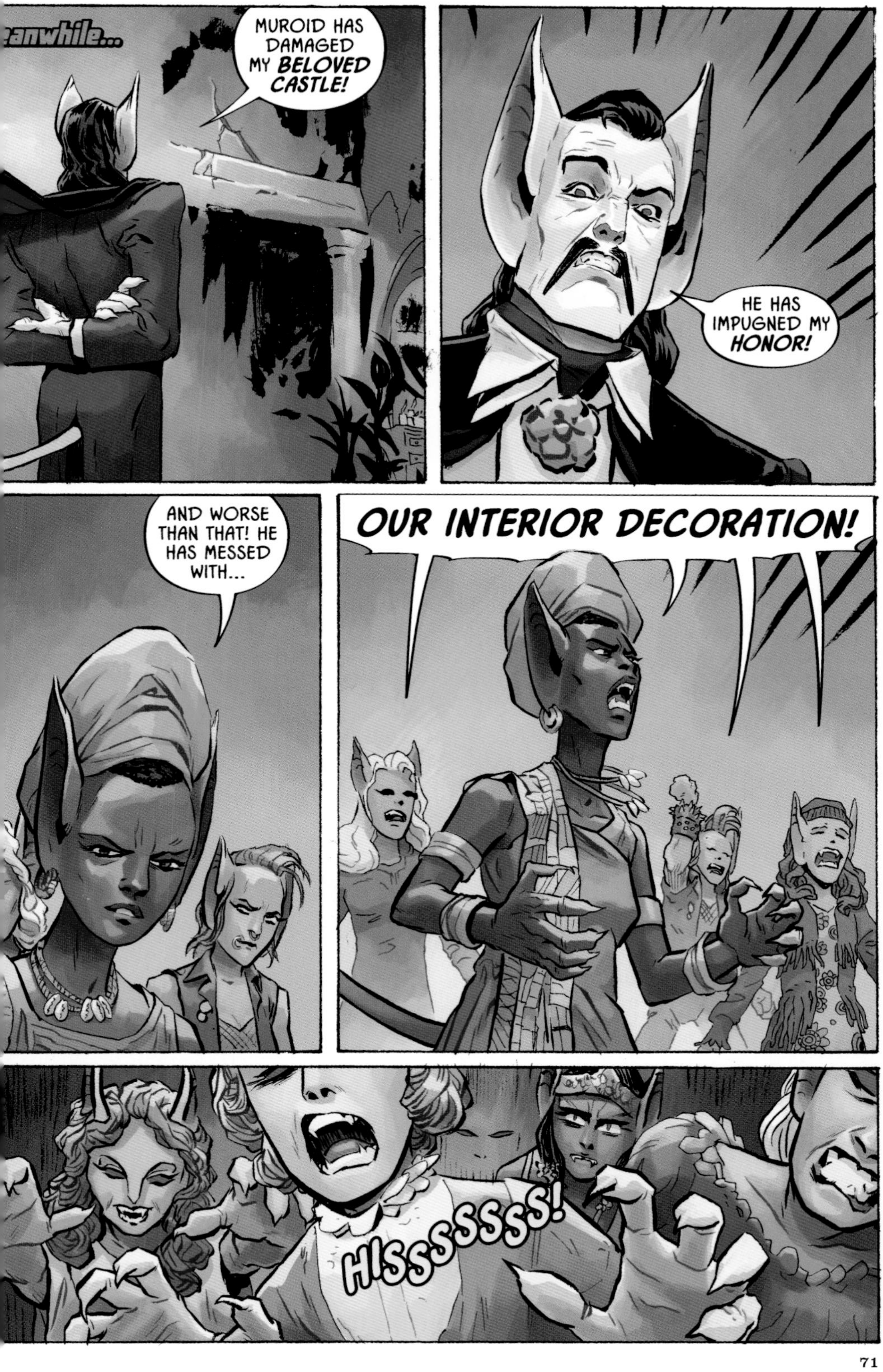
anwhile...
MUROID HAS DAMAGED MY BELOVED CASTLE!
HE HAS IMPUGNED MY HONOR!
AND WORSE THAN THAT! HE HAS MESSED WITH...
OUR INTERIOR DECORATION!
HISSSSSSS!

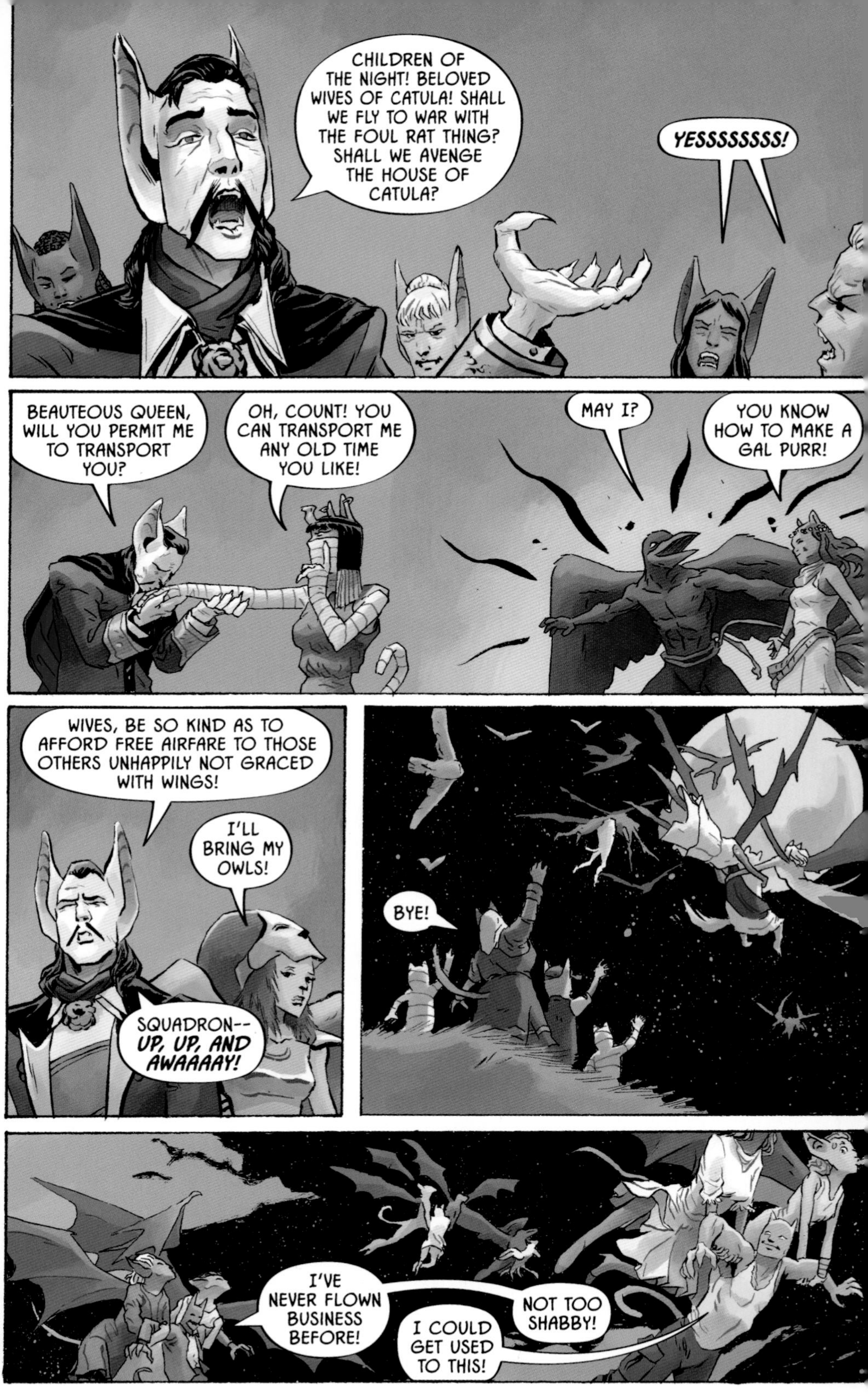
CHILDREN OF THE NIGHT! BELOVED WIVES OF CATULA! SHALL WE FLY TO WAR WITH THE FOUL RAT THING? SHALL WE AVENGE THE HOUSE OF CATULA?
YESSSSSSSS!
BEAUTEOUS QUEEN, WILL YOU PERMIT ME TO TRANSPORT YOU?
OH, COUNT! YOU CAN TRANSPORT ME ANY OLD TIME YOU LIKE!
MAY I?
YOU KNOW HOW TO MAKE A GAL PURR!
WIVES, BE SO KIND AS TO AFFORD FREE AIRFARE TO THOSE OTHERS UNHAPPILY NOT GRACED WITH WINGS!
I'LL BRING MY OWLS!
SQUADRON-- UP, UP, AND AWAAAAY!
BYE!
I'VE NEVER FLOWN BUSINESS BEFORE!
NOT TOO SHABBY!
I COULD GET USED TO THIS!

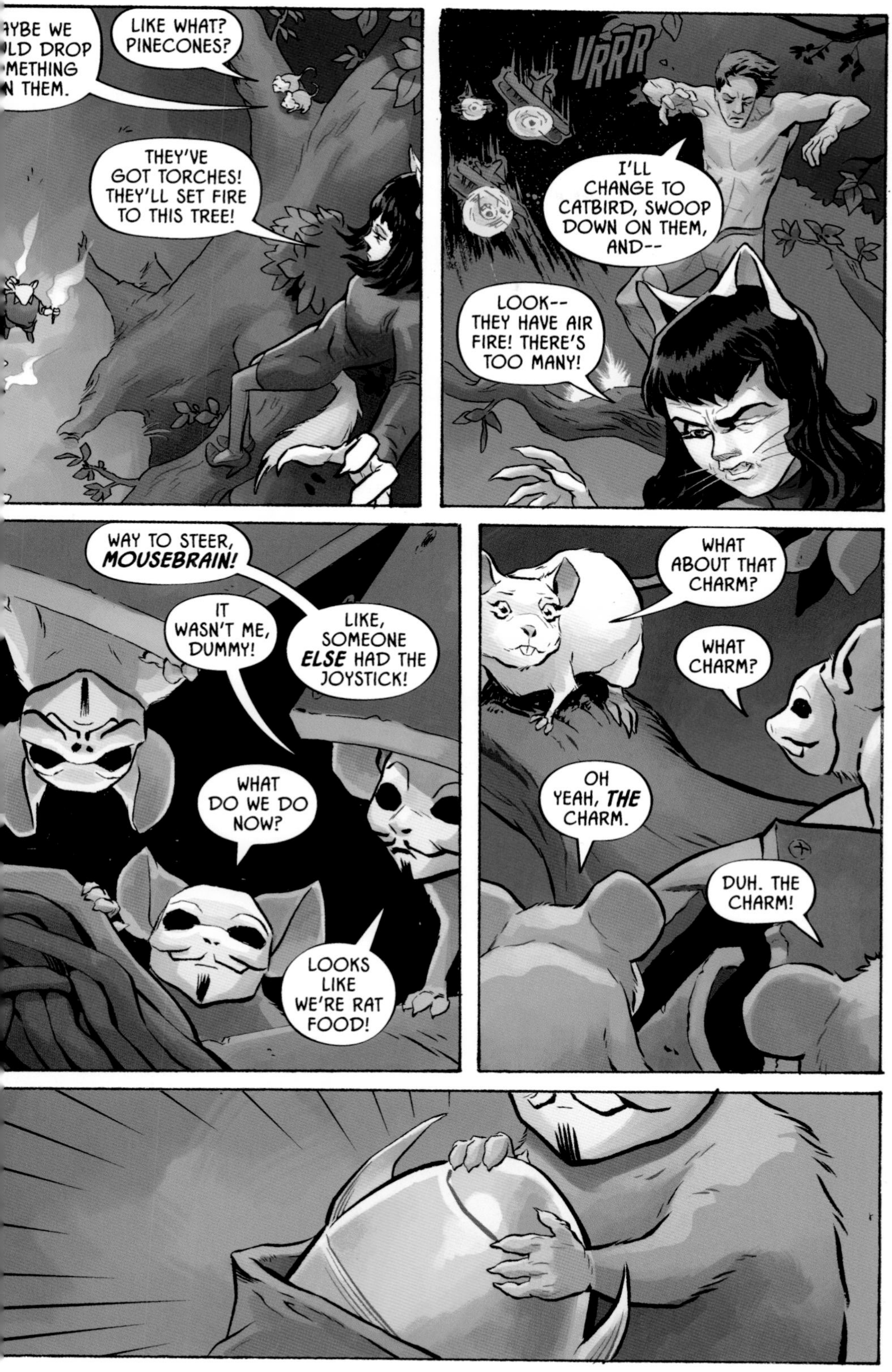
AYBE WE
LD DROP
METHING
N THEM.
LIKE WHAT? PINECONES?
THEY'VE GOT TORCHES! THEY'LL SET FIRE TO THIS TREE!
VRRR
I'LL CHANGE TO CATBIRD, SWOOP DOWN ON THEM, AND--
LOOK-- THEY HAVE AIR FIRE! THERE'S TOO MANY!
WAY TO STEER, *MOUSEBRAIN!*
IT WASN'T ME, DUMMY!
LIKE, SOMEONE *ELSE* HAD THE JOYSTICK!
WHAT DO WE DO NOW?
LOOKS LIKE WE'RE RAT FOOD!
WHAT ABOUT THAT CHARM?
WHAT CHARM?
OH YEAH, *THE* CHARM.
DUH. THE CHARM!

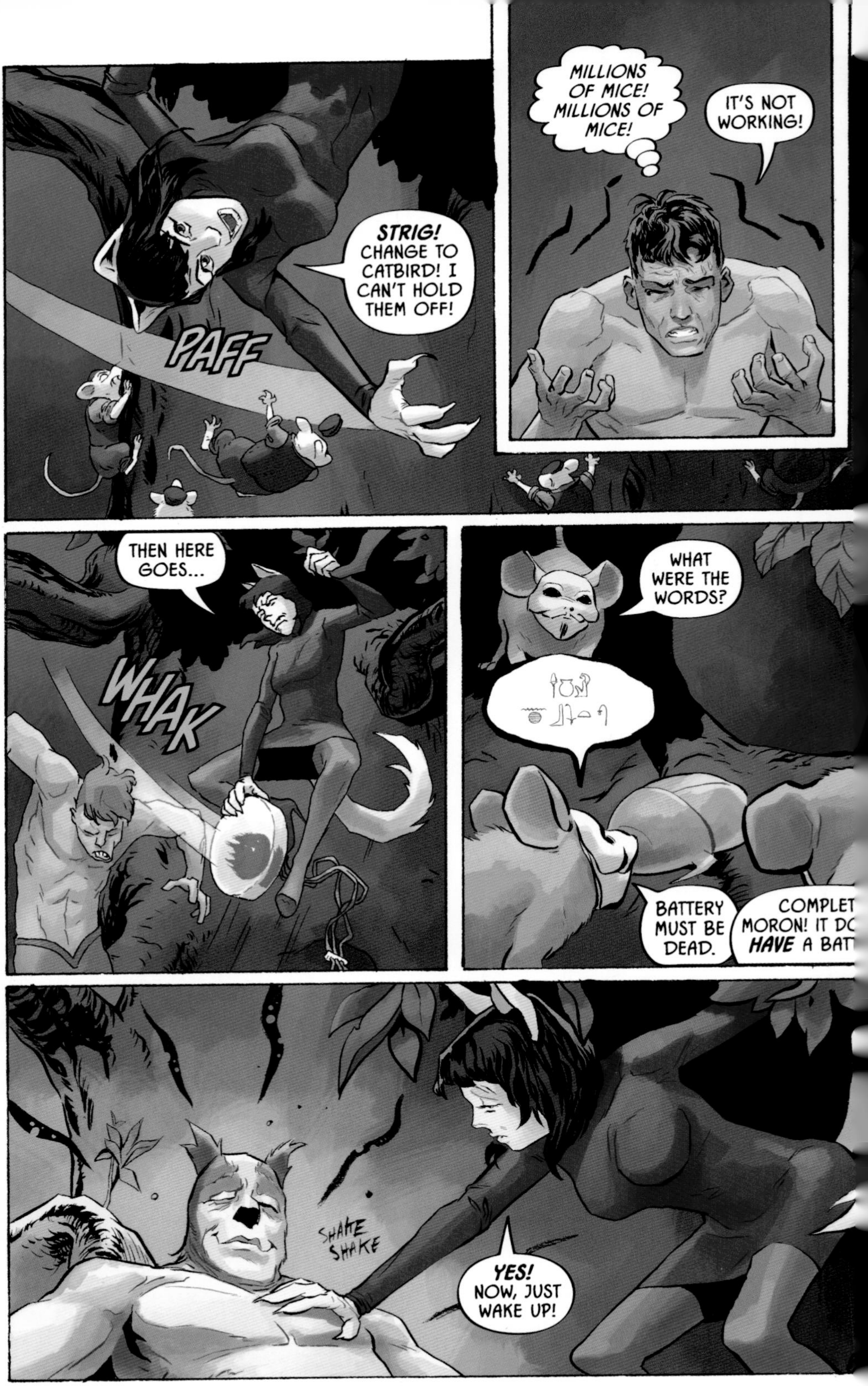
MILLIONS OF MICE! MILLIONS OF MICE!
IT'S NOT WORKING!
STRIG! CHANGE TO CATBIRD! I CAN'T HOLD THEM OFF!
PAFF
THEN HERE GOES...
WHAK
WHAT WERE THE WORDS?
BATTERY MUST BE DEAD.
COMPLET MORON! IT DO HAVE A BAT
SHAKE SHAKE
YES! NOW, JUST WAKE UP!

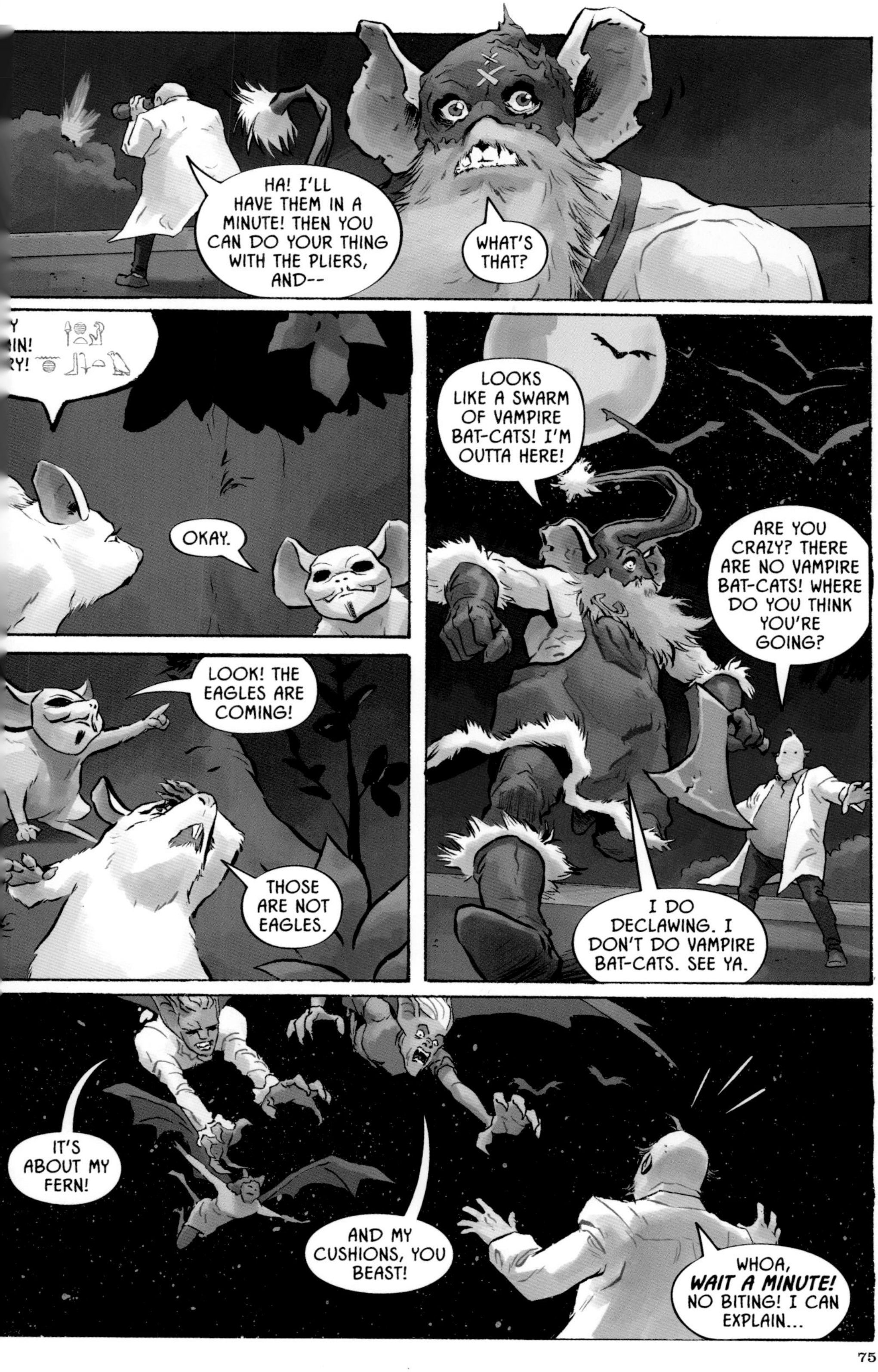
HA! I'LL HAVE THEM IN A MINUTE! THEN YOU CAN DO YOUR THING WITH THE PLIERS, AND--
WHAT'S THAT?
OKAY.
LOOKS LIKE A SWARM OF VAMPIRE BAT-CATS! I'M OUTTA HERE!
ARE YOU CRAZY? THERE ARE NO VAMPIRE BAT-CATS! WHERE DO YOU THINK YOU'RE GOING?
LOOK! THE EAGLES ARE COMING!
THOSE ARE NOT EAGLES.
I DO DECLAWING. I DON'T DO VAMPIRE BAT-CATS. SEE YA.
IT'S ABOUT MY FERN!
AND MY CUSHIONS, YOU BEAST!
WHOA, WAIT A MINUTE! NO BITING! I CAN EXPLAIN...

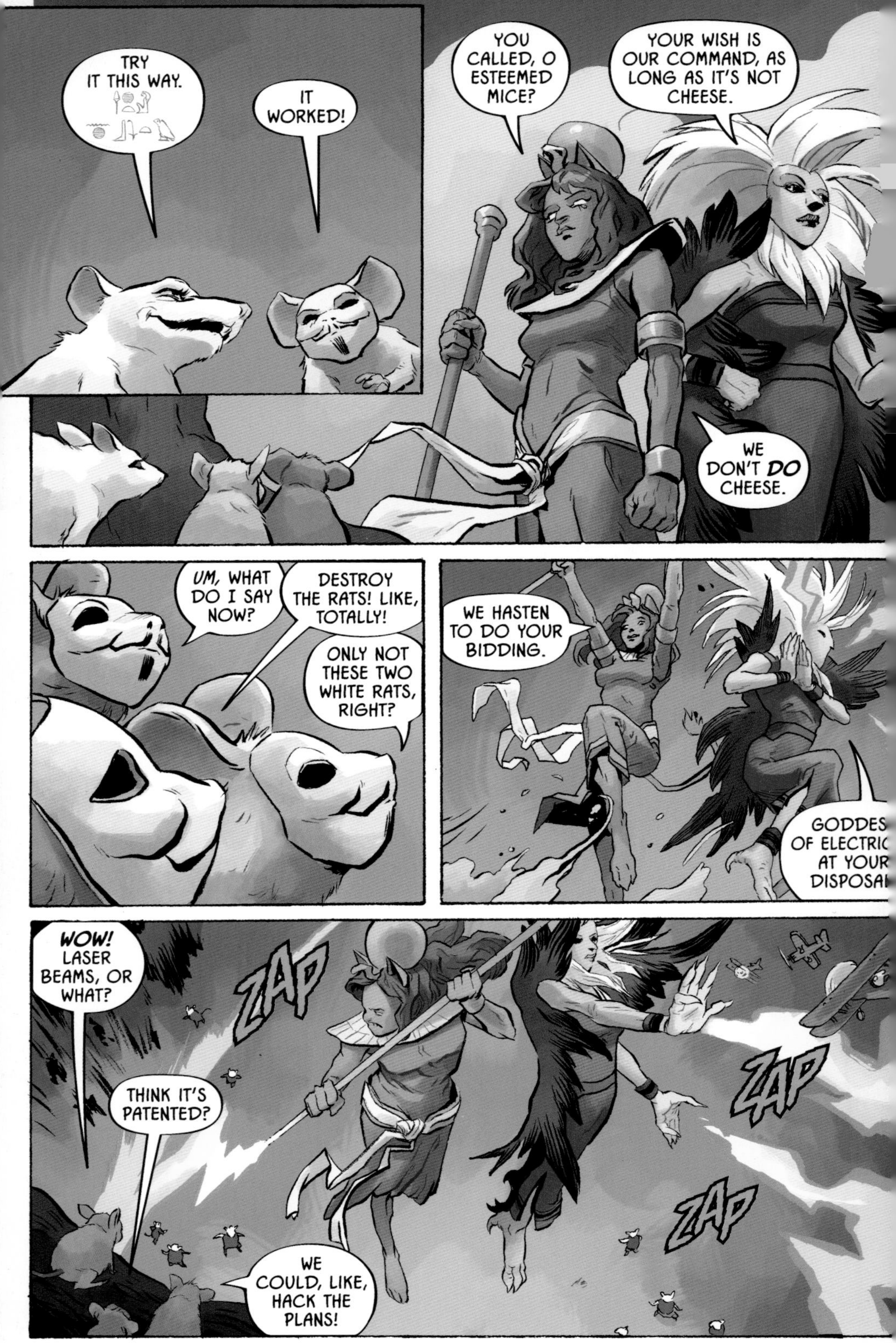
TRY IT THIS WAY.
IT WORKED!
YOU CALLED, O ESTEEMED MICE?
YOUR WISH IS OUR COMMAND, AS LONG AS IT'S NOT CHEESE.
WE DON'T *DO* CHEESE.
UM, WHAT DO I SAY NOW?
DESTROY THE RATS! LIKE, TOTALLY!
ONLY NOT THESE TWO WHITE RATS, RIGHT?
WE HASTEN TO DO YOUR BIDDING.
WOW! LASER BEAMS, OR WHAT?
ZAP
THINK IT'S PATENTED?
ZAP
ZAP
WE COULD, LIKE, HACK THE PLANS!

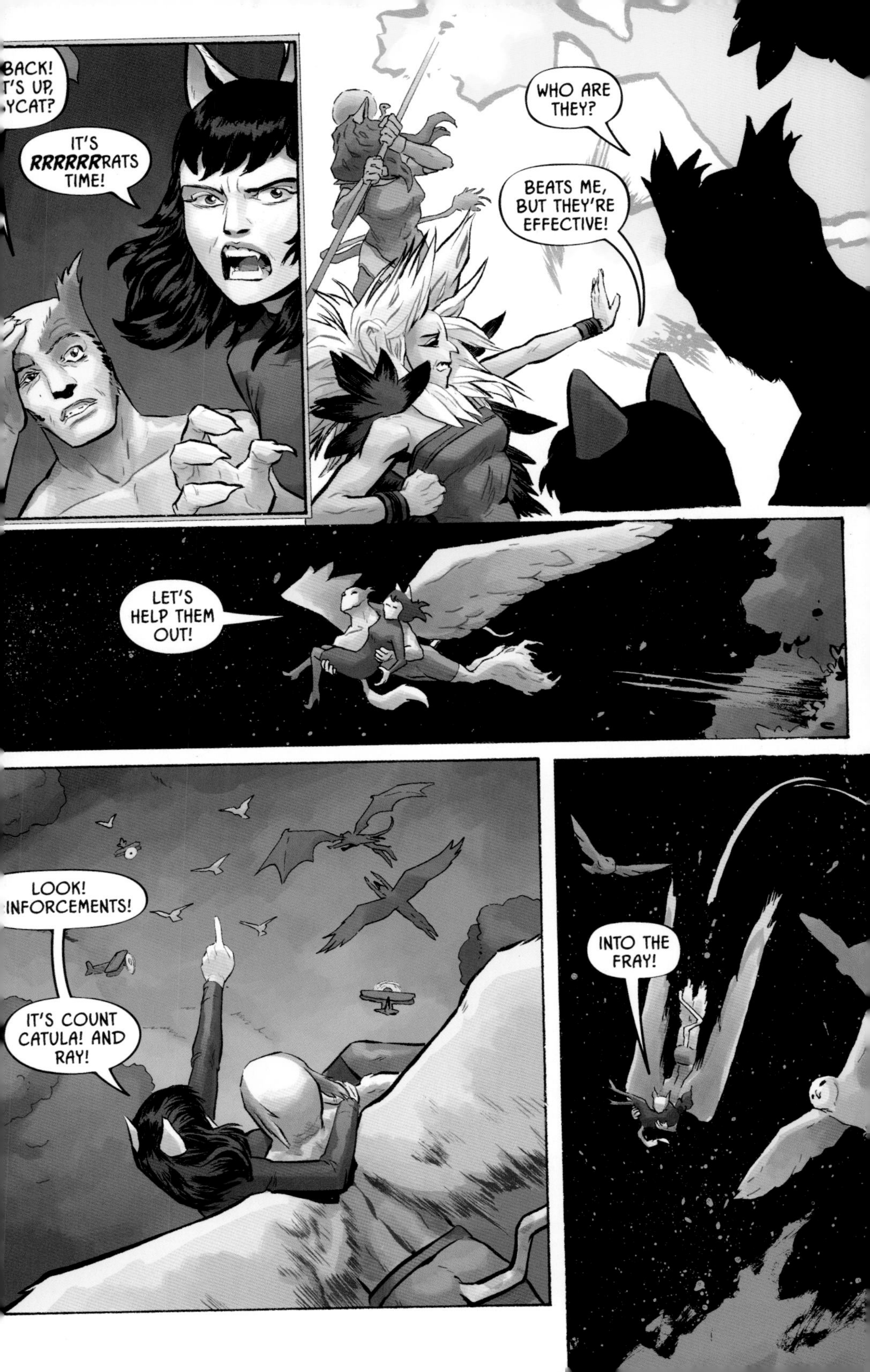
BACK!
T'S UP,
YCAT?
IT'S RRRRRRRATS TIME!
WHO ARE THEY?
BEATS ME, BUT THEY'RE EFFECTIVE!
LET'S HELP THEM OUT!
LOOK!
INFORCEMENTS!
IT'S COUNT CATULA! AND RAY!
INTO THE FRAY!

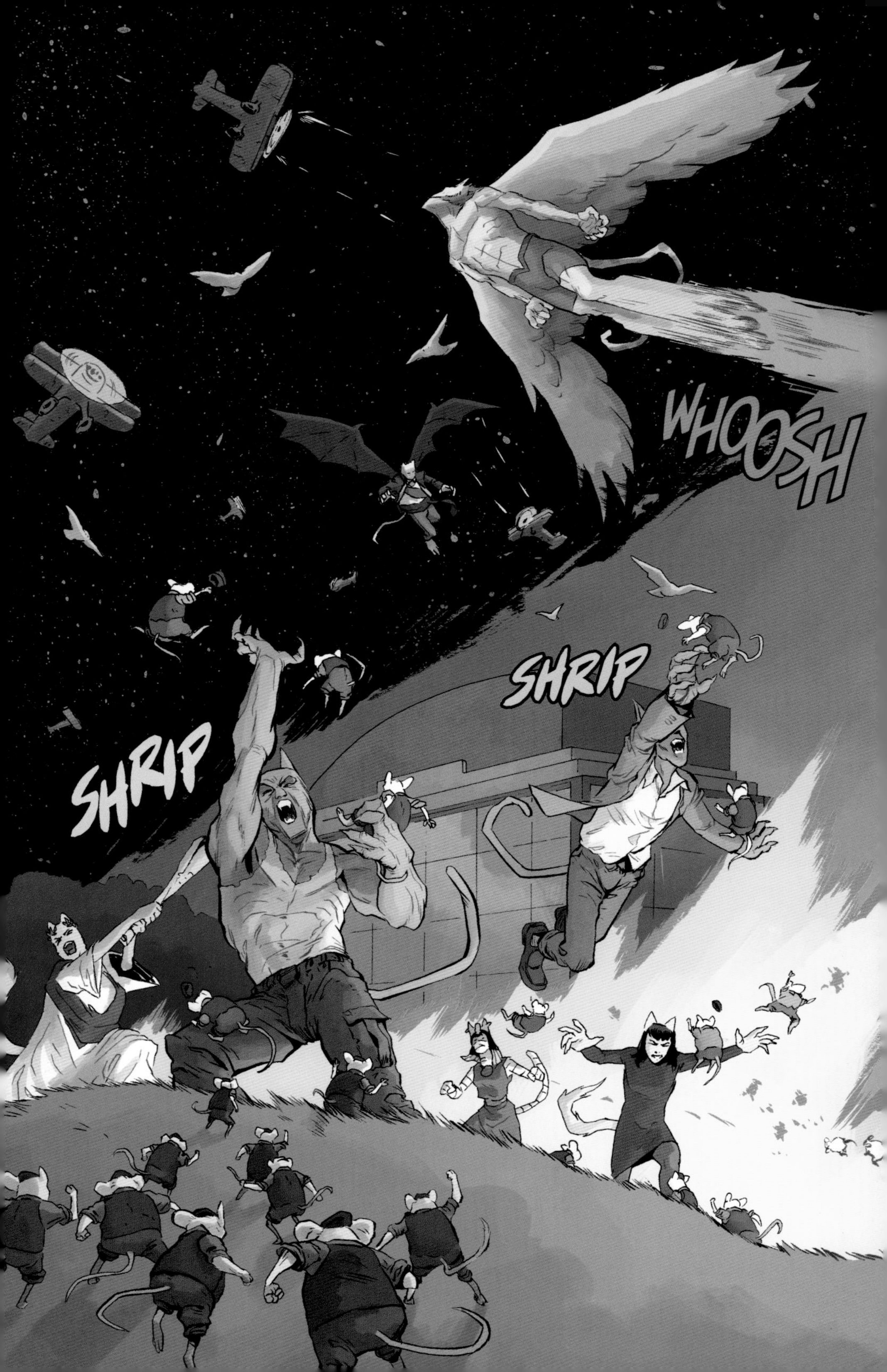
WHOOSH
SHRIP
SHRIP

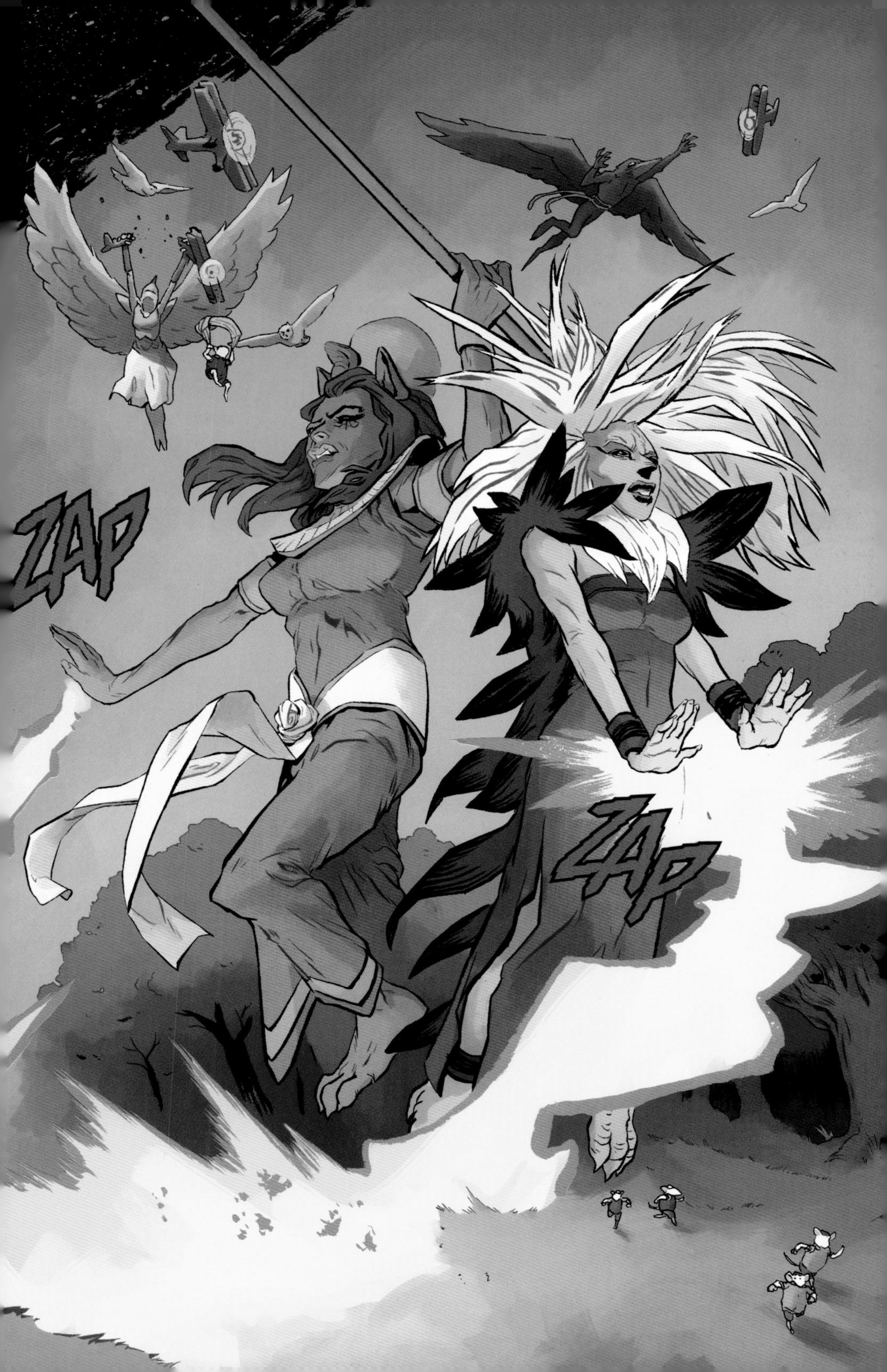
ZAP
ZAP

THREE AGAINST ONE! *UNFAIR!*

SLAM

I HAVE BEEN OUTFOXE OR OUTCATTE1 OR OUTBATTE1 WHATEVER!

I SHALL ESCAPE IN MY RATMOBILE!

I MAY HAVE LOST THE BATTLE...

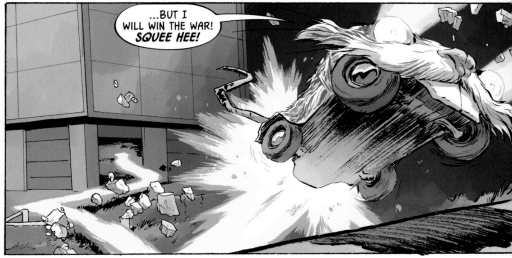

...BUT I WILL WIN THE WAR! *SQUEE HEE!*

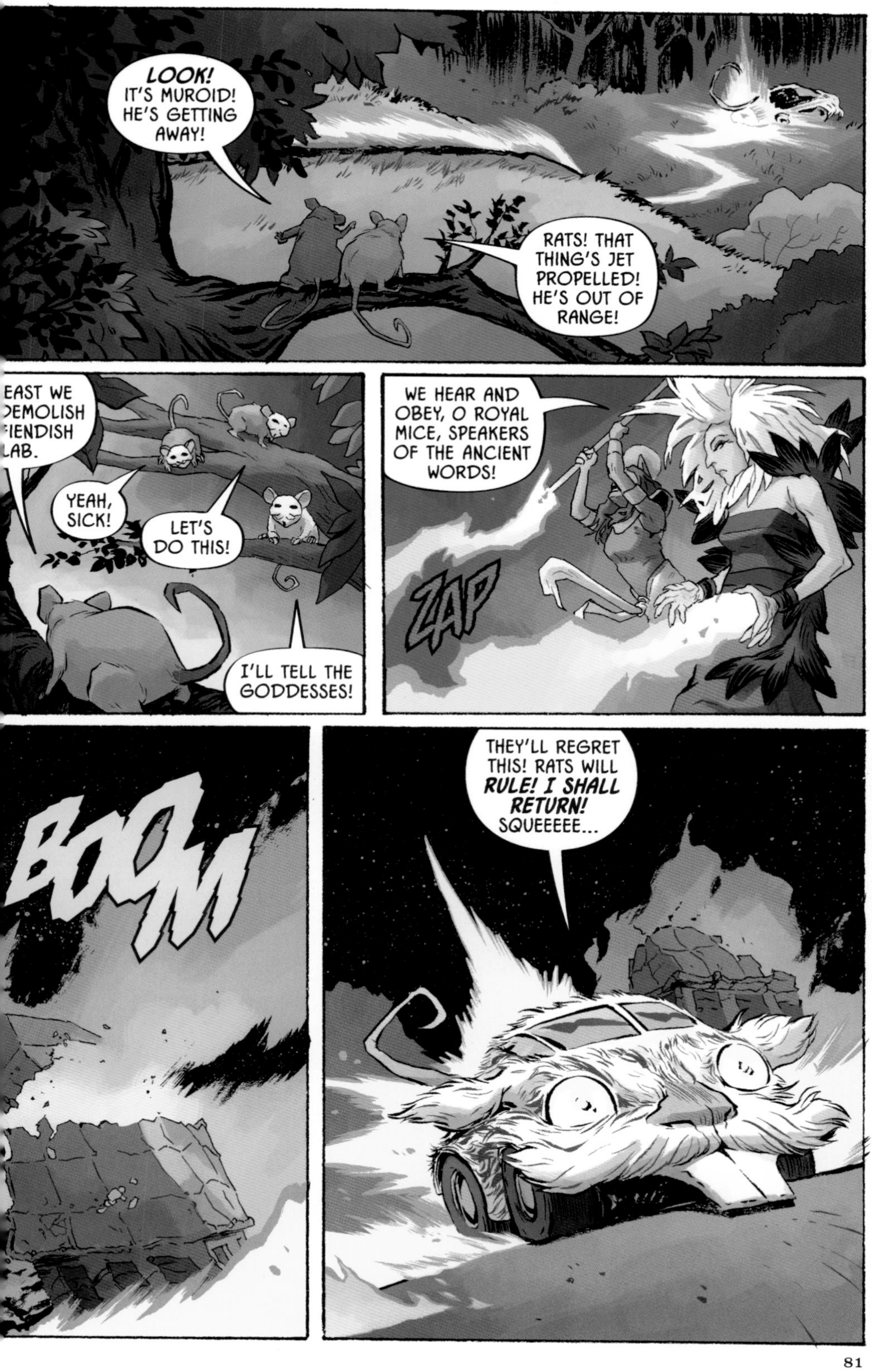
LOOK! IT'S MUROID! HE'S GETTING AWAY!
RATS! THAT THING'S JET PROPELLED! HE'S OUT OF RANGE!
EAST WE DEMOLISH FIENDISH LAB.
YEAH, SICK!
LET'S DO THIS!
I'LL TELL THE GODDESSES!
WE HEAR AND OBEY, O ROYAL MICE, SPEAKERS OF THE ANCIENT WORDS!
ZAP
BOOM
THEY'LL REGRET THIS! RATS WILL RULE! I SHALL RETURN! SQUEEEEE...

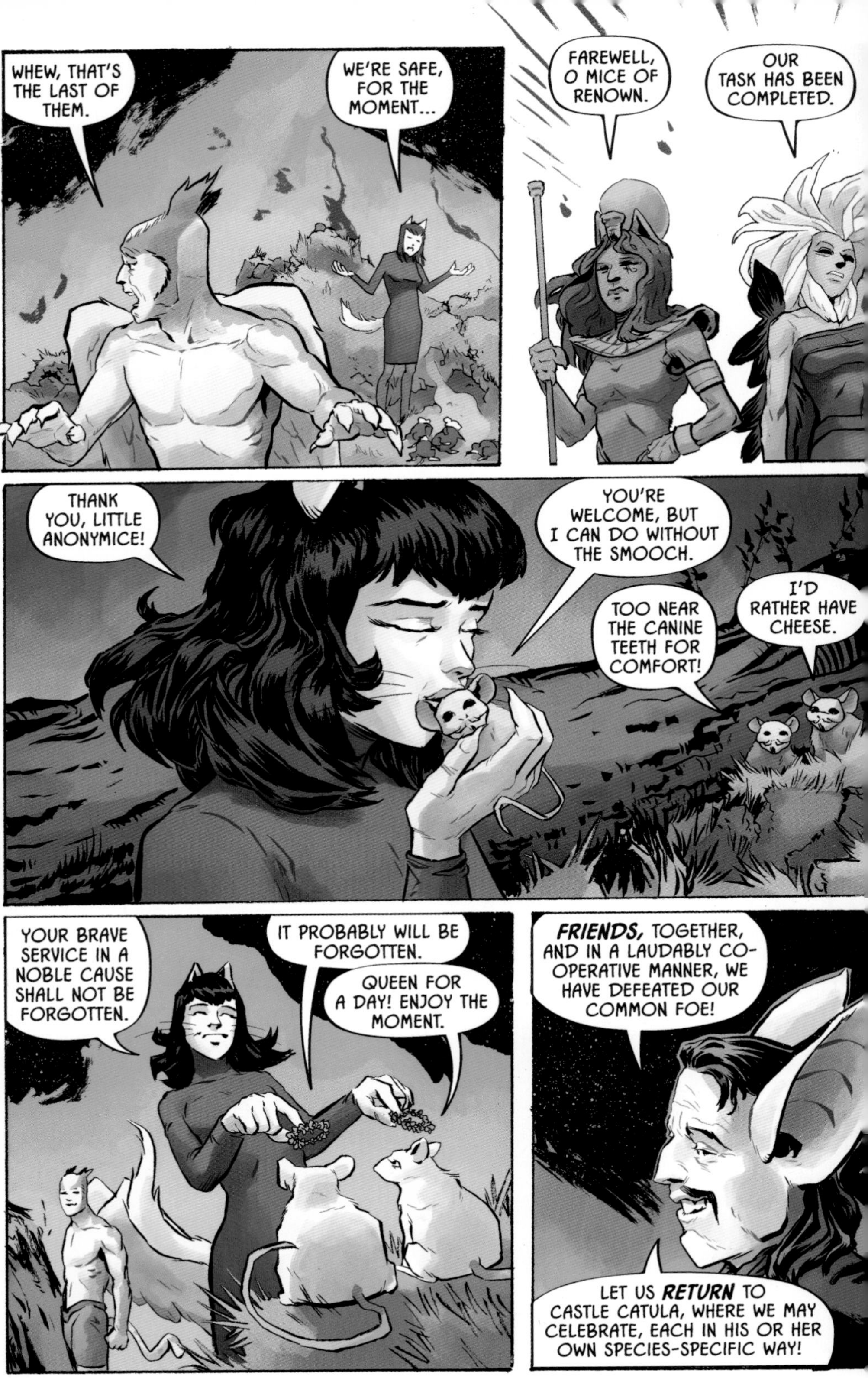
WHEW, THAT'S THE LAST OF THEM.
WE'RE SAFE, FOR THE MOMENT...
FAREWELL, O MICE OF RENOWN.
OUR TASK HAS BEEN COMPLETED.
THANK YOU, LITTLE ANONYMICE!
YOU'RE WELCOME, BUT I CAN DO WITHOUT THE SMOOCH.
TOO NEAR THE CANINE TEETH FOR COMFORT!
I'D RATHER HAVE CHEESE.
YOUR BRAVE SERVICE IN A NOBLE CAUSE SHALL NOT BE FORGOTTEN.
IT PROBABLY WILL BE FORGOTTEN.
QUEEN FOR A DAY! ENJOY THE MOMENT.
FRIENDS, TOGETHER, AND IN A LAUDABLY CO-OPERATIVE MANNER, WE HAVE DEFEATED OUR COMMON FOE!
LET US RETURN TO CASTLE CATULA, WHERE WE MAY CELEBRATE, EACH IN HIS OR HER OWN SPECIES-SPECIFIC WAY!

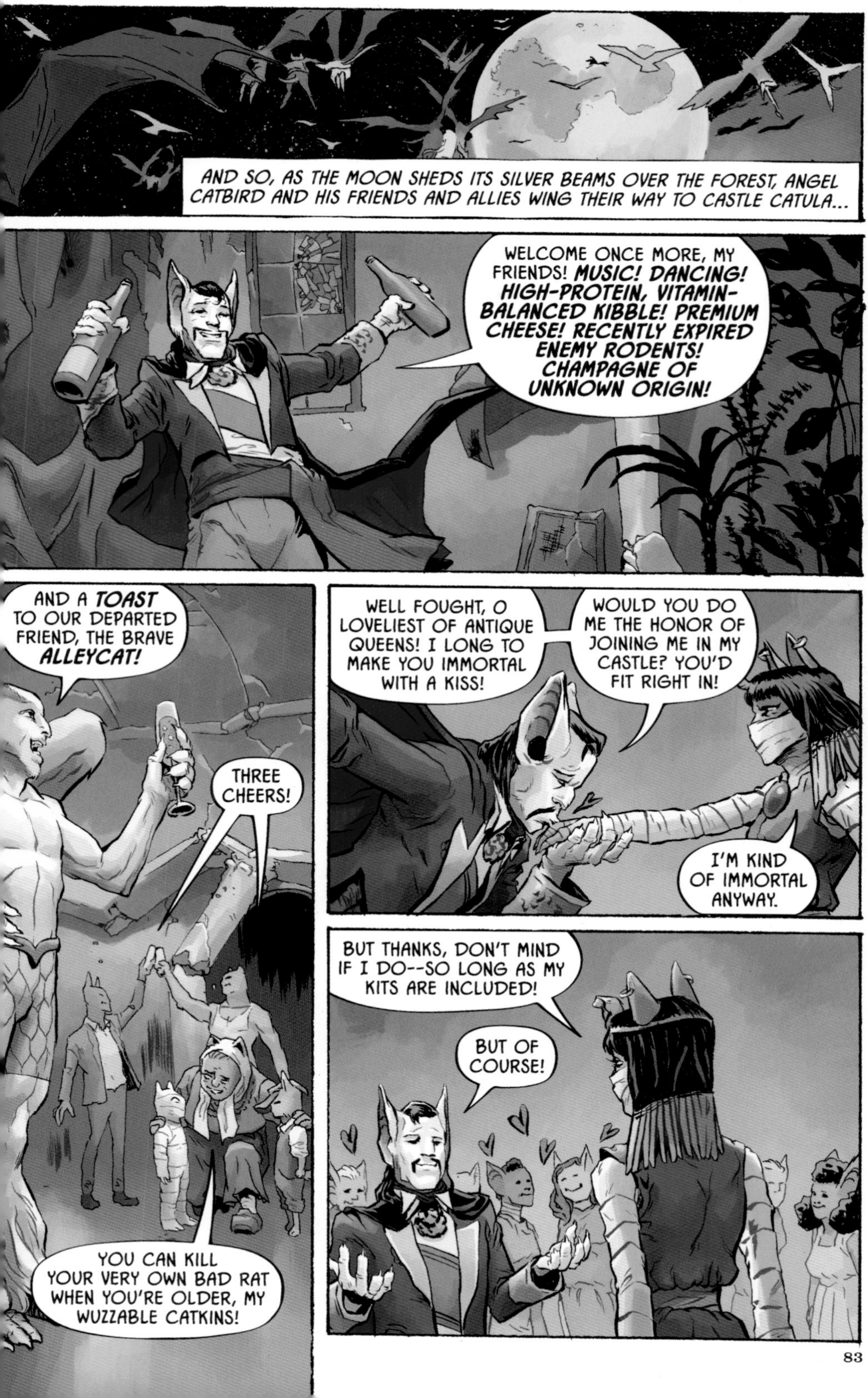

AND SO, AS THE MOON SHEDS ITS SILVER BEAMS OVER THE FOREST, ANGEL CATBIRD AND HIS FRIENDS AND ALLIES WING THEIR WAY TO CASTLE CATULA...
WELCOME ONCE MORE, MY FRIENDS! MUSIC! DANCING! HIGH-PROTEIN, VITAMIN-BALANCED KIBBLE! PREMIUM CHEESE! RECENTLY EXPIRED ENEMY RODENTS! CHAMPAGNE OF UNKNOWN ORIGIN!
AND A TOAST TO OUR DEPARTED FRIEND, THE BRAVE ALLEYCAT!
THREE CHEERS!
YOU CAN KILL YOUR VERY OWN BAD RAT WHEN YOU'RE OLDER, MY WUZZABLE CATKINS!
WELL FOUGHT, O LOVELIEST OF ANTIQUE QUEENS! I LONG TO MAKE YOU IMMORTAL WITH A KISS!
WOULD YOU DO ME THE HONOR OF JOINING ME IN MY CASTLE? YOU'D FIT RIGHT IN!
I'M KIND OF IMMORTAL ANYWAY.
BUT THANKS, DON'T MIND IF I DO--SO LONG AS MY KITS ARE INCLUDED!
BUT OF COURSE!

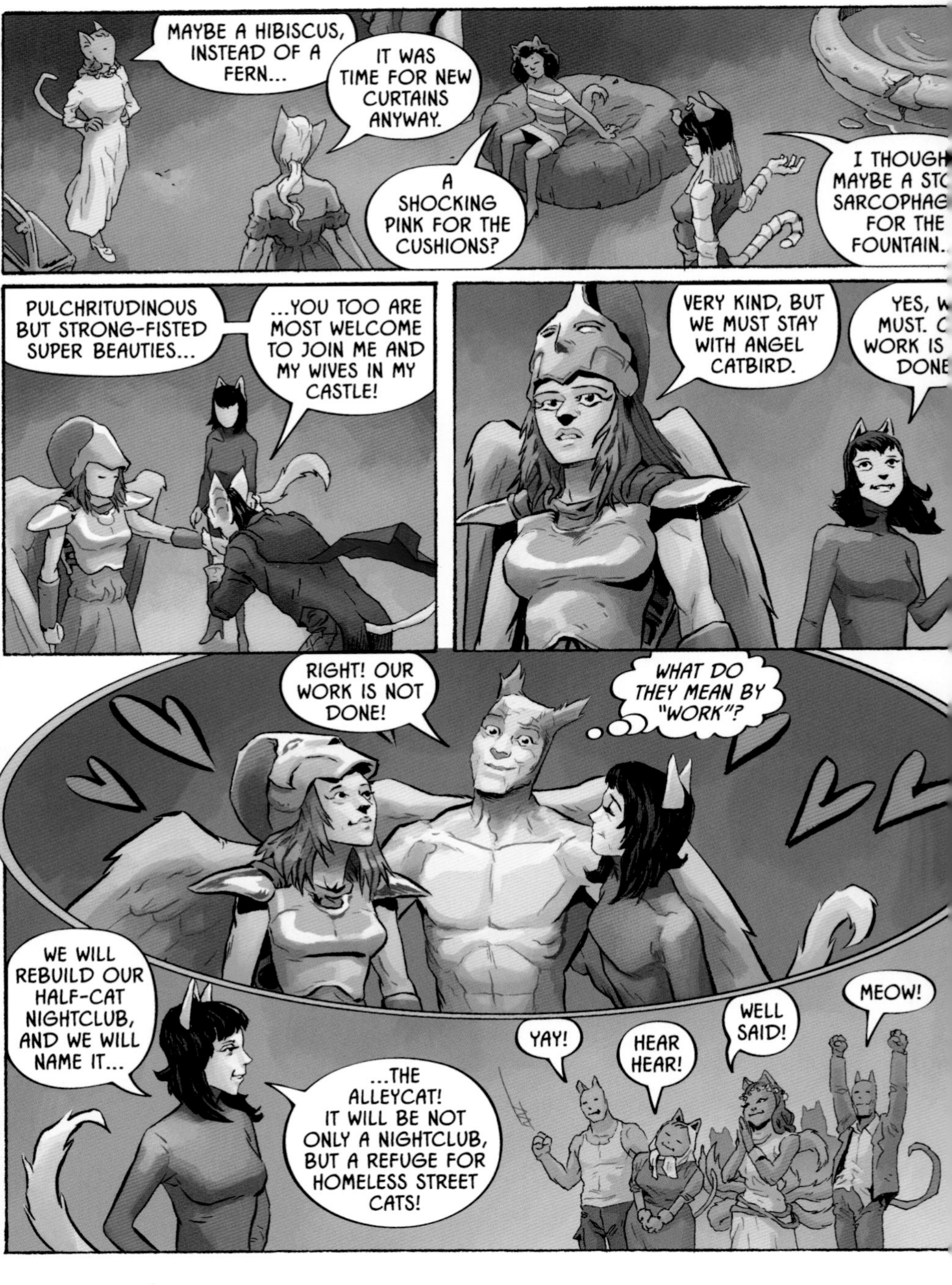
MAYBE A HIBISCUS, INSTEAD OF A FERN...
IT WAS TIME FOR NEW CURTAINS ANYWAY.
A SHOCKING PINK FOR THE CUSHIONS?
I THOUGH MAYBE A STO SARCOPHAG FOR THE FOUNTAIN.
PULCHRITUDINOUS BUT STRONG-FISTED SUPER BEAUTIES...
...YOU TOO ARE MOST WELCOME TO JOIN ME AND MY WIVES IN MY CASTLE!
VERY KIND, BUT WE MUST STAY WITH ANGEL CATBIRD.
YES, W MUST. O WORK IS DONE
RIGHT! OUR WORK IS NOT DONE!
WHAT DO THEY MEAN BY "WORK"?
WE WILL REBUILD OUR HALF-CAT NIGHTCLUB, AND WE WILL NAME IT...
...THE ALLEYCAT! IT WILL BE NOT ONLY A NIGHTCLUB, BUT A REFUGE FOR HOMELESS STREET CATS!
YAY!
HEAR HEAR!
WELL SAID!
MEOW!

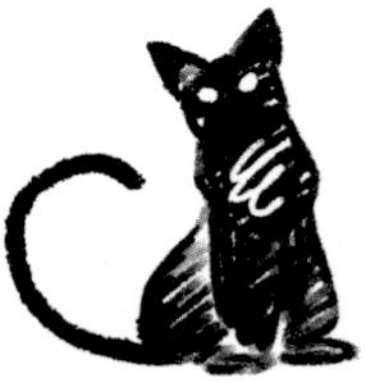

ALLEY CATS

Alley cats—or feral or community cats—need a clubhouse of their own! Some can b tamed, but many never get accustomed to human contact. And while they may see closer to being wildlife than pets, we owe them humane treatment, just as we do a other animal. Keep alley cats and birds safe! Read more at www.catsandbirds.ca

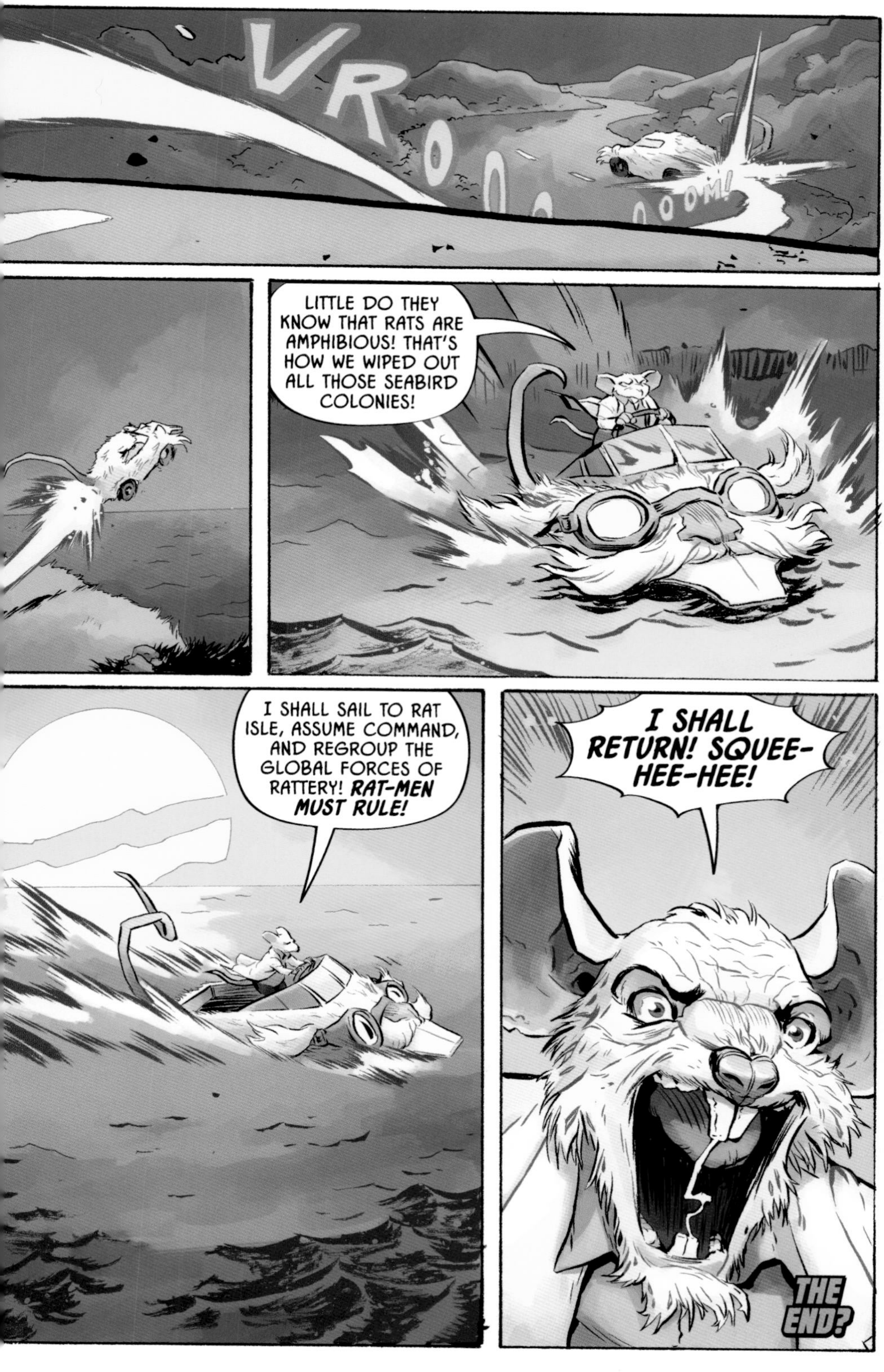
VROOOOOOOM!
LITTLE DO THEY KNOW THAT RATS ARE AMPHIBIOUS! THAT'S HOW WE WIPED OUT ALL THOSE SEABIRD COLONIES!
I SHALL SAIL TO RAT ISLE, ASSUME COMMAND, AND REGROUP THE GLOBAL FORCES OF RATTERY! RAT-MEN MUST RULE!
I SHALL RETURN! SQUEE-HEE-HEE!
THE END?

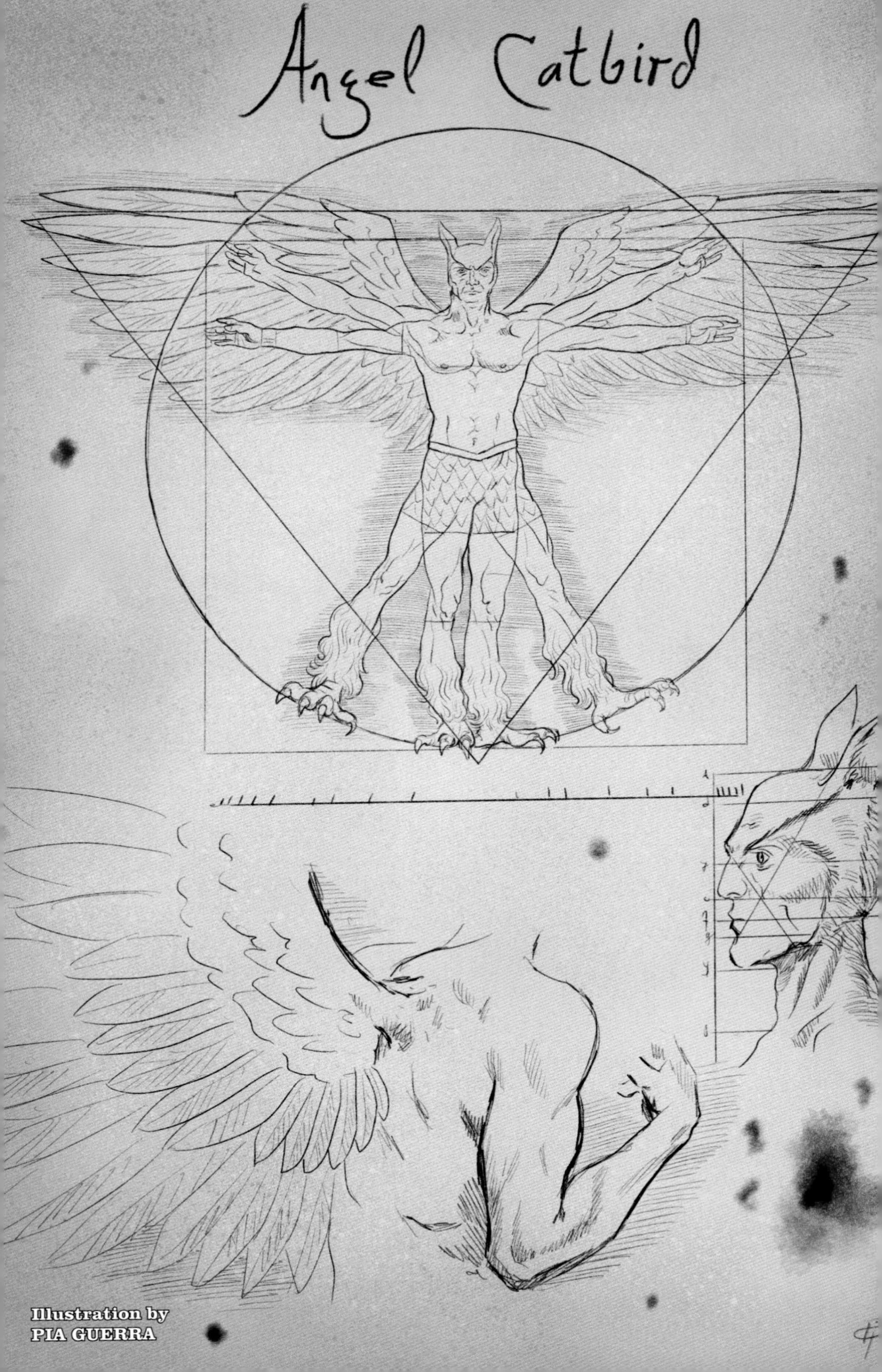
Angel Catbird

Illustration by
PIA GUERRA

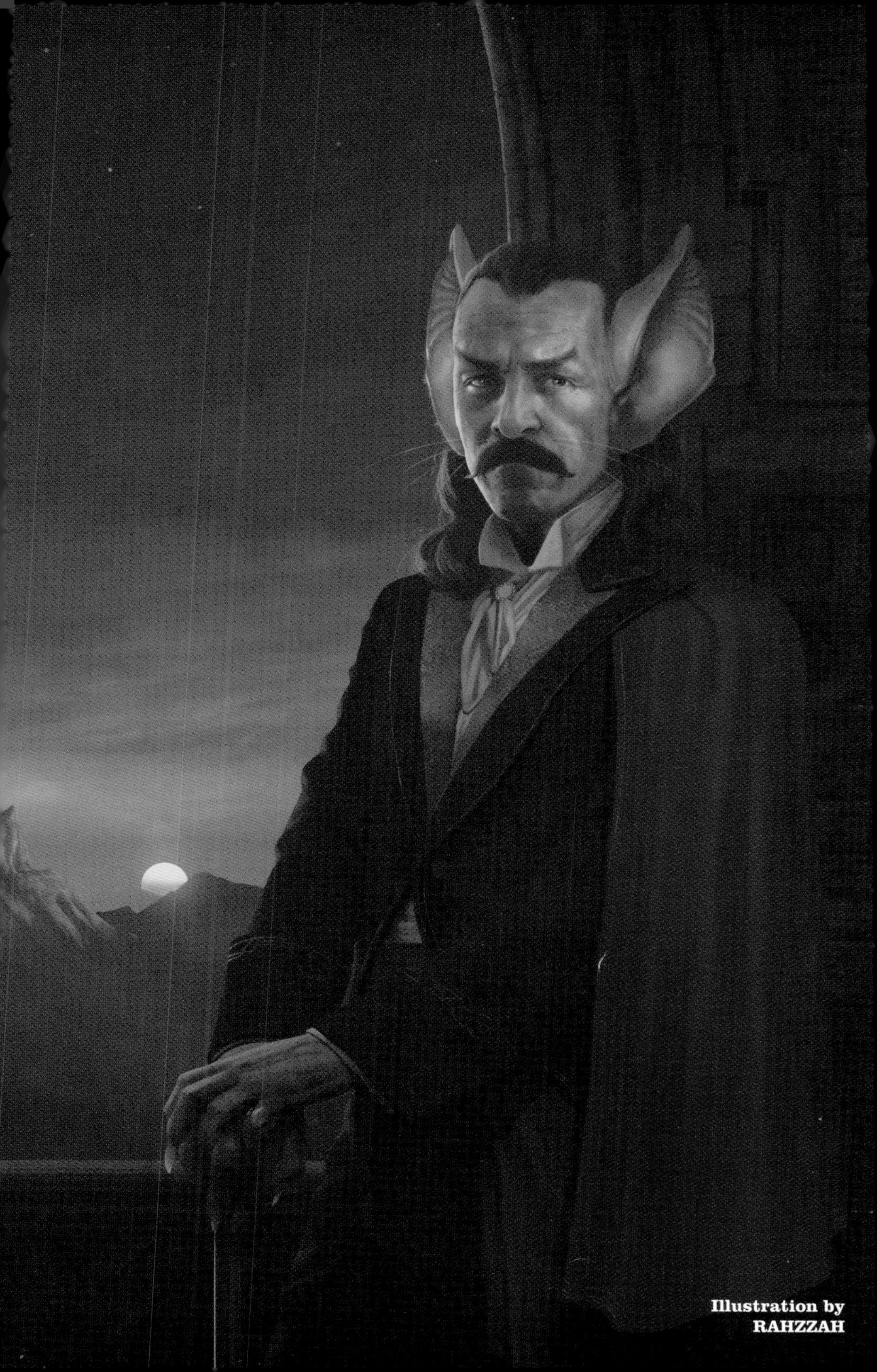

Illustration by
RAHZZAH

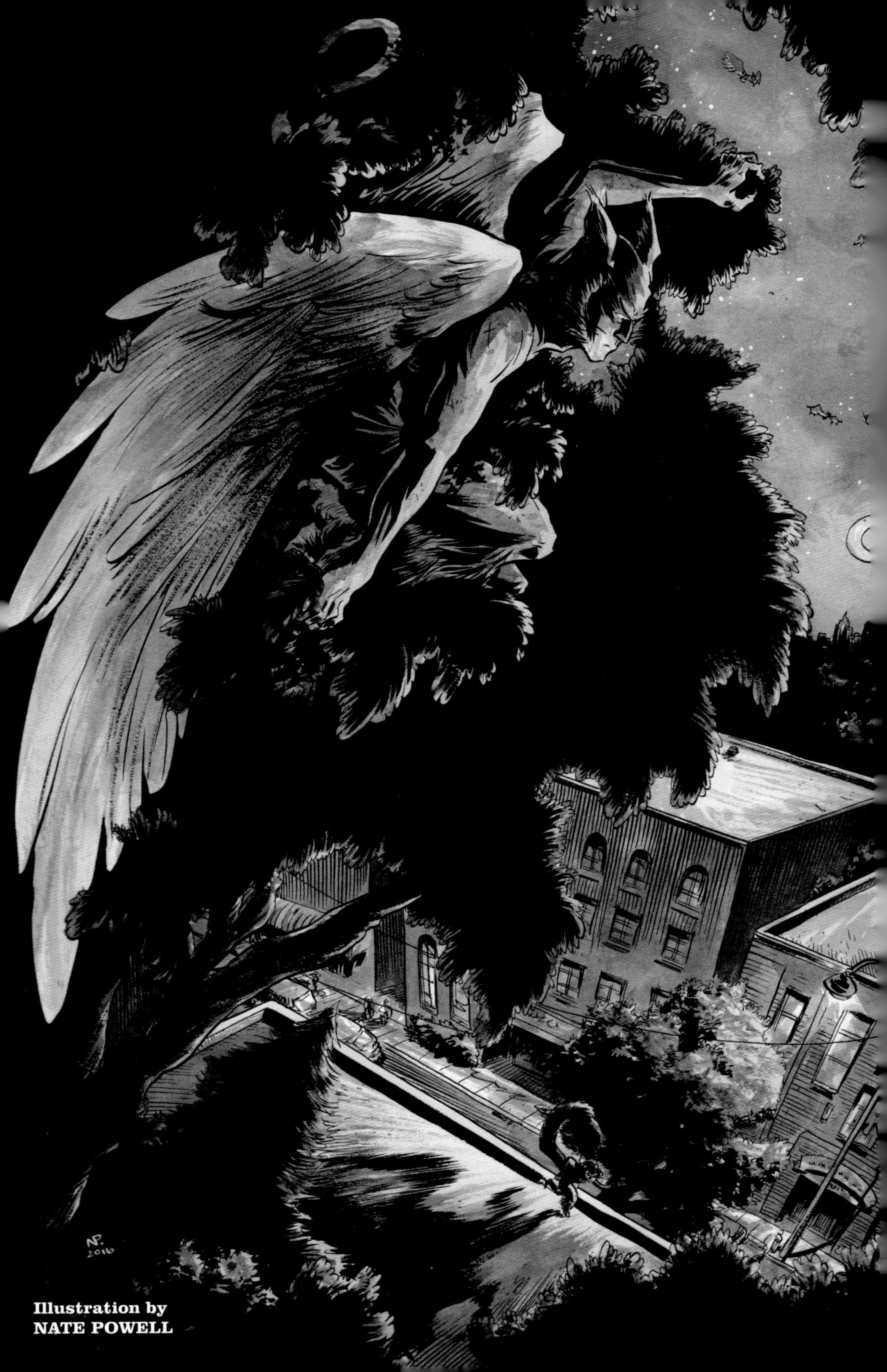
NP.
2016

Illustration by
NATE POWELL

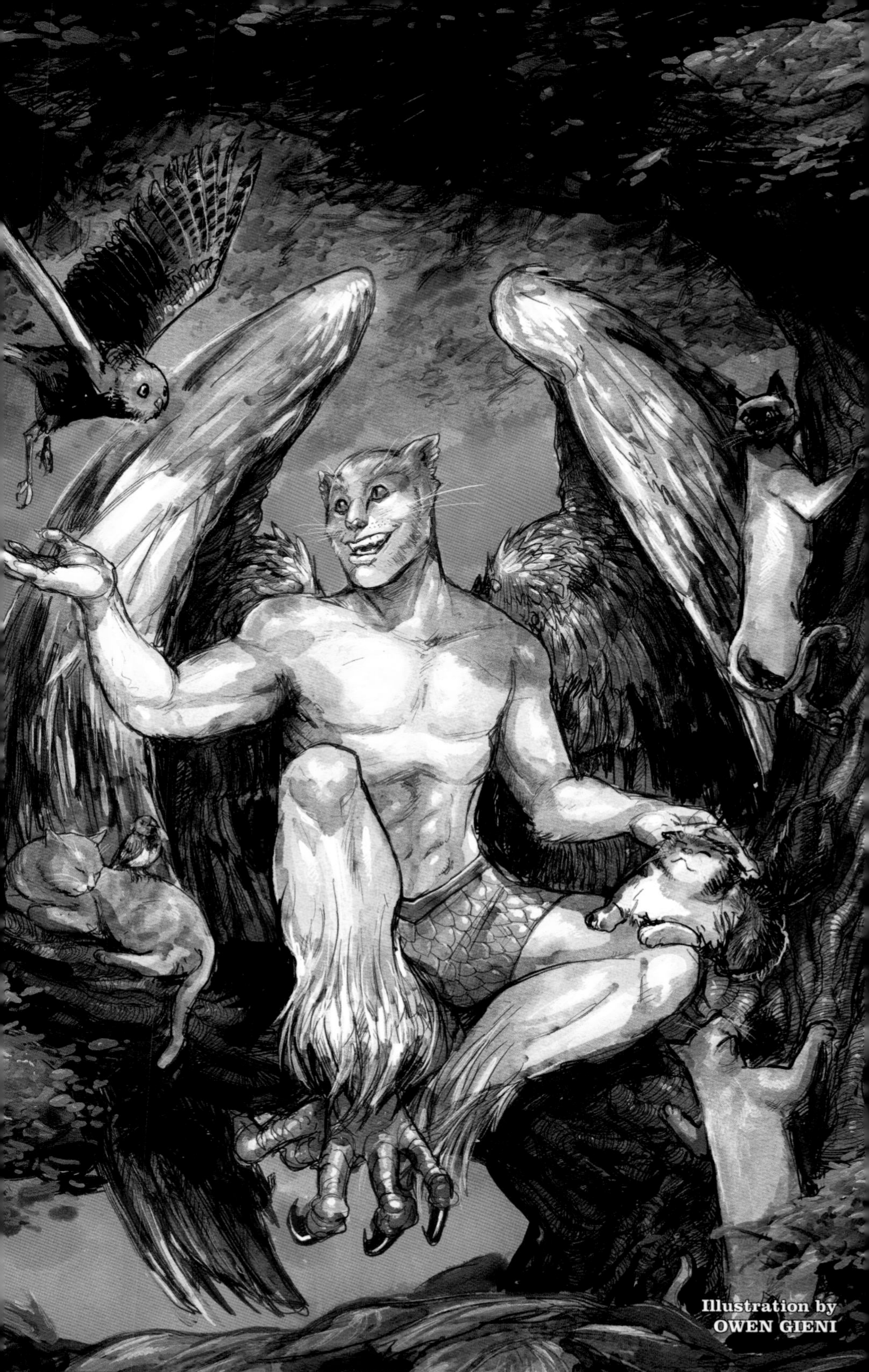
Illustration by
OWEN GIENI

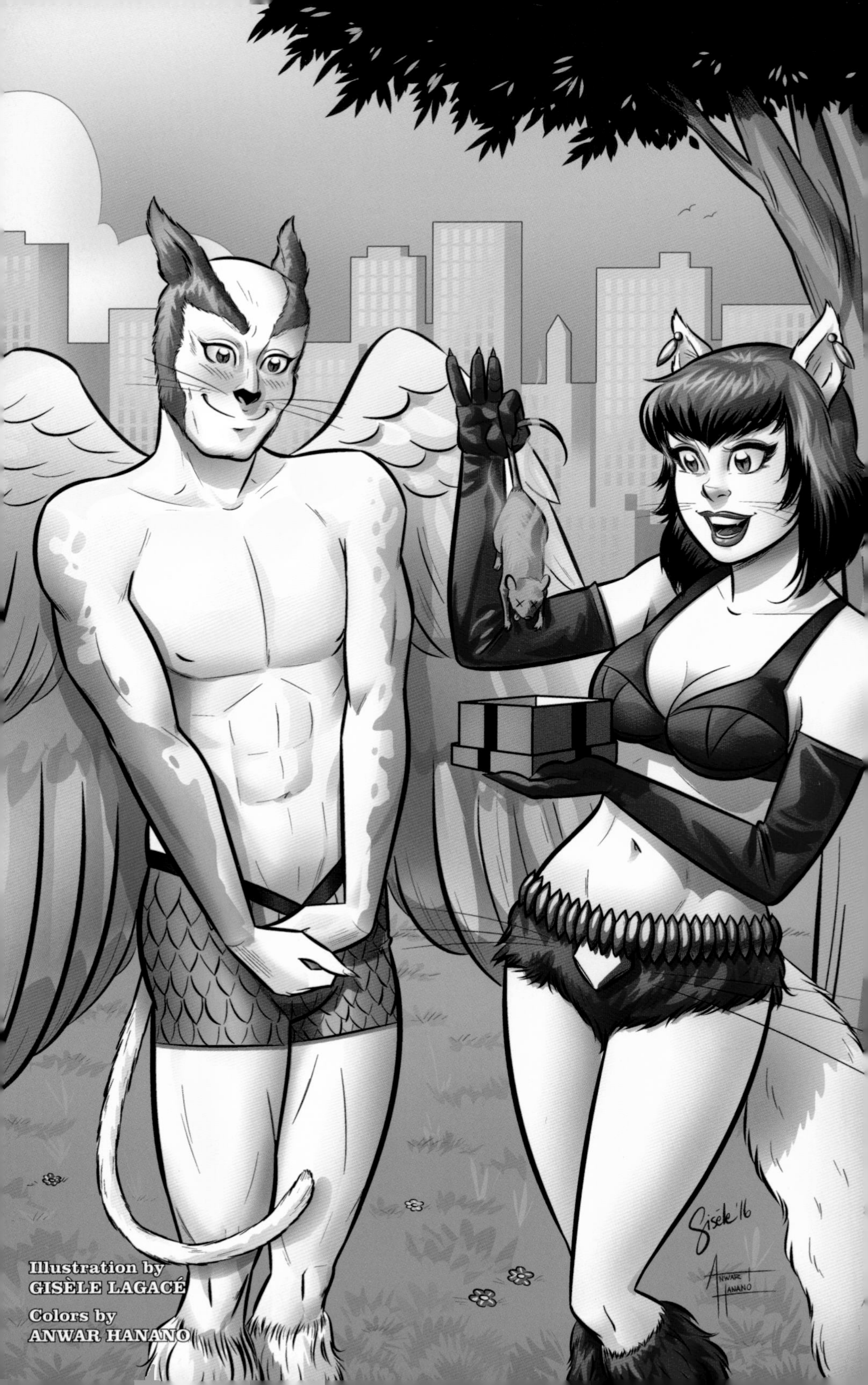
Gisèle '16
ANWAR HANANO

Illustration by
GISÈLE LAGACÉ

Colors by
ANWAR HANANO

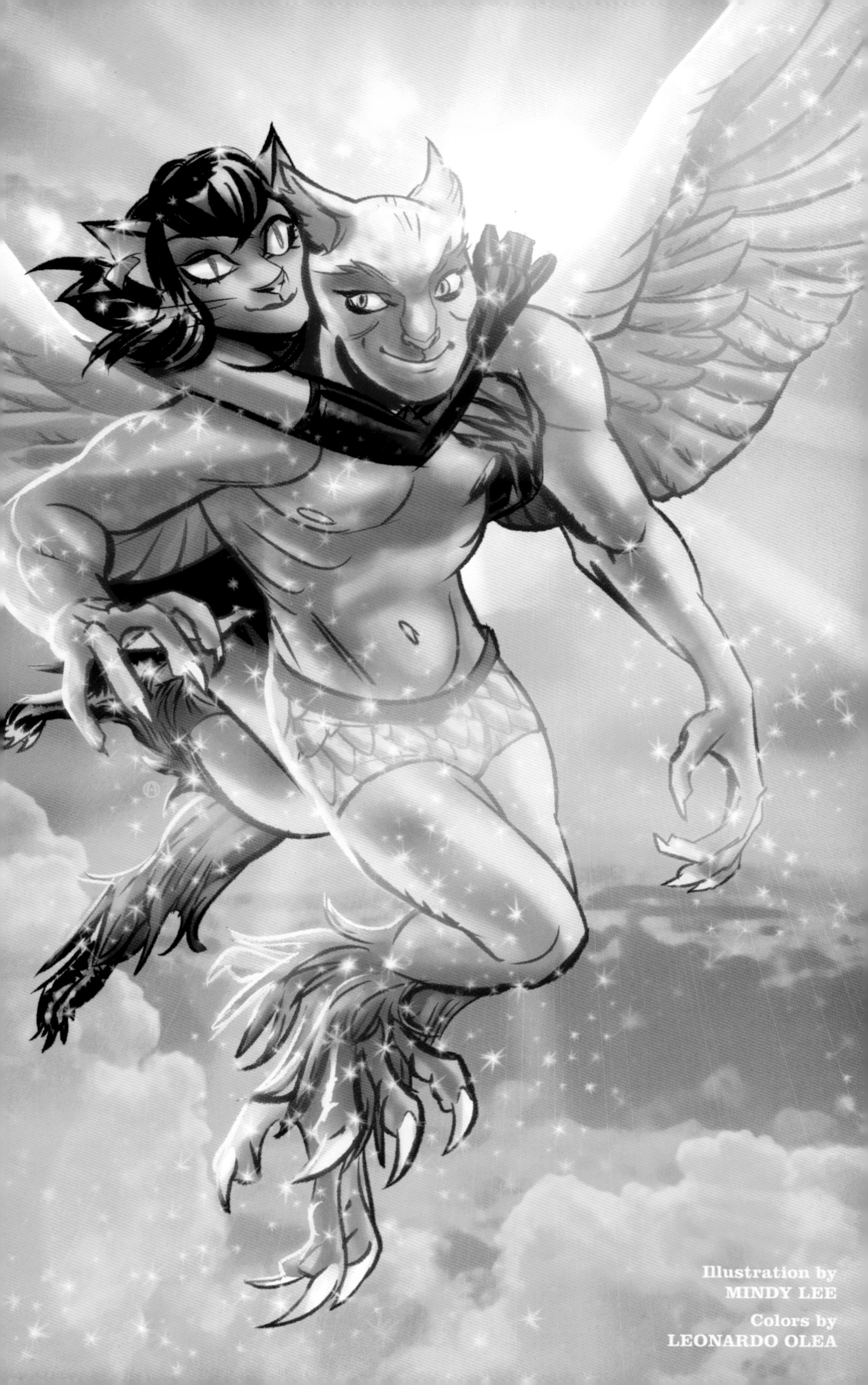

Illustration by
MINDY LEE

Colors by
LEONARDO OLEA

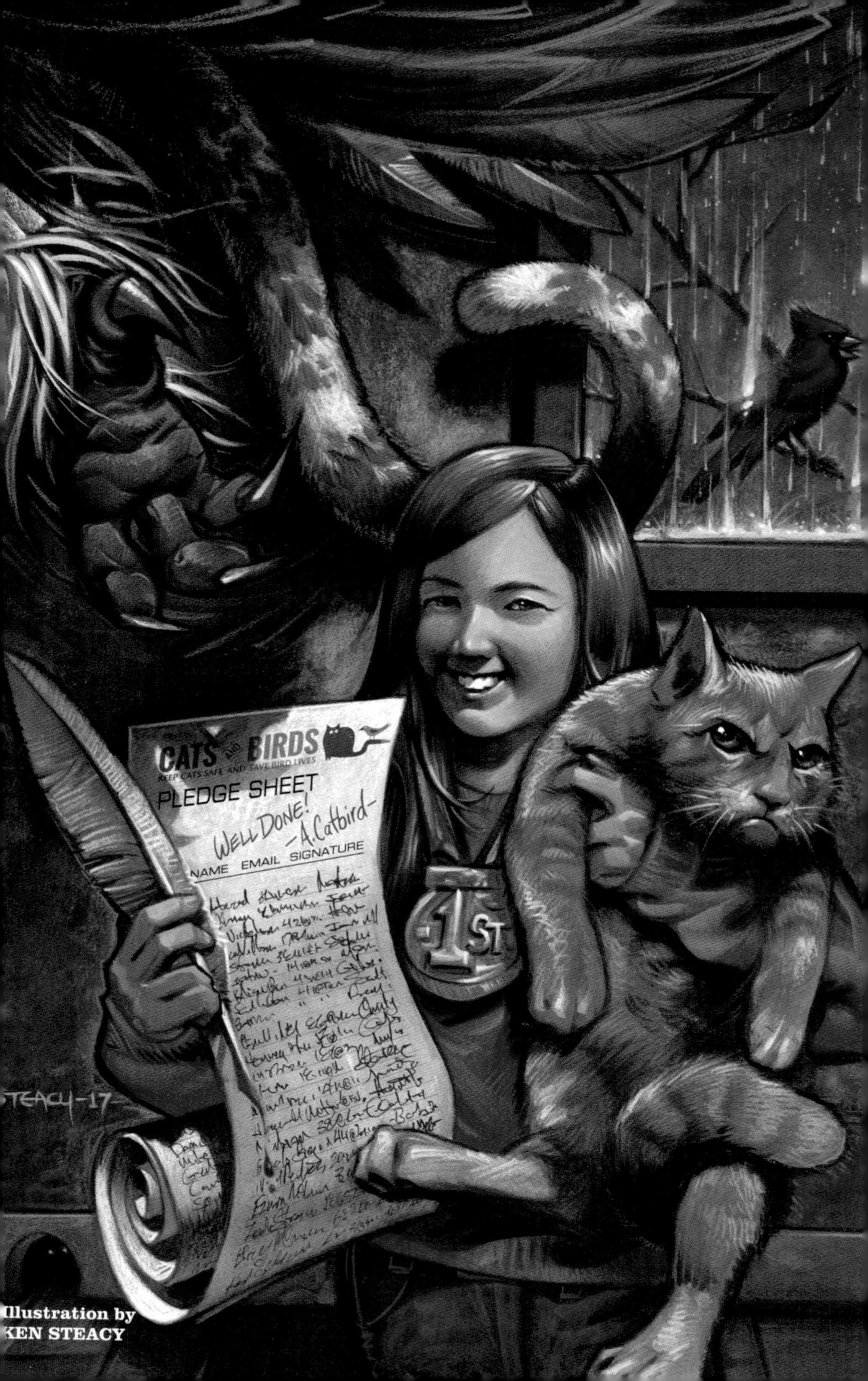
CATS AND BIRDS
KEEP CATS SAFE AND SAVE BIRD LIVES
PLEDGE SHEET
WELL DONE!
-A. Catbird-
NAME EMAIL SIGNATURE
1ST
STEACY-17

Illustration by
KEN STEACY

ANGEL CATBIRD ™

SKETCHBOOK

Notes by

Johnnie Christmas

ANONYMOUSE

The Anonymice are one of my favorite
additions to the series!

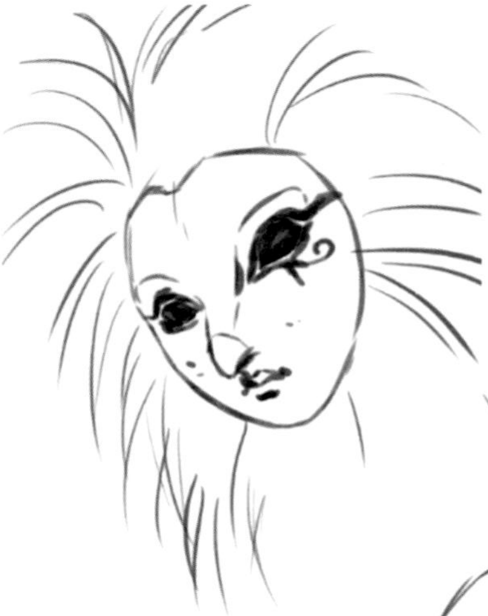

For volume 3, we reworked Nekhbet (the old designs are in volume 1's sketchbook). Margaret wanted to bring in the punky, spiked plumage of real-life Egyptian white vultures, as well as the suggestion of a beak and their miraculously dark eyes.

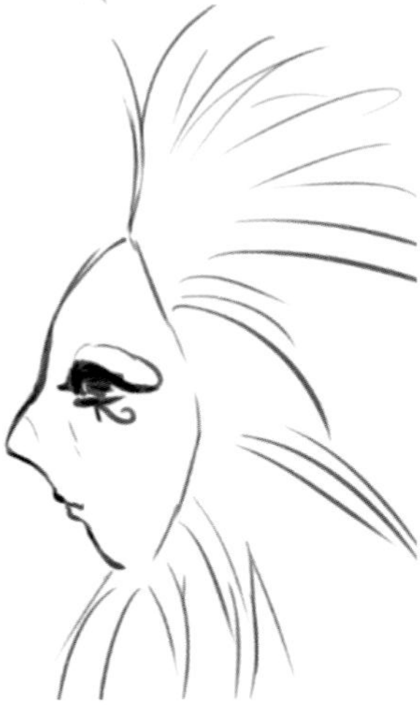

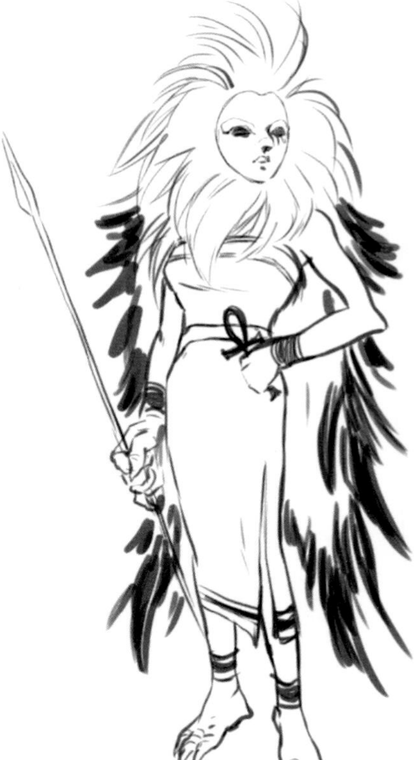

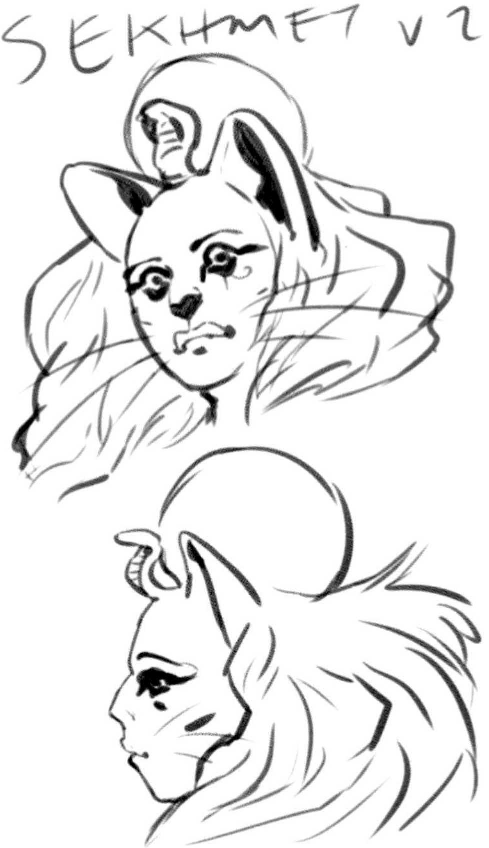
SEKHMET V2

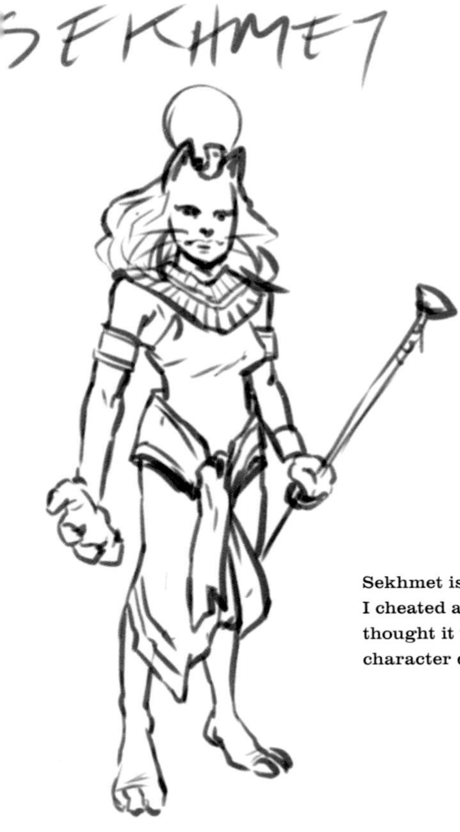
SEKHMET

Sekhmet is one of my favorite characters to draw. I cheated a bit and gave her a male lion's mane. I thought it would make for a more dramatic character design, so I went with it.

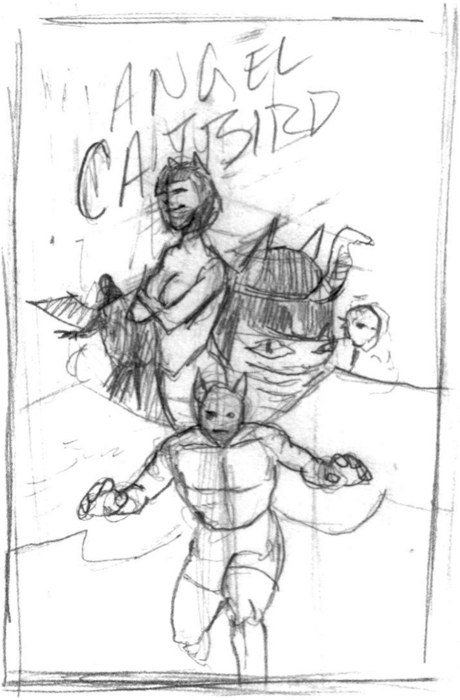
ANGEL
CATBIRD

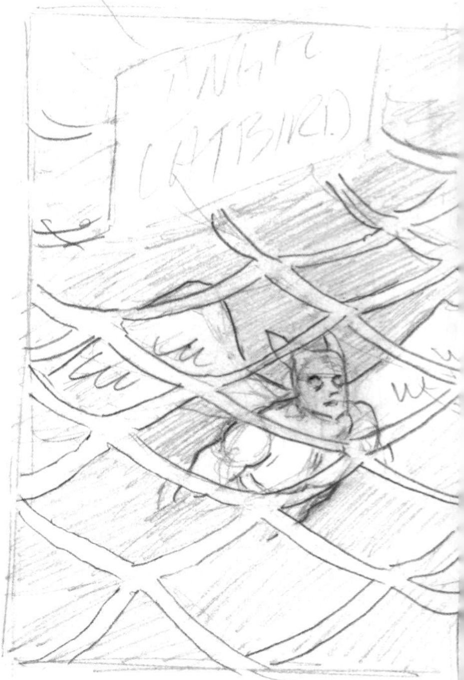
CATBIRD

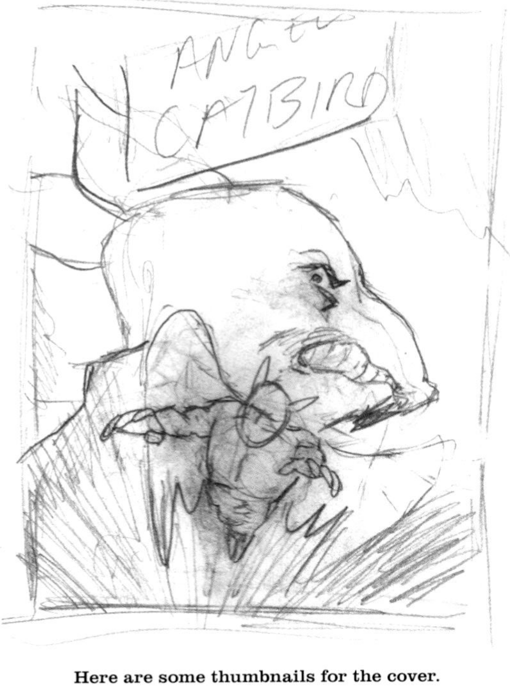
CATBIRD

Here are some thumbnails for the cover.

1. Montage of Angel and some of our main characters.
2. Angel emerging from the dark, captured but unbroken.
3. And a final-showdown-style cover with Angel in the foreground flying headlong into the fray. Muroid looks over, ominously baring his teeth.

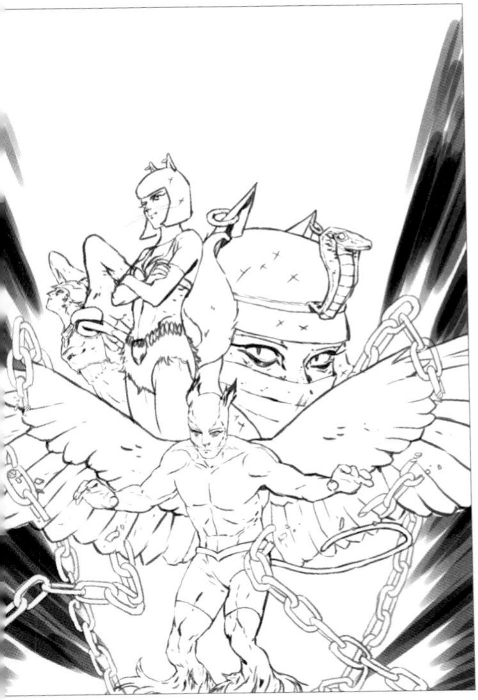

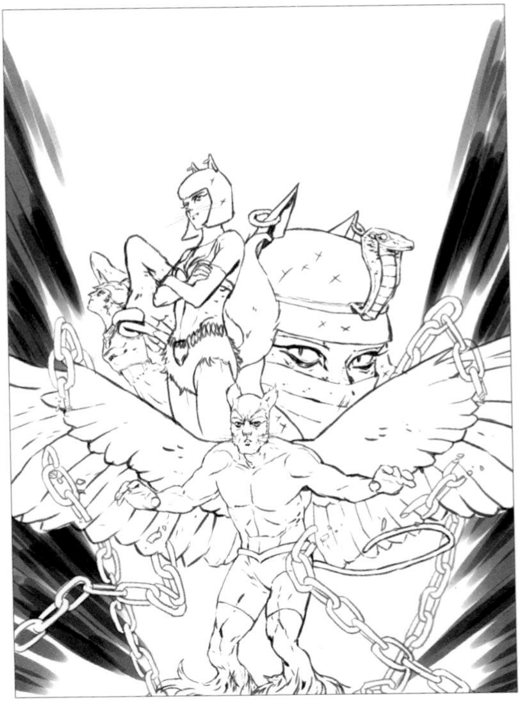

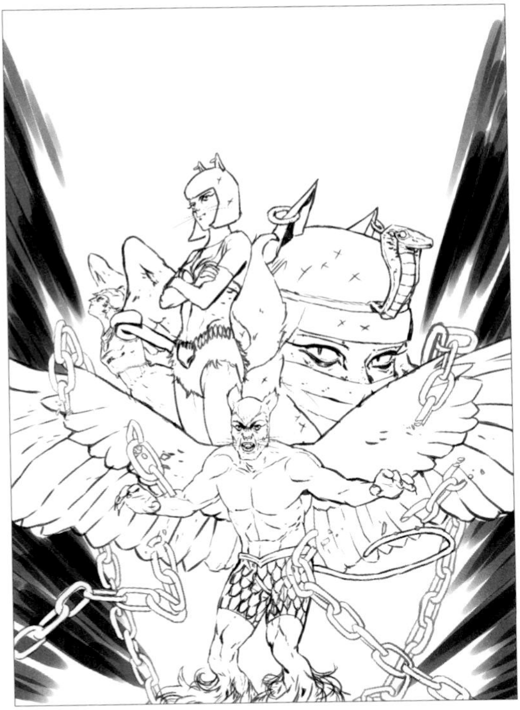

We went with the montage version. There were a few changes to Angel's facial expression along the way and the addition of chains.

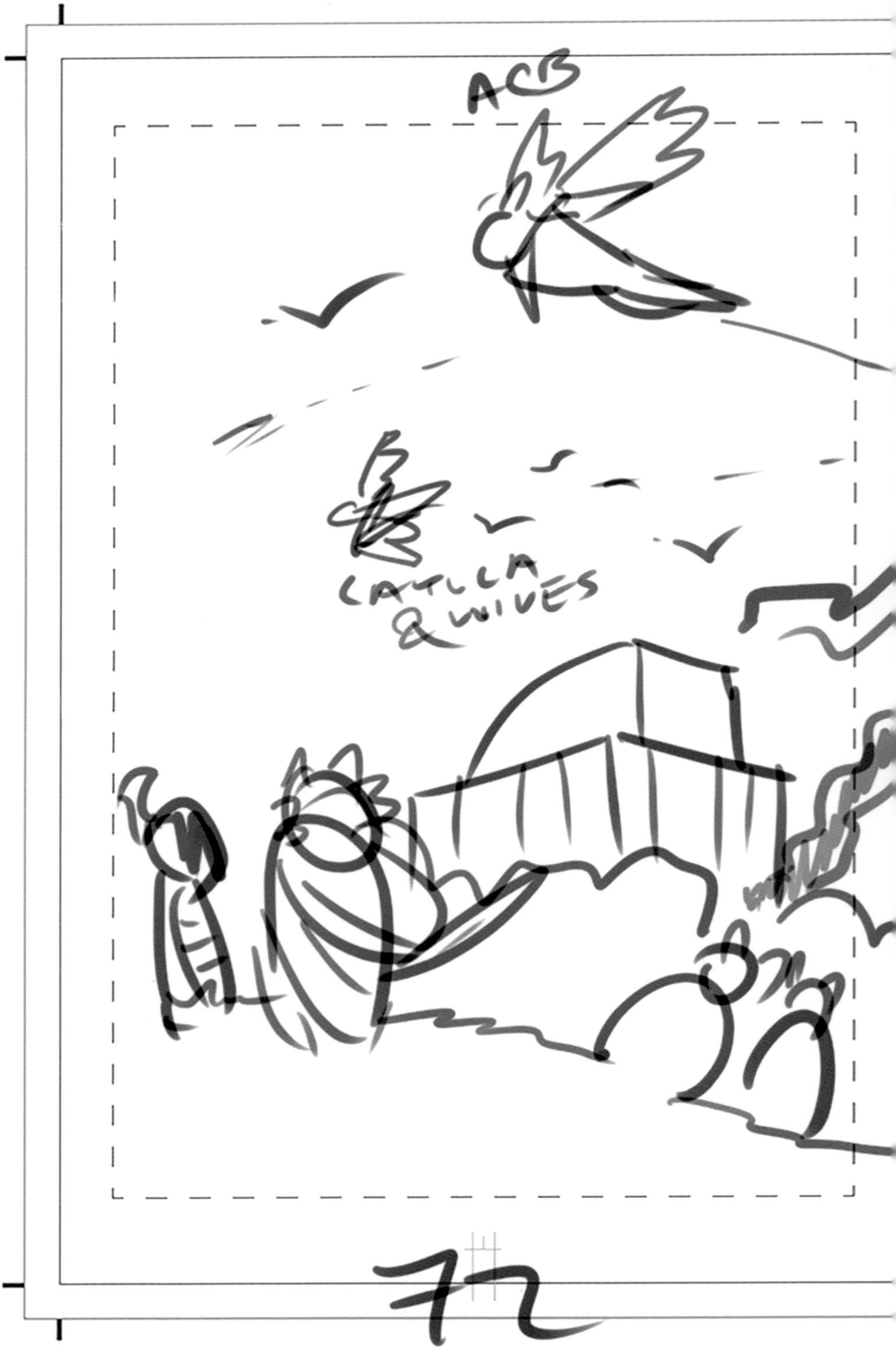
ACB
CATULLA
& WIVES
72

Here's a thumbnail of our big action fight spread. It's important to nail down the composition and action of the page at this stage.

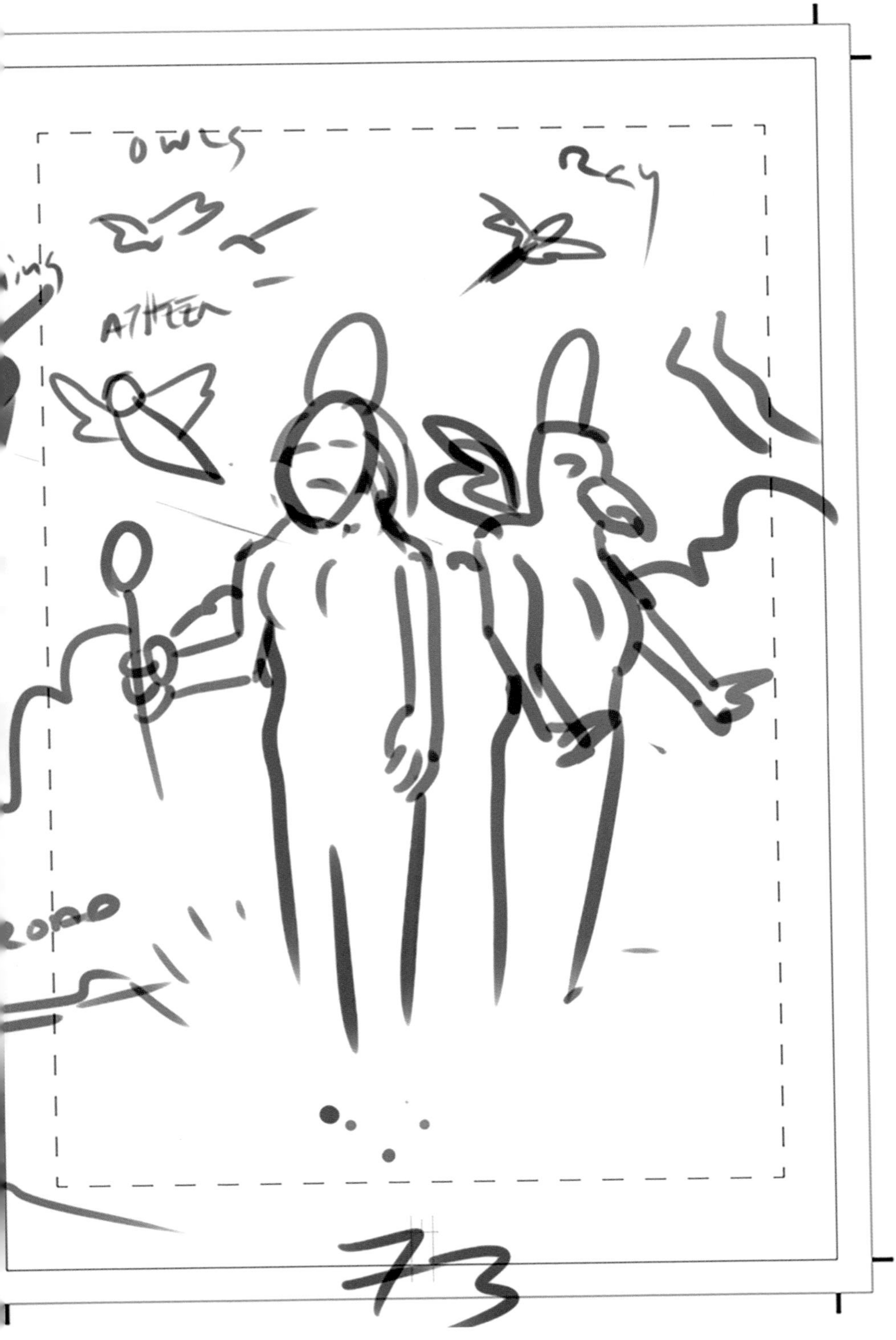
OWLS
73

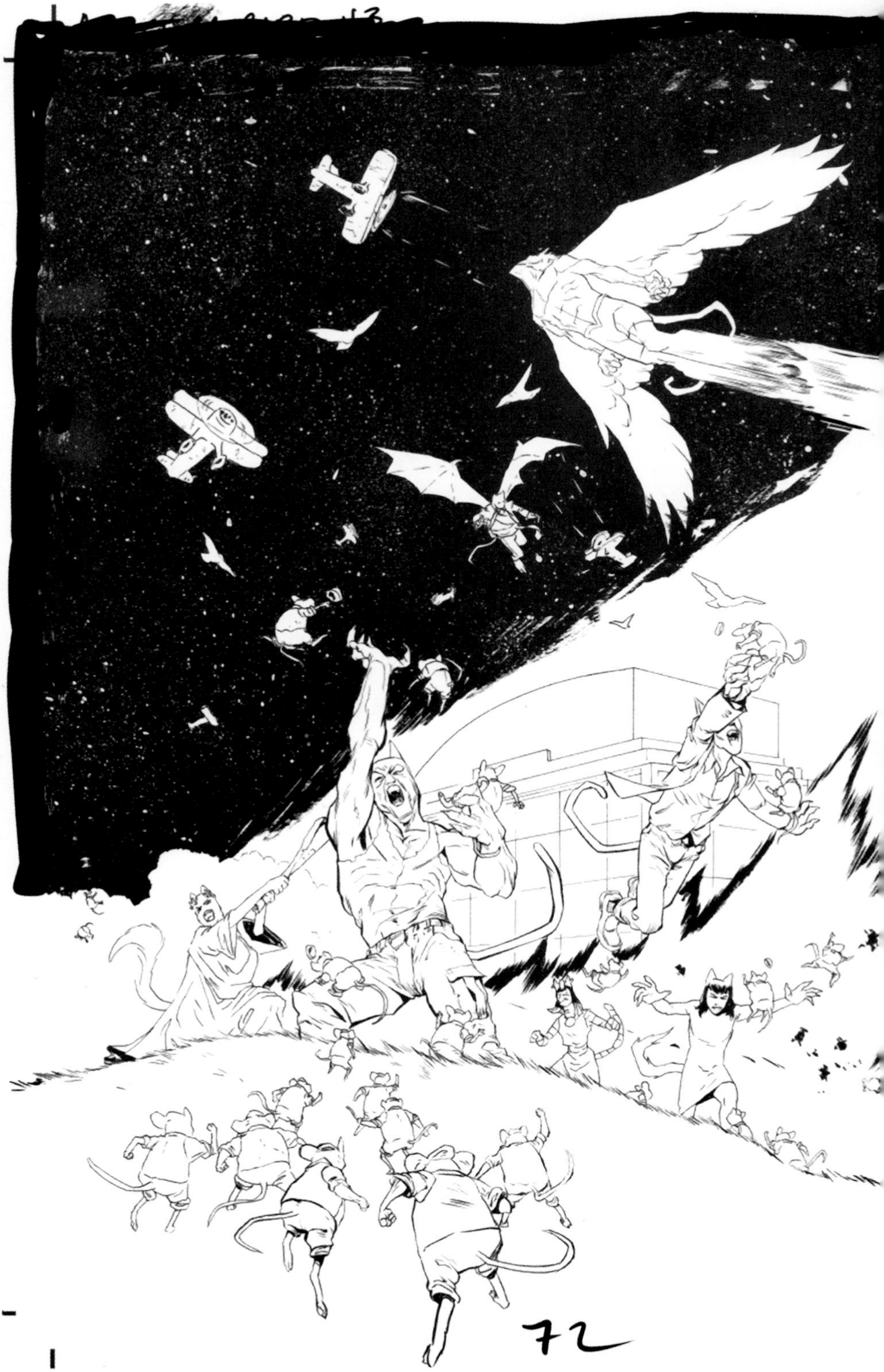
72

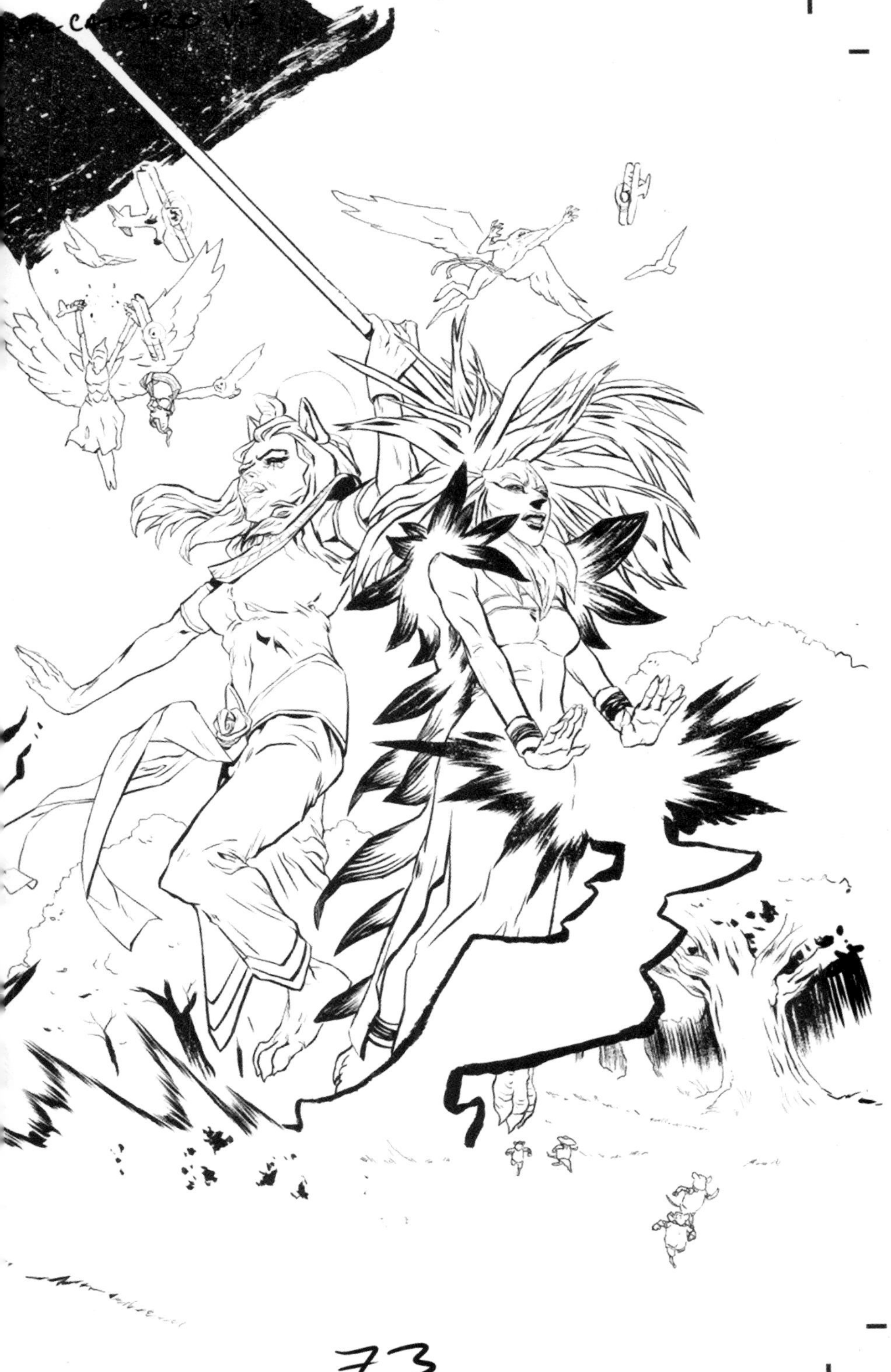
73

And here's the same spread, but with final inks. At this point I handed it off to Tamra to work her wonderful color magic on the page.

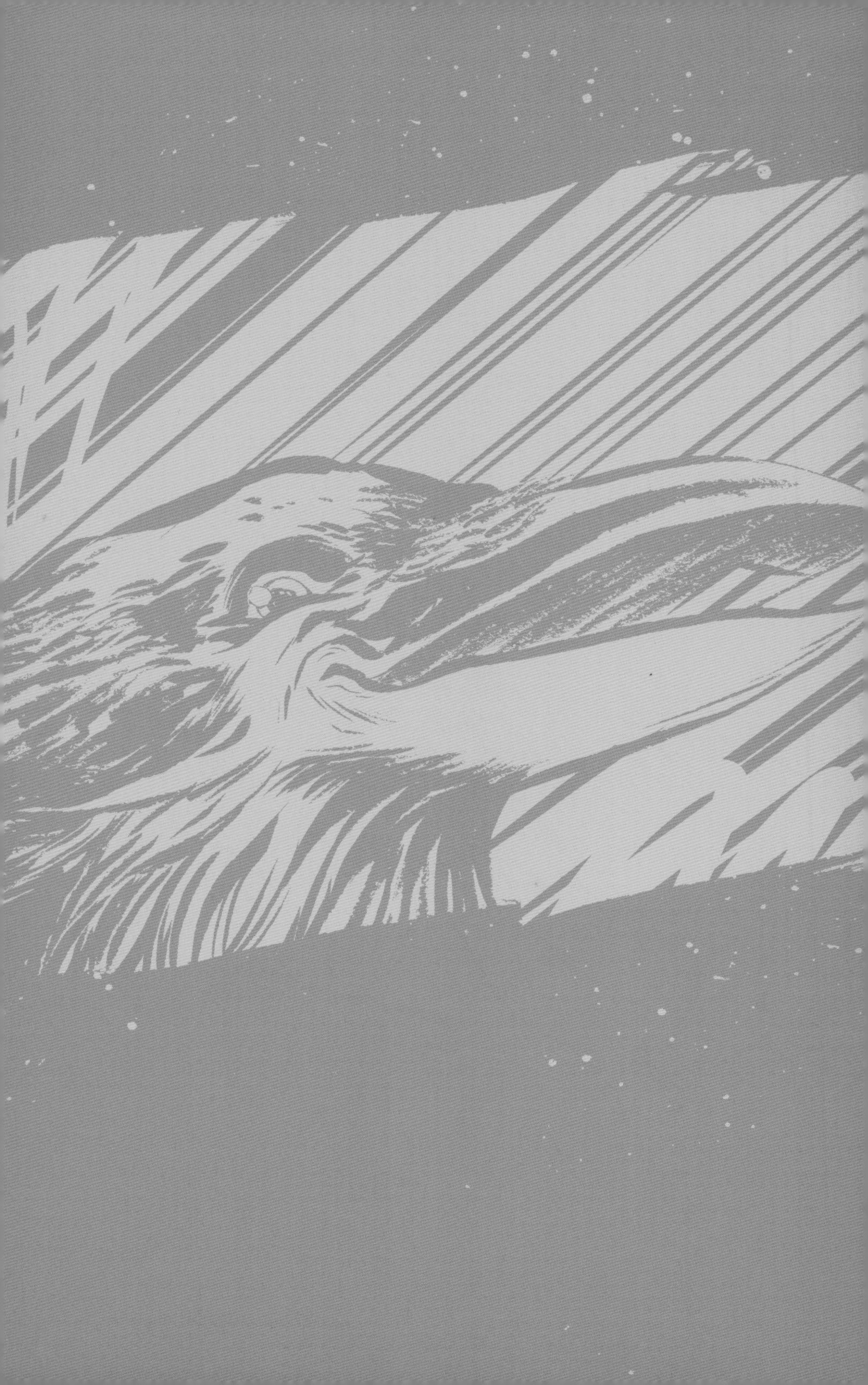

MARGARET ATWOOD

Margaret Atwood was born in 1939 in Ottawa and grew up in northern Ontario, Quebec, and Toronto. She received her undergraduate degree from Victoria College at the University of Toronto and her master's degree from Radcliffe College.

Atwood is the author of more than forty volumes of poetry, children's literature, fiction, and nonfiction, but is best known for her novels, which include *The Edible Woman* (1969), *The Handmaid's Tale* (1985), *The Robber Bride* (1993), *Alias Grace* (1996), and *The Blind Assassin*, which won the prestigious Man Booker Prize in 2000. Her latest work is a book of short stories called *Stone Mattress: Nine Tales* (2014). Her newest novel, *MaddAddam* (2013), is the final volume in a three-book series that began with the Man Booker Prize–nominated *Oryx and Crake* (2003) and continued with *The Year of the Flood* (2009). *The Tent* (mini-fictions) and *Moral Disorder* (short fiction) both appeared in 2006. Her most recent volume of poetry, *The Door*, was published in 2007. *In Other Worlds: SF and the Human Imagination*, a collection of nonfiction essays, appeared in 2011. Her nonfiction book *Payback: Debt and the Shadow Side of Wealth* was adapted for the screen in 2012. Ms. Atwood's work has been published in more than forty languages, including Farsi, Japanese, Turkish, Finnish, Korean, Icelandic, and Estonian.

...graph by LIAM SHARP

JOHNNIE CHRISTMAS

Johnnie Christmas was born in Río Piedras, Puerto Rico, and raised in Miami, Florida. He attended the Center for Media Arts magnet program at South Miami Senior High School and received a BFA from Pratt Institute in Brooklyn, New York, before going on to a career in graphic design and art direction. In 2013 he entered the world of comics as cocreator of the critically acclaimed Image Comics series *Sheltered*. He's also the creator, writer, and artist of *Firebug*, serialized in *Island*, also published by Image Comics. His work has been translated into multiple languages.

Johnnie makes Vancouver, BC, his home.

graph by AVALON MOTT

TAMRA BONVILLAIN

Tamra Bonvillain is originally from Augusta, Georgia, and took an interest in art and comics at a young age. After graduating from the local Davidson Fine Arts Magnet School in 2000, she majored in art at Augusta State University. She later attended the Joe Kubert School, and upon graduating in 2009, she began working full time as an assistant and designer for Greg Hildebrandt and Jean Scrocco's company, Spiderwebart. During this time, she also began to take on work as a comics colorist, eventually leaving the company to pursue a career in the comics industry full time. In the years since, she has worked for many major comic publishers, including Dark Horse, Dynamite, Boom, Image, and Marvel. She is currently the colorist for *Rat Queens*, *Wayward*, and several other titles.

Keep Cats Safe
& Save Bird Lives

Catios are a great way to give your cats the benefits of the outdoors without the risks to them and local birds and wildlife!

Cats allowed to roam freely are exposed to risks from cars, diseases, parasites, fights with other cats, dogs, and wildlife, and malicious humans, not to mention getting lost.

Learn more and take the pledge to keep your cat safe and save bird lives at: **www.catsandbirds.ca**

 Environment and Climate Change Canada   Environnement et Changement climatique Canada